AIN'T THAT A MOTHER

POSTPARTUM, PALSY,
AND EVERYTHING IN BETWEEN

AIN'T THAT A MOTHER

ADIBA NELSON

**BLACK
STONE**
PUBLISHING

Copyright © 2022 by Adiba Nelson
Published in 2022 by Blackstone Publishing
Cover and book design by Alenka Vdovič Linaschke

Some names and identifying details have been changed
to protect the privacy of individuals.

Printed in the United States of America

First edition: 2022
ISBN 978-1-7999-3226-0
Biography & Autobiography / Personal Memoir

Version 1

CIP data for this book is available
from the Library of Congress

Blackstone Publishing
31 Mistletoe Rd.
Ashland, OR 97520

www.BlackstonePublishing.com

To my mother:
If life is what you make it,
you've taught me how to make it beautiful.
My cup runneth over.

To my daughter:
You are and will forever be
my favorite-favorite . . .
and my why.
I am so glad you chose me.
Love you this much!

To Jacqueline:
You embodied the very essence of this book—
Strength, tenacity, undying love for your son,
and facing every challenge head-on.
Ain't that a mother?
You fought long and hard, prima.
Hasta la proxima vez, te quiero.

To Little Adiba:
We did it, baby girl.
We did it.
Step into the sunshine, boo.
You're safe.

TABLE OF CONTENTS

INTRODUCTION

I'm so glad you've decided to pick up this little ditty about some woman you may or may not know in real life! But my guess is that you *do* know this woman—you know me. Because in so many ways, I am you. I've had the thoughts we're not supposed to have as women and moms and daughters. I've done the things we're not supposed to do as women raised in the church, Black women, moms of daughters, women in general. And I've lived. The difference between you and I is that I just decided to tell the whole freakin' world about it. They didn't call me motormouth when I was a kid for nothing.

I've also experienced some very real shit in this lifetime, and before you swan dive into what at times may feel like a cesspool of grief, let me tell you a little bit about what you're about to embark upon. Feel free to grab some Kleenex for tears, an extra pair of underwear in case you pee your pants laughing, and a glass of wine just because. In *Ain't That A Mother*, you will come on a journey with me through the following life experiences:

Postpartum Depression
Miscarriage/grief
Emotional abuse

Self-worth/self-love issues
Poverty
Attempted suicide
Infidelity
Divorce
Sexual assault
Special needs parenting and all that comes with it

It's a lot, I know. But if you can go down this road with me, I can promise you there's not an alligator waiting to eat you at the end. That's what I call the poor outcome I experience when I go down a road I knew I had no business going down. We're just going to take a sometimes less than stellar jaunt through my life. There will be moments that feel like the most delicious glass of Veuve Clicquot, and times that feel like a cocktail made up of nothing but Colt 45, Old English, and Mad Dog 2020. But however it feels, let's raise a glass to going down the road, on the journey to ourselves.

PS—There will also be a healthy dose of f-bombs, a couple of MFers, and definitely a handful of GDs. What can I say? I'm a potty mouth and writing this book felt more like talking to my girlfriends than writing a good chunk of my life story. So, think of it more like we're best buds swapping stories over wings and wine. Basically, we go together now.

PPS—Also, some names have been changed to protect identities.

Love you, byeeeeeeeee!

THE BIG BANG

"Foundation."

Her chubby five-year-old fingers could barely fit around the bottle cap, but she worked every little ounce of muscle she had as she handed me my bottle of mocha-hued Cover Girl foundation. I dabbed it into place, watching my daughter watch me through the large vanity mirror. It reminded me of when I was a little, in any number of the New York City apartments Mom and I lived in, sitting on the lid of the toilet, watching my mom put her makeup on. I would look at my mom and often wonder how someone got to be so pretty. Long, thick, wavy black hair (that always seemed to feather itself) framed her face, with skin that was the same color as the *café con leche* she would drink every morning, little beauty marks dotting her cheeks, and cheekbones that could cut glass. She grew up on the tiny island of Vieques, known for being just off the coast of Puerto Rico, its bioluminescent bays that literally glow at night, *el coquí* (the cutest, tiniest "singing" frog that serves as Puerto Rico's "national animal"), *y las quenepas*—the sweetest, juiciest fleshiest little ball of fruit you will ever taste in your entire life. The sticky sweetness that runs down your chin and all the way up your arms to your elbows as you try to pry them out of their soft green skins will transport you to childhood joy. And yes, they do call Puerto Rico "La Isla Bonita," *pero* trust me, you'll go for the sandy beaches, but you'll stay for the *quenepas*.

The other thing about Puerto Rico, Vieques included, is that it is a heartbreakingly poor island. Now for those of you that don't know, there's poor, and then there's po'. If you're poor, you might occasionally use food stamps, or have to wear hand-me-downs instead of the latest trends. Maybe you live in the nicest apartment complex in the shadiest part of town; but if you're *po'*, honey, that's a whole different story. Your clothes are handmade by your grandmother using hand-drawn brown paper bag patterns. You trade beans for live chickens with your neighbor and you live in a two-room shack. Then you "upgrade" to an abandoned *panaderia* that has been empty for years, and then upgrade again when your grandparents start building a cinder block house where the shack used to be. You eventually have a four-bedroom house that houses ten of your cousins that now live with you *and* your grandparents, and everyone is sharing a bed, and a room.

My mom was po'.

She was also a self-described tomboy—a girl who liked climbing mango trees and sitting on the rooftop with her boy cousins. She also said she was skinny as a toothpick, bucktoothed, and awkward. I couldn't picture that as I watched her meticulously apply mascara to her already luscious lashes. Inner corner to outer corner, top to bottom, every single lash was covered. A tomboy would not be that glamorous. She often described herself as ugly. I didn't see any of that when I watched her get ready in the morning. To me, this woman who put makeup on just to be in the house "because you never know who is going to stop by," was a beauty queen.

I wondered what Emory thought of me as she helped me get ready—my brown skin, the same color as a Hershey's Milk Chocolate bar, braids piled high on top of my head, and a gap between my two front teeth that she got a kick out of trying to put her index finger through.

"Concealer," I said, and she handed me the long tube of red lip gloss, smiling a big cheesy grin. My kid had jokes.

"You really think I'm going to put red lipstick under my eyes? Try again, homeslice." I took the red lipstick out of her chubby little kid fingers and wagged it at her, in a joking, scolding manner.

Laughing so hard her body shook, she found the tube of concealer and handed it to me. When Emory laughs her whole body laughs. She either leans way back or doubles over, shaking like a grandpa who has just told (what to him is) the joke of the century. Her shoulders bounce up and down, her eyes squint shut, and no sound comes out for about twenty seconds, and then BOOM—this sound reminiscent of Eddie Murphy in *Beverly Hills Cop*! It's pure gold, I tell you—pure gold.

We went through this routine of "doctor and assistant" until it was time for me to do my hair. But then she pointed to her lips and made a kissing sound.

"Babe, I already have my lipstick on."

She made the sound again and then pointed to the small container of red glitter sitting on my vanity. Of course she remembered the glitter—my kid loves any and everything that sparkles. How could she *not* remember the glitter?

"Oops! You're right! Okay—hook me up!"

This was her favorite part, and she squealed as I unscrewed the cap. I leaned toward her, and with as much concentration as she could muster, she took her tiny index finger, dipped it in the ultra-fine red glitter, and patted it on until my lips were fully covered.

When she was done, she sat back, looked at my face, and then made the American Sign Language sign for "beautiful." Before Em received her first communication device we had to find some way for her to talk to me, tell me what she wanted, what she needed, what she was thinking. So in addition to our gesticular communication, I also taught her some very simple sign language, and beautiful was one of the first signs she learned—because she needed to know that she was beautiful.

"Thank ya, babycakes! Now let's do my hair! Can you get out my bobby pins and that bright pink flower in the drawer?"

Up until this point my braids had been sitting in a high bun on top of my head, and when I let them down, Emory instinctively put her hands in them to untangle them. She was *obsessed* with hair. My hair, my mom's hair, she'd even reach out and put her hands in some white lady's hair once when we were out at Target.

Awkward? Yes.

Did I stop her? Meh—not so much. We'll call it payback for all the white ladies who just "had to touch my hair" when I was a kid. And for that white lady who, just last week while I was shopping in Target, tried to touch my afro because it "looked so soft." Luckily, I have excellent bob-and-weave skills, so she missed her opportunity.[1]

Emory watched patiently as I twisted my braids into vintage victory rolls on top of my head, placing a bobby pin every few inches until the entire thing was secure.

"Flower." I held out my hand for her to give it to me, but she pulled her hand back and said "NO!" and pointed to herself.

"Honey, you can't wear the flower—I need it for *my* hair."

Again, she greeted me with a firm "NO!" and then pointed to me, and then to her own hair.

"Oh! You want to put the flower in my hair for me?"

"YEAH!"

Okay. Let me just pause here for a second. It is one thing to let your child with poor muscle tone and low fine motor skills put glitter on your lips. It is something else altogether to let that same child place a flower clip into your hair, which is attached to your tender-headed scalp. This child was likely to snatch me bald with one ill-timed, uncontrollable move. I mean, it's not like the beauty industrial complex designs hair accessories with disabled people in mind[2]. So yeah, I needed a minute

---

1. Side note to white ladies reading this: SOLANGE LITERALLY TOLD YOU—DON'T TOUCH MY HAIR. She wasn't kidding. It's the twenty-first century. Act like you know.
2. Yes, I'm looking at YOU, Goody, Conair, and Scünci.

to think about this request. I looked at this girl who loved me and wanted nothing more than to place this damn flower in my hair. My scalp was already twitching but alas, I gave in.

"Okay, you can do it. BUT! You must place it right where I'm pointing, and let the clip go when I say, 'let go.' Deal?"

"Yeah!"

I took the flower from her hand to pinch open the clip, and then replaced my fingers over hers in order to keep the clip open. I watched her in the mirror as she slowly and methodically placed the flower about two inches below where I was pointing to. She sat back and looked at her handiwork, beaming with pride, and I knew that that flower was staying right where it was. My scalp was intact, and my baby had placed the flower. We were good.

And then my mom walked in.

Now, y'all. I love my mama. I do. This woman has at times worked three jobs, just to put food on the table. She has the most random, inexplicable, ill-timed sense of humor, and is as cynical about love and relationships as the day is long. But she is my rock and I love her. However, at the time, she was also a minister. An opinionated minister[3], who had thoughts and ideas about—oh, so many things. She had raised me with the belief that it's not ladylike to curse in public, so I definitely was not surprised she had gone this route. If there was a rule book about proper "ladylike" decorum, she was all about it. I held my breath as she walked in and surveyed the scene. Me and Emory seated at the vanity, me in my leopard print robe, Em in a T-shirt and pull-up, my bra and panties on the bed, with my fishnet thigh-highs strewn nearby, and my fiancé reading a book on the other side of the bed.

"Hi! Hi! Hi! Hi!" Emory screamed excitedly. If she was ever a mama's girl, you wouldn't know it when my mom walked in. At that very moment me and my red glitter lip glory ceased to exist.

"Hi, mama! How are youuu? Are you helping mom dooo . . . ummm . . ."—turning to me—"um . . . is she helping you get ready?"

---

3. Oxymoron, anyone?

"Yep! She is!"

My mom turned her attention to me. "Ay, Adiba! Really? Do you think that's wise? I mean—*¡las preguntas!*"

One thing you should know about my mom: when she's annoyed with me, she'll switch to Spanish in a heartbeat. I used to think it was just her thing, but I do it now too.

"Ma—if she has questions, *voy a contestar las preguntas.*"

"But Adiba—*tan joven!*"

"Yeah, Ma . . . she's young. And if my memory serves me correctly I was the same age when you told me all about how babies were made and pulled out a *Playboy* magazine to show me what a penis looked like, so don't go getting all Virgen de Guadalupe on me now!"

I was dying of laughter—on the inside. My mom's face let me know that I might have tiptoed a little too far over the line.

"*Mira!* Watch ya mouth!"

"Yes, Ma. Anyway, what are you doing here? I told you I have a sitter coming."

I glanced over at Emory who was lost in la-la land, pushing her fingers through the holes of my fishnets.

"I'm going with you."

"Say what now?"

I just knew this woman was joking. She couldn't be serious. Even Em stopped mutilating my tights to stare at my mother in shock and awe.

"But why? Like . . . WHY? You don't need to be there. Seriously. Like, for real—don't come."

"*Mira* . . . I'm coming *y no me puedes parar.*"

"I can stop you if I go flatten your tires really quick!"

"It won't matter. I'm riding with you!"

Then this woman, my mother, gave me that sweet Latin mother smile that is code for "try to stop me and I'll break your face." I was stuck. There was literally no way out of it—she was going to see what she saw and think whatever she was going to think.

"Fine. But sit far away—where I can't see you."

"Girl, stop worrying about me and get dressed—we're gonna be late!"

Eyes rolling so far back in my head I saw stars, I slid my long, thick brown legs into my thigh highs one at a time, thanking God on high for the genius who thought to rubberize the tops of thigh-high hosiery. Next came my high-waisted panties with the word "BANG" bedazzled across the ass. Then the bra, my polka-dot dress, black pumps with rhinestones down the heel, and my black vintage handbag.

Emory watched me as I did a once-over in the mirror. Her legs crossed at the knee like a little lady, only to display the scar that ran the length of her left thigh. She'd had surgery when she was two years old to correct her hip joint which was 80 percent displaced. With her legs crossed you couldn't tell that her left leg was almost an inch shorter than her right leg. Her right arm rested on the armrest of her wheelchair, while her much smaller left arm sat limply at her side, her hand flexing and relaxing at its own whim—evidence that she was born with Erb's palsy (a brachial plexus injury to her left shoulder and arm). But her eyes—they danced and lit up like a baby discovering colors for the first time, as I crossed the room and twirled in front of her. My skirt whirled and billowed out and she laughed.

"How do I look?" I asked her.

Again, she made the sign for "beautiful" and grinned ear to ear.

She thought I was beautiful.

I knew she was beautiful.

I bent down to rub noses with her and then realized I'd forgotten something. I ran into the kitchen with my mom pushing Emory in her wheelchair behind me. I quickly flung open the refrigerator to grab a cucumber, a banana, an eggplant, and a carrot, and then snatched open a kitchen drawer to grab my whisk. All the while Emory was cracking up—she knew what was up. My mom on the other hand, not so much.

"What in God's good name are you—"

"Aht! No questions. You decided to tag along. Fine. But you don't get to ask questions!"

My mom had absolutely no idea what she was getting herself into.

Honestly, neither did I. But it was too late to turn back now. I was bent over rubbing noses with Emory (our goodbye routine) just as the sitter walked in.

"Oooooh! Okay! I see you! Hot date?"

I looked at Em and winked as I made my way out the door.

"Yeah—somethin' like that."

*

Two hours later, I was standing backstage angry whispering to no one.

"Goddamn it. This woman doesn't listen! I told her to sit where I couldn't see her—and there she is! Right. Fucking. THERE."

I wanted to vomit. I was nervous. And I had to pee. And I was hot. Why the fuck was I so hot all of a sudden?

And then I heard it. There was no turning back. Shit, shit, shit, shit, shit.

"Please welcome to the stage, about to pop her burlesque cherry, our resident nutty, naughty housewife—The BIG. Bang. *McGillicuddy*!"

The crowd cheered, the house lights went down, and Etta James' "I Just Wanna Make Love to You" poured out of the speakers. I broke through the curtains in full BIG Bang mode and began my routine, making sure *not* to make eye contact with my mother who had rebelliously perched herself front and center—right next to my fiancé. I peeled and deep-throated my banana to the noise of a roaring crowd. Do y'all understand how difficult it is to mimic fellatio on stage when your fiancé and mother are seated side-by-side, ten feet in front of you? I grinded on a whisk and bared my ample bosom, stretch-marked belly, and cellulite-dotted thighs to a packed house. I shimmied, bumped, and grinded my way all over that stage, and the crowd loved every second of it. As Etta sang her last note, I grabbed the offending banana, took a bite, gave the audience a wink, and sashayed my ass off that stage. And then straight up the back stairs, out the back door, and into the bar parking lot, where I stood in nothing but pasties and panties, puking up that same damn banana. One of the local burlesque legends, who had been outside getting some air, held my hair back and gave me water to wash my mouth out with. She regaled me with stories about her debut, and how nobody had ever puked during their debut. "Maybe you're starting a new tradition," she said, holding her infamous Hula-Hoop at her hip. Olivia Twisted, with her bright blue eyes and platinum blond hair piled high on her head, stared at me with her giant grin. I think she was simultaneously proud and concerned because, I mean, who deep throats a banana on stage only to puke it up three minutes later? When I finally came up for air, my mother was standing right in front of me, in that dark parking lot. It was just me, Mom, and Olivia. And then in the blink of an eye, it was just me and Mom. Olivia ducked out with a quickness. *Dammit!* I thought to myself. I was stuck.

"Mom?"

Silence.

Shit. Anyone with a Latin mom knows that silence is never a good thing. You'd rather be dodging rogue *chanclas*[4] than have your mother say nothing at all. She moved toward me and I instinctively stepped back, *porque tú sabes que* if your mom is quiet and moving toward you, it is highly likely that you're about to catch a quick slap upside your head.

"*Me cago en na, mujer!*"[5] Literal translation: I shit on nothing. "Come here!"

And with that she gave me the biggest, most enveloping hug I think she'd ever given me. I stood there, a chunk of banana in the corner of my mouth, not moving, barely breathing, and wondering who this woman was.

"I'm so proud of you!" she whispered into my ear.

I let out a sigh of relief. "Ma, I felt so liberated and exhilarated on that stage—but also sexy, and powerful, and fierce. I felt like nobody could tell me a godda—I mean got-dang thing! It was *so real.*"

---

4. Flying flip-flops that Latin mothers love to utilize in their so-called discipline techniques

5. Literally the dumbest Puerto Rican curse phrase in existence. Why we use it, I don't know, but walk into any Puerto Rican household and you'll hear somebody hollerin' it. I promise you.

"Yeah . . . I get it now . . . This burlesque thing is bigger than you. It's not even really *about* you, is it?" I shook my head. She was right. It wasn't about me at all. It was about all the women that looked like me—the dark-skinned women, the fat women, the women with gaps in their teeth, the women with naturally kinky hair—the women society and the media and every TV show and movie in existence had turned into a running punch line—these women needed to see themselves in that space. It was about my daughter seeing her mother, who didn't look like the "beautiful women" she saw on TV, claim and own her beauty and her sexiness for herself, regardless of what the world had to say about it. It was about her knowing intrinsically, because not only had I talked the talk but was now walking the walk, that our bodies are beautiful and perfect and lovely just as they are—fat, brown, disabled—however we present in this world. It was about her knowing *that* specifically.

Then she looked me dead in the eye. "What I don't get is why the produce? I mean, did you have to do that with the banana?"

"That wasn't me, Ma. That was Bang. That girl is a freak!"

*

That night after my fiancé and I got home and relieved the babysitter, I snuck into Emory's room to watch her sleep like I did every night. She was the most beautiful thing I'd ever seen, and I questioned God, like I did every night, as to how and why he saw fit to bless me with such an amazing child. Her body betrayed her daily. Her body movements are often uncontrollable, so there is always a twitch of some sort happening. Her left leg is shorter than her right, her left tibia is twisted, and her right foot supinates, so ankle-foot orthotics are a must in order to keep her feet in alignment, and her left orthotic always comes with a lift to make up for the length discrepancy. Her left arm, from shoulder to fingertip, is severely underdeveloped, is limited in mobility, and finger dexterity seems like it takes the concentration of a thousand MENSA members. Her heart, however, overcompensated with enough love to float a hot air balloon. This child, my Emory, was, and is, joy personified. I wondered if she knew that *she* was the "why" behind burlesque, that this was the last bastion of my self-love/body love journey. Allowing others to see my body as it was, in full flesh, without me sucking in (which I had been accustomed to doing 24-7 since my ballet/cheerleading/sorority days), and with all my jiggly parts live and in action was . . . a lot. It meant finally and authentically accepting all the parts of my physical self that society told me I should hate. Up to that point I had talked a good talk. Now, for the sake of my child, and maybe (perhaps, OKAY, definitely) for the child still residing in me, I had to walk the walk. And it felt like instinctively, she knew this. Like instinctively she understood that my baring all, without fear and without shame, was so that I could empower her to embrace her own body, without fear and without shame.

I kissed her on her forehead, slinked back out of her room, and tiptoed to my room, not wanting my heels to make any noise on the floor. I plopped myself down in front of my vanity and began the undoing of The BIG Bang McGillicuddy. Eyelashes off. Flower out. All fiftyleven bobby pins removed from my hair. Glitter lips wiped away. And finally, the pasties. As I peeled the pink diamond ring pasties off my breasts and tossed them onto the vanity, I thought about the night that had just ensued. Had I really just deep-throated a banana, done a little bit of a bump-and-grind on a kitchen whisk, and flashed my ass in a pair of see-through panties with the word "BANG" emblazoned across it in rhinestones, in front of a roaring crowd? I sure as fuck did, and it was hands down the best night of my entire life. I did that shit. Jesus Christ himself couldn't tell me *nothin'*! I stared at everything laid out before me, thought back to the roaring crowd and my daughter asleep in her bed, my mother's words, and I knew.

She was my why, and she was worth every second of it—banana puke and all. And I mean honestly, if I wasn't going to be the one telling my daughter to go out there and own her entire self for herself, who was? My mom?

Tuh. That lady had her own stories to tell.

THE FERRIS WHEEL
OF INFIDELITY

"I don't tell my story."
"Why?"
(pause)
"Because it's already over."
—a conversation between my mother and I

There are these things that are silently whispered about within Black and Afro-Latin communities called "generational curses." Some Puerto Ricans call it *"el fufu."* Things that take place over and over again, generation after generation. Ghosts from your grandmother's past, and her grandmother's past, and so on and so forth—all carrying the remnants of poor decisions that were oftentimes heaped upon them, (without permission), like the lasso of an ill-fated life. They couldn't escape it if they tried, and that inability to escape changed everything until it made its way to you. Maybe you've noticed these remnants in your own family? Do you and all your aunties date the same kind of man? Do all the firstborn sons go to jail at some point in their life? Is domestic violence "a thing"? If so—welcome to the club, but let's *not* stay a while, mmkay?

As a young child, I was always in "grown folks' business" and so I heard about these curses. I knew that my mother's father cheated on his wife with my nana, and that's how my mom got here. I knew that my father's father had cheated on *his* wife with my grandmother, and that's how *he* got here. And all three women, my mother and both grandmothers, for one reason or another, ended up being a single parent. Whether by continued infidelity, death, or survival, *el fufu* continued.

Now, if I wanted to use my social work knowledge and apply empirical data, I would tell you that families of color are statistically more likely to be led by single parents. I would tell you that according to the Casey Foundation[6], African American families have the highest number of single-parent households, holding the reins at 65 percent. And I would tell you that this, in and of itself, is its own unique kind of generational curse, stemming from the days of slavery when the men of the family were routinely separated from their families, and either sold or killed. And I could tell you that that absence of the Black father in the home was strategic and systematic, and that so many of us Black women are unknowingly playing our role in a curse that had absolutely nothing and everything to do with us.

And after all of that, I could tell you that, armed with all of that research and knowledge, I simply did not want to be another statistic.

But you're not here to read stats. We're talking about generational curses.

When I was one and a half, my mother, like her mother had done twenty years before, found herself completely swept off her feet by a man. By the time I was two, we were living with Johnny[7], a mailman, who already had a wife and daughter in Harlem, which he had conveniently forgotten to mention.

But in my two-year-old mind, Johnny was the bee's knees. He was funny and silly, and all the things television tells you a Daddy is supposed to be. He played with my hot wheels cars with me and bought me my most prized possession—a black T-top Trans Am that when you pulled it back until it clicked and then let it go, it would take off zooming through the house. When in the city, he would put

6. Stats taken from the Anne E. Casey Foundation KidsCount Data Center, years 2008–2017

7. Name changed to protect his identity, though honestly, this asshole deserves zero protection from whatever the universe throws at him

me atop his shoulders and carry me around, like a queen looking out over her land and royal subjects. He bought me my first pet, and when my mom accidentally killed it[8], he bought me a replacement. He took me to baseball games almost every weekend, teaching me everything about the game. Under his tutelage I grew to love Gary Carter and Mookie Wilson and Doc Gooden, Darryl Strawberry and Keith Hernandez—only the greatest Mets players to ever play the game. He used to let me count the gray hairs in his head. He was my dad, and I loved him more than I loved anything at that time— maybe even my own mom.

When I was five years old, Johnny moved us to a huge house in Queens Village, New York City. Our family rented the top two floors, and for the first time in my life, I had my own room. I covered the pale yellow walls with posters of Menudo and Michael Jackson. I had a record player that spun everything from MJ's *Thriller* album to Alvin and the Chipmunks' Christmas album and my personal favorite, Disney's *Alice In Wonderland*. I even had my own television! I was living the dream of a kid just being a kid.

Until I wasn't.

When I was six Johnny and my mother came to pick me up from my paternal grandmother's house. I was so excited to see them that, in front of my biological father, Brian, I ran up to Johnny with an enthusiastic "Daddy!"

Before I realized my mistake, Brian looked at me, my mother, and then Johnny with a look he typically reserved for *only* my mother—a sour mix of disdain and disgust. And then the yelling ensued. Johnny and my father were in each other's face, with Johnny standing just a few inches taller than my father. They yelled and nose-to-nose'd each other until my grandmother got them to knock it off.

We left in a hurry, with my mother apologizing to my grandmother, and my grandmother telling my mother not to bring Johnny

---

8. A parakeet named Tommy that my mother accidentally smooshed between the bathroom door and the radiator.

back to her house. That afternoon my mother and Johnny took me to Flushing Meadow Park, where we laughed and took "family pictures" in the grass under the Unisphere . . . but there was a shift. I felt it. The car ride home was too quiet.

Over the next two years I witnessed the demise of the childhood I had come to love. That fight was just the beginning. For reasons I may never know, Johnny, like my father, began to use cocaine, which then turned into crack. But *unlike* my father, he also turned to another woman. If you're keeping track, that makes three—his wife, my mother, and side chick #2. We moved from our two-story, beautifully furnished apartment in Queens Village into a room in my nana's crowded apartment in the Bronx projects, and later to a small, unfurnished two-bedroom apartment in Flushing. This apartment was directly across the street from Flushing Botanical Gardens, which fed into Flushing Meadow Park—the same place we'd taken those "family pictures" a couple of years earlier. We had no furniture because Johnny had put it all in storage, and then used the money my mother gave him to get it out of storage, to buy drugs. We had no food because Johnny lost his job. And eventually we had no Johnny because in the heat of an argument he picked up the one piece of furniture we did have, a chairless, marble-topped dining room table, and threw it at my mom.

I heard it before I saw it.

A week or so later, my mother and I moved into a room in a boarding house, and she didn't date anyone for a long time—four years to be exact. Not until we moved to Arizona.

Then there was Martin, Leroy, and Miguel—all married or engaged. Every. Last. One of them.

She would go quiet for days after the truth was revealed. With Martin it was about seven months after they started dating that the fiancée popped up. With Leroy she was about two and a half years in before she found out about the wife. That one was particularly gut-wrenching. She bumped into the both of them at the grocery store, and he acted as if she didn't exist. Looked right through her.

She stayed quiet for about two weeks with that one. And Miguel—well, I rallied against him from day one because she knew he was married going into it. But sometimes even a love that isn't yours feels good.

Each time, I watched my otherwise bright and vibrant mother, this woman who danced around the house, blasting Celia Cruz, Marc Anthony and Soul II Soul, go dark and sullen—retreat into herself to lick the wound, and be less than gracious, asking herself "Why me?" and "How could I not have known?"

I watched as time and time again my mother's heart was crushed by these men whom she loved, who didn't love her back. I couldn't understand how and why she kept falling for the same guy over and over again, and I vowed to never let that happen to me. I refused to suck in all of my power so that a man could wave his dick around and feel like hot shit. The curse of falling in love with married men would stop with me. And the curse of having children with married men and then raising them alone would also stop with me.

*

In August of 2008 I fell in love with Jeff. Jeff was divorced. In September of 2008 I got pregnant, and in November of 2009 I found out that, lo and behold, I had been riding in the front car of the family's Ferris wheel of infidelity. Yes, unbeknownst to me, I had met, fallen in what I *thought* was love, and had a baby with a married man. Cue the carnival music.

Now, I'm sure you're wondering exactly how I found out he was married.

At a funeral. I found out at a funeral. And not just *any* funeral. His beloved *grandmother's* funeral.

By their very nature, funerals are the worst. I've never been to one that wasn't dramatic in one way or another—and with good reason. I mean, someone's loved one is no longer on this earth. There should be wringing of hands and gnashing of teeth. Hell, maybe even a wig or two thrown! But unless you're in Tyler Perry's next Madea movie[9] there really shouldn't be any grand revelations that have the potential to completely upend an entire family. A funeral simply is not the place for that.

Except that it was. At Jeff's grandmother's funeral, Jeff's father, Peter, a large, imposing Black man—standing over six feet tall (or at least that's how big he seemed to me), with mostly gray hair and a mustache, felt it was the perfect time and place to make me aware of the fact that Jeff, his son, who I had been dating for almost two years, who I had had a baby with six months prior, was in fact, married. Mind you, I'd never met this man before, but this was the time and place that he thought it was most appropriate to deliver this hot shit sandwich of news.

Now, before we get into what I like to refer to as "the tapioca pudding" moment of my life (unexpected, difficult to swallow, and on some level, you know that nothing in your pudding cup is naturally occurring in nature), I need to give you some history. When I met Jeff, he told me that he had been divorced for the past two years, that he had two kids and his own apartment. I felt reassured by these facts. No risk of the curse here! So, one thing led to another, I put on Jill Scott, Plan B didn't work, and next thing you know I was pregnant. A few short months later he moved in with me, his kids began to spend three to four nights a week with us, and every few months, just before lights out I'd go into his son's room and sit next to him on the bed, doing my best to attempt to have a chat. I'd try to talk about the day with him, ask him how he was feeling—anything. I was trying to connect in any way I could. We'd stare at the navy blue painted walls (never at each other), him picking at the blanket, me chewing the inside of my lip, and inevitably I would end up having the following conversation with Jeff's eleven-year-old son:

"Hey, Frankie! Are you ready for bed?"

9. Upon the writing of this chapter, I discovered that Tyler Perry had *A Madea Family Funeral* coming out in 2019. While completely coincidental, I can't help but wonder if it even compares to my real-life dramedy.

"I guess," Frankie said, looking forlorn, his feet dangling over the side of his bed, gaze fixed on the navy blue wall across from him. His shoulders were rounded and slumped, as if he carried the weight of ten thousand worlds on them, and I noticed that the skin on the sides of his thumbs was red and irritated—like he'd been picking at it.

"What's wrong?"

"It's not fair that my parents aren't together anymore. I mean . . . I'm not trying to be mean or anything . . . but it's your fault," he said.

"What? Frankie. I know divorce is hard. I know it is. Especially when you're young, but I had nothing to do with your parents' divorce. They were divorced long before I came into the picture. I didn't even know your dad in 2006," I replied.

"But they're not divorced."

"Frankie, honey . . . they are. I know it's hard to accept, and I promise you it will get easier as time goes on. I promise you."

"No. Listen to me. They're. Not. Divorced. And you're the reason they can't be together."

He said this without pause and without hesitation. I didn't hear a trace of anger in his voice, a catch in his throat—nothing. It was just a simple, matter-of-fact statement—as if he was telling me we were out of cheese. I paused before responding because (a) that was an odd way to say something so incendiary; and (b) *why* would he say something so incendiary? I mean, that's a pretty big rock to lob into someone's pool—the ripple effect could do major damage to those nearby. I decided he was just an angry child, and let his statement lie right there in the middle of the room. Finally, I spoke.

"Oh, babe," I sighed. "I don't know what else to tell you other than I am not. I didn't even know your dad in 2006. I met him over the summer (2008). Try and get some rest. Good night."

And with that, I would turn out the lights, close the door, and give Jeff the play-by-play of our conversation. He didn't even flinch when he informed me they'd taken the divorce pretty hard.

Y'all.

I'd been gaslighting a kid!

Now fast forward about fifteen months after meeting Jeff, and maybe one month after yet *another* "it's your fault, no it's not" conversation with his children, and I found myself sitting in his deceased grandmother's home. We had put her in the ground no more than two hours beforehand, and Jeff had left me alone with his father and Emory, so naturally this was the perfect time to flip my WHOLE LIFE upside down. Naturally.[10]

Peter sat in the armchair across from me, perched on the edge (almost like a cat waiting to pounce), watching me pat Emory's back as she fell asleep on the couch. Continuing to stare at her, never at me, he spoke out into the air, to me.

"She's a beautiful girl."

His deep voice in the otherwise quiet house startled me. The television was on, but the volume was fairly low. I shot my head up to look at him, and he chuckled and held a hand up, as if to apologize for startling me. I made eye contact with him and smiled. It was the first time we'd ever been alone in a room together, and the first time we really ever made (and held) eye contact. After a few seconds it made me uncomfortable and I cleared my throat, returned my gaze to Emory, and managed to croak-whisper out a response.

"She really is, thank you," I replied.

"You know, I don't hate you," Peter said. He was still staring at me and speaking in as much of a hushed tone as a man with a booming voice can muster.

I laughed nervously. "Oh! Um, I didn't think you did, but that's good to know."

"I just wish Jeff would do things the right way."

"What do you mean?" I said, still patting Emory's back.

"Well, I just wish that he had gotten his divorce before you got pregnant," Peter said.

Say what now? I thought to myself.

---

10. Did I mention this was my FIRST TIME meeting him? Yeah, also THAT PART.

"He did get his divorce! They've been divorced since 2006."

"Uh, no, ma'am."

"Uh, yes sir. Jeff told me that he and Bunny[11] got divorced in 2006."

"No, ma'am. They did not get divo—"

Pause.

I was not about to let this man whom I'd *just* met, at a funeral no less, finish his fucked up (albeit true) sentence. No sir. He didn't get to blow up my life just because he was sad. That being said, this is the tapioca I mentioned earlier—unexpected, indigestible, and not even *close* to natural. I wanted to vomit.

Continue.

"And how do you know this?" I interrupted, sounding annoyed.

"Because my wife, Jeff's stepmother, represented Bunny in the divorce, and the day they were supposed to finalize everything, Jeff showed up and started crying, begging and pleading with her not to go through with it. Saying that he loved her and the kids and didn't want to tear the family apart. So, she didn't sign. They didn't finalize. They never divorced. My wife was very upset. Anyway, *they're still married.*"

What he said next sounded like some Rod Serling, *Twilight Zone* type shit in my ears.

"*We thought you knew.*"

You know that scene in *Get Out* where Daniel Kaluuya is sitting in the armchair and everything goes silent, the camera zooms in on his face and he has just one solitary tear rolling down his cheek, right before he enters the Sunken Place? Yeah. That was me—minus the tear because I was not about to give this man the satisfaction. But I *was* descending, rather quickly, into what felt like a limitless, soundless, tapioca-filled void. By this time, I had stopped patting Emory's back, as she had fallen asleep to this man's fucked up version of a bedtime

---

11. So, her name isn't really "Bunny" . . . but really you could insert any fruit or cuddly animal name here and it would work.

story, and I sat there bewildered. In my head, I flipped over the glass coffee table in front of me, put my foot through the television screen, and punched Jeff's dad square in his lie-tellin' mouth. But in reality:

"Can you excuse me, please? I need to make a phone call," I said.

I didn't even wait for his response. I just got up and left the room, leaving Emory sleeping under the watchful eye of the man who didn't hate me, but was quite comfortable blowing my world ALL the way up. I walked into Jeff's grandmother's parlor, surrounded by pictures of her and her late husband (the irony, I know), and called my best friend, Faith, in Scottsdale.

"Hello!"

"Hey."

"What's wrong?"

"Jeff's married."

"I'm sorry. It sounded like you just said Jeff's MARRIED."

"I did. JEFF'S MARRIED."

"*What?*"

"Yeah."

"Motherfucker."

"Mother. Fucker."

*

To say I was devastated is an understatement. In my head I was Angela Bassett lighting aaall his shit on fire and daring him to say something. I mean—WTF? Who does that? And why had Jeff done it to *me*? In reality, I was trying to rationalize staying with a married man so that at least the generational curse of single parenting might finally end with me:

"I love him, and he loves Emory. If I give him time, he can get a divorce, and then we can be a happy family."

"Everyone makes mistakes—I can't expect him to be perfect. And forgiveness is a thing. It could actually bring us closer together."

"He may still be married to her, but he's been with me for the last two years. Obviously, he loves *me*. The divorce will just be a formality."

Y'all.

This is not the time to "Girl!" me. There are things we do in life that are based on our personal history, and there are things we do in life that are based on our desires for the future. And I couldn't see a future where I was a single parent, but I also couldn't see a future as someone's side chick. I couldn't see myself struggling through life the way my mother had. I didn't want food stamps, three jobs, living with family members, and eternal heartbreak. For the most part, I'd done things the "right" way. I went to college, got the degree, even graduated top of my class! This wasn't supposed to be *my* lot in life. Society dictates that when you do things the right way you get the big house, nice car, loving husband, 2.5 kids, and a Golden Retriever named Fred. In hindsight, that is all such an elitist way of thinking. I can recognize and admit that now. But at the time, no. This wasn't supposed to be happening to me. This was not supposed to be my life. That being said, it clearly was. My fancy four-year degree and cum laude status guaranteed me nothing but a piece of paper. It offered shelter from nothing. Not even from the hatred of children whose lives I was tearing apart. I now understood why his kids kept telling me it was my fault, and I understood why the first time I met Bunny, she tried to kick my ass when I was five months pregnant and telling her not to curse in front of the kids,[12]. I understood why she all but jumped over the hood of her car to get to me, and why Jeff had to hold her back to keep her from ripping me limb from limb. I understood the fire in her face, the rage in her soul, the deep, deep anguish in her heart. I would imagine that when you see your husband (the man you've been with since your early twenties, made two children with, and endured all of his bullshit and abuse) make a whole new family with another woman, and *that* woman tries to tell you how to behave in front of your own children—I would imagine that a proper ass whooping is justified. Y'all, I had it coming and I didn't even know it. But now, I understood.

---

12.   Side note: If you are carrying the child of someone's husband, don't ever, ever, ever, ever, EVER fix your mouth to tell that woman how to raise HER children. You *might* get body slammed. And while I don't condone violence . . . I *will* side-eye you.

I also understood that I now had a decision to make. Do I stay or do I go? If I go there will be trouble, and if I stay it will be double. Shout out to The Clash.

If I stayed, I was knowingly making a decision to stay with a married man and live a lie, *but* staying also allowed my daughter to be raised with her father in the home—something I never had. If I told him to leave I risked getting into a huge fight with him in front of my daughter (and his children) and being a single parent, but ultimately being able to tell my daughter (one day) that her mother knew she deserved more, refused to settle for less, and stayed true to her heart ultimately doing the right thing.

But what *was* the right thing?

Was it right to tear my daughter away from her father because he lied? I mean, I could leave him, but they could still have a relationship, right? Right? I mean, I'm a smart woman and I am of the mindset that when it comes to ending relationships when children are involved, it is imperative that the children feel the least effects of the separation, meaning *their* relationship with the other person should not change. But what if your entire relationship with that person was based on a lie? Can you trust that *your child's relationship with them* will be based on truth, love, and honesty? Can you trust that when your child asks "Daddy, why are you and mommy not together anymore?" that he will answer honestly? Or would I be reduced to the bitch who left because I was mad? I knew Jeff adored Emory, but did he love her enough to tell her the truth? Conversely, was it right to stay with Jeff, allow him to correct his wrong, and raise my daughter in a home with both parents?

I was at a crossroads.

I confronted Jeff, and while he initially denied it (numerous times), he finally came clean. Things weren't okay. I wasn't okay. But in the end, single parent guilt won out, my daughter's happiness was more important than anyone else's—mine, Bunny's, even Jeff's other children. Like I said earlier, there are things we do in life that are based on our personal history, and there are things we do in life that are based on our desires for the future.

*

I had PROMISED myself that the generational curses would end with me, but sometimes the history you're born into and the history you make turn out to be the same goddamn thing. And that shit bites like a motherfucker.

What I'm saying is that, in hindsight, I think I knew. In the deepest part of my gut, I knew that either he wasn't divorced or that he was in a relationship. *Something* was up. I didn't trust that voice that kept saying "Girl, he does NOT make four thousand dollars a week *and* drive a broke-down hooptie. What else is he lying about?" Or the voice that said, "He's divorced . . . but you can't go upstairs to his apartment because 'it's messy'? Really? GIRL." But like so many of us, in our desperate quest to be loved, feel loved, and make love, I ignored the voice in my head telling me to run in the opposite direction, and ended up running straight into the lion's den.

Why didn't I trust my gut? What the fuck had I been looking for?

Well, I suppose the same thing I think my mother, and her mother, and my father's mother were all looking for. The same thing that caused us to make irresponsible decisions, ensuring that the Manigault-Rosario curse lived on.

I think we were all looking for a deep, abiding, unyielding love for ourselves.

You see, I don't think any of the women running through my veins ever truly loved themselves. I'm sure they thought (and respectively, think) they did, but they didn't. Not in a genuine, authentic way. Not in a way that scoffs at the idea of "needing a man," and only takes one because she wants one. Not in a way that seared the concept "I am worthy of more" or "I am enough" into their brains. And certainly not in a way that ever allowed them to look into a mirror and see the beauty they birthed, the beauty in the resilience of their souls, despite their struggles. The beauty lying deep in their bones, in the marrow, in the double helix of every cell in their body—because those cells were transformed by the trauma heaped upon them without permission when they were busy looking for love, or simply trying to survive. And those trauma-infused cells came together to birth me. And then I added some of my own trauma to the DNA sequence and birthed a girl-child of my own. The weight of this is not lost on me.

And if I can help it, my daughter won't ever know such a curse even exists. She will not know that there is a Ferris wheel of lies and deception holding a seat with her name etched in gold because I am filling her up. I am smothering her with physical love and affection, and filling her soul and heart with adoration and pride—none of which my mother or grandmothers had from their mothers. And to be honest, none that I had either. The women that came before me were taught to survive in a world that did not want them—whether due to slavery, civil rights, or infidelity—and they were imprinted with the notion that to love your child is to teach them how to survive. This is what my mother imprinted on me, and for what it's worth, they were not wrong in this imprinting. It was necessary for the time and circumstances.

I should say that to an extent, I am also imprinting "love is survival" into Emory because I mean, let's keep it real, this world is *still* not ready or even welcoming to disabled folks, and it's *still* trying to figure out what to do with and how to love Black women, so yes, as a parent I *do* have to impart survival as a form of love into my child. But I also have to temper it with food for her soul. For the women in my family, there was a deep chasm where physical touch and affection and adoration were supposed to be. So, with Emory, I smother her. I cover her face in kisses. I tell her every day how much I love her and how I think she is the most amazing human being I've ever known. I knee slap to an obnoxious degree at every single one of her jokes and act absolutely terrified when I push her wheelchair into a dark room and she hollers out "BOO!" as if to scare the ever-loving shit out of the person who brought her into that dark room in the first place. I gush over every science fair project and classroom presentation and allow her to call every damn person in my phone to tell them about her accomplishment because dammit, my baby is proud of herself and they're going to be proud too. I tell her every day, as she is being loaded onto the school bus, that she is smart and kind and that she has the power to determine what kind of day she is going to have based on the choices she makes. When she gets older I'll start doing some role-playing with her to help her learn to spot a lie. For her this is extra important. Someone will take one look at her wheelchair and communication device and assume she's a pushover. I want them to know, but more importantly, I want *her* to know that no, she is absolutely *not* a pushover. I want her to know that with just a few touches on her communication device she can tell homeboy or homegirl to "get to steppin'" and when they try to rebuff her directive she can follow it up with "I said what I said."

This is important. She, more than any of us, needs to know her own power, her own love, her own beauty.

So I do, and will do all of these things to fill her cup to the point of overflowing so that she will never go seeking approval or validation in the arms of a person who will not respect her enough to love her properly, love her wholly, love her and her alone. I do this so that the Ferris wheel might finally stop turning.

I do this because it wasn't done for me, and this curse has got to end.

MEETING JEFF

"Pam! Girl, what time is it?"

"'Bout time for us to close these damn doors and lock up this restaurant so we can go the hell home! Deebie, what you gettin' into tonight?"

"MY BED, girl. I am *exhausted!* Working that double today took everything I had—all I wanna do is crawl into bed and sleep," I wailed, as I wiped down yet another booth in my section of the only Ruby Tuesday's in Katy, Texas.

"Well think again, my love, 'cause brotha-man walking in is *yours.* I'm wiping down the bar."

I turned around half annoyed, half curious about who was walking in because the lilt in Pam's voice was a little higher than usual. At this point in our lives, we only got excited for two reasons: big dollars or big D. I couldn't tell if either was true just looking at this man, but he *was* cute, and he *was* my type. As he passed through the double doors of the restaurant I noticed that though he wasn't super tall, he had this energy about him that made him seem like he was six feet two, when he was probably closer to five foot ten. It was like his presence entered the room before he did. My girlfriend calls that Big Dick Energy—and he had it (THE ENERGY! I had no idea what this man had in his pants). His skin was the color of the caramel candies my grandma kept in her crystal candy dish, and he had dark, piercing eyes that hid behind the longest, curliest eyelashes I had ever seen. I was trying to go about my business cleaning my booths but found myself distracted by his shiny bald head that reflected the lights in the restaurant, and his perfectly trimmed and lined up goatee. Yeah—this man was delicious. And as he and all his Big Dick Energy sauntered up to the bar I thought to myself, *Okay, I see you brotha-man. It's hella late and we're about to close, but* I. See. You.

"Are you guys closed?"

I glanced at Pam who could not be bothered, as she meticulously wiped down every wine glass on the bar.

"No," I answered. "Not yet. Sit wherever you like. I'll be over with a menu in just a moment."

Because karma's a bitch, this man sat right down at the far end of the bar. I had to laugh as Pam rolled her eyes at me as I cruised by her with a menu and a glass of water for our guest.

"Welcome to Ruby Tuesday's! Have you been here before?." I put on my "leave me a big tip since you're keeping me here past closing" voice.

"Nah, what's good?" he asked, looking right into my hot, and now blushing face.

I won't lie to you. I felt that look all up and through my thighs. It had been a hot minute since I'd even kissed a man, and this look was enough to make my nipples cut glass. I leaned in a little closer to, you know, show him the menu favorites.

"Well, everyone loves the shrimp, and this chicken dish is very popular, but the special today is the salmon."

Pam, never one to miss a beat, quipped, "Uh-huh. Fish is always popular. *Everyone* loves fish."

I shot her a look because I knew exactly what she was doing, and so did he. Before I could say a word, this man let out a laugh that echoed throughout the entire empty restaurant, and Pam said nothing as she continued to meticulously wipe down the already spotless wine glasses.

"Well, then that settles it. I'll have the salmon, with a side of rice pilaf and broccoli. And a side salad."

"Great. Can I interest you in a glass of wine to complement your meal?"

"What do you suggest?" he says, and once again, his eyes look straight into my soul. I stared right back, never losing eye contact as I rattled off the list of white wines.

"I'll take the Estancia."

"Okay. I'll be right back with that."

I wanted to walk away but my feet wouldn't move. It sounds ridiculous but it really was like one of those moments out of a Molly Ringwald movie. You know, where she's face to face with the hot guy and she's staring at him, nibbling on her bottom lip, and he's just staring back at her smirking, and the silence is finally broken when one of her witty, quirky friends comes along and says something to snap them out of the orgasm they're about to have from their intense eye-fucking session . . . well that was this and I was Molly and he was Jake and Pam was the witty friend who offered up this lovely gem:

"Am I pouring wine or are you two gonna keep staring at each other like prepubescent twelve-year-olds?"

I immediately abandoned my eyegasm and rushed around the bar to pour his wine. As I brushed past Pam to bring him his glass of Estancia I whispered, "Bitch, I can't stand you."

She lovingly whispered back, "Love you, boo!"

I placed his order and continued to clean the restaurant, coming back to him with his food, and to check on him. Make no doubt about it—this brotha had something to him. There was an air of confidence that was intriguing, but also slightly off-putting. But when you haven't been kissed in months, clean teeth can be intriguing. He told me he made anywhere from $2000 to $4000 a week selling furniture, (while I was barely able to scrape together my $1100 mortgage, $300 car payment, utilities, and food between my school social worker job and waitressing), was divorced, and had two children—a boy and a girl. He showed me pictures of his children from his previous marriage. His son was his doppelganger, and his daughter looked as sassy as the day is long—her squinty eyes and side smirk daring you to step to her just a little bit sideways so she could hit you with "Yo mama!" He assured me she was *every* bit that sassy.

"Do you have any children?" he asked.

Apparently a thirty-year-old woman with no children is a rarity. I can't lie. It's not that I didn't want them, but since I hadn't had any by then, I'd resolved that I probably wasn't going to have any, and was very okay with being everyone's favorite auntie.

"Honey, I'm a school social worker by day, and a waitress by night. When would I even find the time to get myself knocked up?"[13], I quipped.

"Oh, come on! There's always time for fun!"

"I don't know about all that, sir. But I do know there's always time to pay your bill," I said, as I slid his billfold across the bar to him.

"Oh, that's how you gonna do me?" he laughed.

"Um, I haven't done you yet, sir. When I do, you'll know. Now can you please pay your bill so we can go home?"

Y'all, I don't know what the hell had gotten into me! Who did I think I was *blatantly* flirting with this man—a customer no less—like this? Ha! Let me not lie. Y'all know exactly who I thought I was. I was a woman thinking about the possibility of getting *him* into *me*. If this man wanted to, he could report me to my boss for blatant sexual harassment, and I could lose my job, my house, my car—all of it— all behind some D. However, I had an instinctual feeling that was not going to happen, and I was right. He stared at me and I stared back. He let out a slow chuckle while opening the billfold.

"How do you pronounce your name? I see it here on the receipt."

"Ah-dee-bah."

"That's beautiful. What does it mean?"

---

13.   In hindsight, THIS is where I jinxed myself.

"Cultured. Writer. Poet. Gift of God."

"Interesting. Are you cultured?"

"I think so."

"Are you a writer?"

"No, but I am a poet."

"Nice. Are you a gift of God?"

"Time will tell."

He squinted his eyes at me, and I heard Pam let out a loud huff behind me. My girl was beyond ready to go home. He quickly placed his money in the billfold and handed it to me. Our fingers touched and I promise you I felt an ovary quiver. Who was this man? Why was I being so flirty? Why was my ovary having a seizure? WHAT WAS HAPPENING? I walked away to cash him out and I knew he was staring at my ass. Shoot, I would too. My booty is rotund. I slid it across the bar to him (the billfold, not my booty), thanked him for dining with us, and invited him to come back and see us again. As I walked around the bar and past him, he stopped me.

"Excuse me."

"Yes?"

"I never told you my name."

"I never asked."

"Touché. Well, it's Jeff."

"Nice to meet you, Jeff."

"Listen, here's my number. If you ever need a new bed . . . or anything . . . let me know. I'd be happy to show you around the floor."

"The floor? I thought you were trying to show me the bed?!"

He stared at me, quizzically.

"Oh. Wait. You mean the sales floor."

"Yeeaaah."

"Yep. Got it."

I took the torn piece of paper with his number on it and shoved it in my apron pocket. I was mortified. Had I *really* just assumed that this fine-ass man that I had *just* met was trying to talk me into his bed by using clever innuendos? Did I have no couth? No home training?

No good sense left in my body? And the wild thing about it all is that *this* mortified me, but I was balls to the wall when it came to letting him know that "when I did him, he'd know." *Aye Dios Mio, Adiba . . . you a hot-ass mess,* I thought to myself as I heard Jeff chuckling—again.

"You're funny."

"Yep, that's what the rumor is. Have a great night!"

And with that, I spun on my heels and hustled to the kitchen to drop his dishes off and save what was left of my dignity, though I was pretty sure I'd scraped it into the trash with what was left of his dinner. Pam came bounding in.

"Bitch, what was that?"

"What was what?"

"That! That 'that's what the rumor is' bullshit! Homeboy was trying to holler at you! Are you gonna call him?"

"Um, probably not. I dunno. Maybe? Probably not."

"Probably not, my ass. You betta call that brotha and let him knock the cobwebs off your coochie! You out here playin' keep away with the goodies and he's tryin' to play tag."

I cracked up. I could always rely on Pam to (a) tell it like it was, and (b) put her own "Pam spin" on it.

I looked at Pam and yawned. "Girl, let's go. It's late. And I'm tired."

"And . . . you gotta go wash your panties."

"I can't stand you, Pam."

*

When I took my apron off that night, something fell out of the pocket and landed under my bed. Too exhausted to get on my hands and knees and find out what it was, I washed my face and crawled into bed. I didn't give the end-of-night's events a second thought. However, the morning wanted to make sure I didn't forget. As I sat on my toilet the next morning, bleary-eyed and with screaming feet, I glanced at my bed as I peed and mapped out the day ahead. My eyes settled on a folded-up piece of paper resting on the carpet underneath it. It all came rushing back to me like a movie flashback scene. "Are you a gift of God? Time will tell. Oh! You mean the *sales* floor! You're funny! That's what the rumor is."

All of it. There it was, rushing right in like a storm I forgot was in the forecast. I wasn't prepared with Jeff the night before. I was embarrassed because that was definitely not the "ladylike behavior" my mother had drilled into me during my formative years, but my GOD was I giddy about flirting with a man and having him flirt back with me! It had been three months since my divorce but over a year since I'd been with a man. The mere possibility that there could even be the slightest inkling of sex made me wring out my panties. Don't judge. It could be you one day, sitting on the toilet regretting things you said the night before while staring at a phone number balled up on a piece of paper under your bed, as you silently contemplate the merits of casual sex.

Finished with my contemplation, I washed my hands (because I'm not a heathen), walked over to the side of my bed, and got down on all fours. I stared at the balled-up piece of paper and decided this would be a great way to test myself. I told myself if I was still thinking about Jeff in two weeks, I would fish the number out from under my bed and call him. If not, the paper would stay there and collect dust. I got dressed and went on about my day, not giving Jeff, nor the phone number, a second thought. And that continued for a whole 1.75 weeks—until I found myself in much the same situation as when I noticed it the first time. Sitting on the toilet in the morning after a particularly long shift at the restaurant, I turned my head and allowed my eyes to focus on something under the bed. And then there he was—right in the front of my mind like I'd just seen him the day before. Jeff.

Shit! Now I have to call him, I thought to myself. I tried to convince myself that I didn't really want to call him, but since I'd made a deal with myself, I had to honor it. Honestly, though, I *knew* I wanted to call him. I wanted the attention. I wanted to flirt and be flirted with. I wanted to talk to someone other than the kids at my school and the patrons in Ruby Tuesday's. And if I'm being honest with you (and myself), I wanted the D. There. I said it. I was horny as hell, my vibrators were more like light hummers because I'd worn the damn things out, and I desperately wanted someone to sweep out every last "coochie cobweb," as Pam so lovingly called them. So, I called him.

"Hello?"

"Hi! Is this Jeff?"

"Yeah, who's this?"

"Hi, Jeff, it's Adiba—the waitress from Ruby Tuesday's. You gave me your number a couple of weeks ago . . ."

"Ooooooh, yeah! Hey, how are you? I didn't think you were gonna call!"

"I'm good, thanks! Yeah, I've been busy . . . how've you been?"

"Good, good. Just working hard and making sales. And taking classes."

"Classes?"

"Oh, yeah. I didn't tell you—I'm also in culinary school."

"Oh, so you're cute *and* you can cook?" is what I said. What I *thought* was, *Oh my God, Adiba. You're doing it again. Just stop. Be cool, be cool.*

"Girl, I can *burn* in a kitchen!"

"Okay, okay, Mr. Chef! Well, when do I get to taste your cooking?" *Ugh, Adiiibaaaaaa . . . what are you doooiiing?*

"Well, hold up now. I don't cook for just anyone. I gotta see what you're about before I give you all this goodness!"

I felt my face flush with hotness.

"Okay, well, how do you plan to find out 'what I'm all about'?"

"Do you like Vietnamese food?"

"Never had it."

"Whaaaaaaaaaat? Well, that settles it then. Let's meet for an early dinner at the Vietnamese restaurant on Fry Road, around the corner from your restaurant. How does tomorrow sound?"

"Tomorrow sounds great."

"Great. Then I'll see you tomorrow!"

"See you tomorrow. Bye, Jeff."

"Bye, Adiba."

Now, I'd like to pause here for a moment. Remember a little while ago I told you I'd been officially divorced for only a few months, but hadn't been with a man since I'd left my ex-husband a year prior. Well, what I *didn't* tell you is that at no time during that year/year and a half that I was single did I invest in therapy of any sort. I just went on about life like I hadn't endured a very painful divorce and a painfully unhappy marriage. I took absolutely zero time to look at myself and examine how I contributed to the breakdown, what I could have done differently for myself and differently for the marriage, or even contemplated why I agreed to marry someone after dating long distance for a whole three months. Yep. You read that right. I accepted a marriage proposal after dating someone I only saw on weekends for three months. You can judge me for that. I judge me for that. That was probably one of the single dumbest things I've ever done in my entire life, and if you ask ex-husband number one, he'd probably agree. He should not have married me—neither of us were ready, and I may or may not have spent our wedding planning money (which was 90 percent his money) on bills and trying to pay off payday loans (Okay, I *totally* spent the money on covering up my own financial mismanagement). I was his third, but possibly his fourth wife. We were a walking cautionary tale and if we were a commercial, ten out of ten random people on the street would not recommend we marry each other. But, we did it. I did it. And when it was over, I just moved along, full of anger and hurt and rage—and yes, desperation. Should I have found myself a therapist? Hell yes I should have found myself a therapist! *Did* I find myself a therapist? No. No, I did not find myself a therapist. That's not a thing "we do"—or at least that's what I'd always believed, growing up Afro-Latin. You either pray it away, or you pray it away, make an offering to St. So and So, and then pray it away again. *¿Pero sabes que?* In hindsight, had I gone to a therapist I would have saved myself all of the heartache, hangovers, and bad sex that was waiting for me just around the bend—but I wouldn't be the woman writing this book now, sooo score one for doing bad all by myself!

But I digress.

Date day arrived and I danced around my bedroom as I slipped into my nonperiod panties. Jill Scott's smooth-as-good-lovin' voice poured out of the speakers and right into me, filling me with all the sex-goddess confidence you could shake a condom at. I had no intention of having sex with Jeff on our first date, but I did have every intention of making him *think* he would want to have sex with me. I wasn't overt with it—I wore a simple sundress and heels, but I walked into the restaurant with that "yeah you know you want this" swag. Y'all know what I'm talking about—when you *know* your lip gloss is poppin', you smell like white gardenias and dreams come true, *and* your typically unruly hair finally decides to get some act right in it! Friend, you couldn't tell me *nothin'* that day. I was feelin' myself.

And then I was feeling sick. Have you ever experienced that? You walk into the date feeling like "OH HELL YES!" and then take one look at your date and instantly think "oh, God . . . no"? This man showed up to our date in a green polo shirt with stains on it, cargo shorts, and worn-out sneakers. And did I mention he pulled into the parking lot in the most broke down–looking black four-door Honda Civic I'd ever seen? It was rusty, missing hubcaps, had a dent on the side, and it was filthy. Someone had literally written "WASH ME" into the dust on the back window. He had put all of zero effort into our date, and it showed. What happened? Where did Señor Suavecito go? I tried not to (outwardly) judge him because it's not like I was rolling in piles of money, and I certainly wasn't driving a luxury vehicle. My new 2006 Toyota Corolla didn't even qualify as mid-luxury, so I had no room to talk. And my mom always said, "You never know someone's plight," "Don't judge a book by its cover," and all those other things moms say, so I was polite and followed him inside the restaurant. But believe me, in my head the judgment was louder than a catfight on one of those Real Housewives shows.

The conversation was easy, and it flowed. Jeff made me laugh quite a few times, and I found myself inspired listening to him talk about his dream to finish culinary school here and then move to France and study under the greats. He wanted to own his own restaurant one day and eventually earn a Michelin star. He seemed so driven and determined to make it happen that I believed he would. I listened to him talk about his children—how his daughter was sassy and a bit of a tomboy, but sweet as pie—as long as you stayed on her good side. And how his son was smart and handsome, and as funny as the day is long—always ready with a joke. He took so much pride in his children—I could tell by the way he spoke of them that they were his ultimate joy. I asked about his relationship with their mom, his ex-wife, and he didn't go into specifics except to say that they didn't get along very well and that they had been divorced for two years. He did, however, feel lucky that she still let him see his children, and moved into the apartments right across the street from him so that he could be close. He told me about his parents—specifically his mom. She had died when he was thirteen from an aneurysm. She was forty years old at the time, and for that reason he believed that he too would not live past forty. Those good old generational curses can be difficult to break when you've decided there's no point in fighting them.

"Jeff! Don't say that! You're basically willing it to happen if you say that!"

"But it's true. I honestly don't believe I'll make it to forty. I'm not sad about it. It just is what it is."

"It is *not* what it is, Jeff. You have your whole life ahead of you. What you need to do is focus on getting to Paris, opening a restaurant, and earning your first Michelin star."

He paused and smiled at me, his eyes lingering on mine two seconds past slightly uncomfortable, causing me to look down into my food and shyly smile.

"What?" I quietly asked, continuing to pile vermicelli onto my fork and into my mouth.

"You're just really sweet, Adiba. But also, there's a reason I believe this, and it's not just because my mom died when she was forty years old. I'm diabetic. Have been since I was thirteen. I was diagnosed right after she passed. She had high blood pressure; I have high blood pressure. And that mixed with the diabetes, and the fact that I don't always eat the way I'm supposed to . . . well . . ."

I sat there for a moment, taking in all I'd just heard but really unsure of what to think. I had never known anyone that was diabetic, much less dated anyone that was diabetic. All I knew about diabetes was that you had to test your blood sugar by pricking your finger a million times a day—and I only knew that because that's what all the infomercials advertising for no-stick testing devices said. I finally managed to swallow the giant ball of noodles in my mouth, and raised my eyes to meet Jeff's. I held his gaze as I gulped down some water, and then as if on cue, I did what I always did. I donned my trusty cape and transformed into Captain Save-A-Ho.

The need for me to "save him" kicked into action and before he'd even suggested it, I'd made up my mind that there was going to be a second date. Jeff had been through a lot in his life—rough relationship with his father, no relationship with his little brother, loss of a parent at a young age, divorce . . . I don't know if it was the social worker in me that wanted to bundle him up and take him to safety (what was he in danger of?), or the desperation of loneliness that made me want to place myself in a position of being needed so that I could fill up my "self-worth" cup with external validation (oh, hello, therapy. I see you there), but whatever it was, I was going to date this man and make him well and we were going to move to Paris and open five-star Michelin restaurants serving healthy, delicious food that would not only be good for him but would save his life.

Folks, this is where you judge me. G'head. Do it. I'd judge *you* if you told me some delusional shit like that. I'd probably also want to slap you into reality. Which is probably why I didn't immediately tell my best friend about Jeff. I didn't want to be talked out of it. So selfish, I know. I had absolutely no business trying to save anybody, with my working-two-jobs-just-to-barely-make-ends-meet ass, but there I was trying to better someone else's life instead of focusing on how I could better my own. What I needed to be figuring out was how I could move from two exhausting jobs to one fulfilling career. And if I'm being honest, I probably needed to sit my behind on someone's couch and try to begin to figure out how and why I married someone after not even knowing them for a year, separated from them after a year and a quarter of marriage, and then was dating three months after the divorce was final. Something was definitely not right with that picture. But a lifelong habit of deflection, projection, and all-around rejection of certain self-truths is a hard habit to break. So, I dated!

At the end of this date, Jeff did, in fact, say he'd like to see me again. And because I'd already made up my mind that I was going to be his personal Mother Theresa, I agreed to a second date—with a caveat. He was not to show up in dirty clothes, and it was not to be in the daytime. His car did not have air conditioning (did I not mention that?), and him showing up to our first date, in the Houston summertime heat, with no AC blowing, meant that he showed up sweaty, and just a touch musty. (Again—judge me. It's fine. You should totally judge me for looking past all the superficial things. Standards are absolutely a thing—even if they're surface level.) He agreed, and a week later, Jeff took me to a local Italian restaurant where we held hands and talked over candlelight. At one point Tony Bennett's "It Had to Be You" came on, and he stood up, took my hand, and asked me to dance—right there in the middle of the restaurant. I balked at the idea, exclaiming that people would see us. He said that he didn't care that people could see us—he wanted them to see us. He said he wanted people to see what falling in love looked like. How could I say no to that? It could have been a line right out of your favorite Taye Diggs/Sanaa Lathan rom-com! I obliged him and let my head settle on his shoulder. We danced to the entire song and when we sat down, our waiter brought us each a glass of champagne that had been sent over by another couple in the restaurant. I felt like I was in a dream. Nothing like that had ever happened to me—not the dancing in the middle of a restaurant, not the champagne being sent over, and not someone telling me, before I told them, that they were falling in love with me. I was the Queen of Unrequited Love. But not that night. No. That night I forgot all about the beat-up Honda and stained polo of our first date and allowed myself to just wallow in love that was apparently carved out just for me, and the attention I was getting (that I felt I rightfully deserved). I was a good person who had had a hell of a year. I'd earned these good feelings, this champagne, this dance in a dimly lit Italian restaurant.

I'd also earned the intense make-out session we had on my couch when I invited him to my house after dinner. He was an incredible kisser, and asked for consent before asking for consent was considered "sexy." I didn't sleep with him that night though. Remember—I wanted him to *think* he wanted to have sex with me. And he did. So, mission accomplished—sort of. See, I also *couldn't* have sex with him without telling him one crucial thing. I had HPV, and he needed to know that because if we did have sex, even with a condom, there was still a possibility I could pass it along to him. I. Was. Terrified. I mean, it's not like I was having to tell him that I had HIV or herpes[14], but I still had to tell him that I had an STI that was transmittable. I knew that I wanted to have sex with him, but I had to be a grown-up about it first. I called him while en route to Ruby Tuesday's and we talked about what our next date was going to be—trying to decide what we wanted to do, where we wanted to go, and at some point the conversation turned toward sex. Get your heads out of the gutter, y'all. I wasn't having phone sex while driving—though that would be kind of hilariously awesome. Could you imagine the looks on the faces of the drivers next to me? I don't know about you, but I can't have good phone sex without looking like a damn video vixen. It's literally impossible to keep a straight face. But, I digress. We were not having phone sex, we were just discussing whether or not I was on birth control, did he like condoms, what positions did I favor, etc., and I knew I had to tell him right then and there. It was do or . . . don't climax. I wanted to climax.

"Soooo . . . I'm loving this conversation, Jeff. And I could definitely talk to you about my favorite positions all day, but I'd rather show you. Buuuut, I can't show you without being completely honest with you."

---

14.   Please understand that there is absolutely NO JUDGMENT OR SHAME in having HIV or herpes. I just imagine that it would be a much harder conversation to have, in the context of sexually transmitted infections and diseases due to the unfortunate stigma around both of them.

"Okay. What's up? Wait. Lemme guess. You're a virgin!"

"Hahaha . . . Don't you wish! Um, no sir. That's not it."

"Damn! Okay, go ahead."

"Well, I'm kind of embarrassed to tell you. I kind of want to throw up, having to tell you. Before I tell you this, I want you to know that I have not been with anyone since I left my ex-husband. Ugh. I'm gonna puke." I truly felt like my stomach was creeping its way up my esophagus.

"Adiba. Just say it. I'm sure it's not that bad. And whatever it is, we'll deal with it. I'm not going anywhere."

And right then and there I felt my stomach settle and a calm wash over me. I took a deep breath and went into it.

"Okay. So, a couple of years ago, shortly after I got married, I tested positive for HPV. It hasn't gone away, and I am undergoing a procedure called a colposcopy to have a couple of polyps removed from my cervix. I need to tell you this because even with a condom, I could still transmit it to you, and it could manifest in you as genital warts. Ugh. There. That's it."

"That? That was what you needed to tell me?"

"Yeah."

"Girl, that's nothing! I'm not worried about that, and again, I'm not going anywhere. I appreciate you telling me. I really do. But trust me. You have nothing to worry about. I'm fine. You're *definitely* fine! We. Are. Fine. I love you, and I'm not going anywhere."

I drove in silence, listening to his words, tears streaming down my face, not fully able to believe what he'd just said. I was absolutely sure he would end things with me when I told him—not stay and then proclaim that he loved me. He called my name a few times before I let out a sniffly "I love you too." In hindsight, should I have said it back to him? Of course not! I didn't *know* this man. I mean, I knew things *about* this man, but I didn't really know him. What made him tick, what his philosophies on life were, whether or not he believed in God, how he viewed relationships (with himself or others)—I didn't even know his belief system when it came to parenting or how he handled money!

These are all things one should know and be able to fully embrace before proclaiming their love to someone. But here I was, returning the favor because essentially this man deemed my cervical health a nonissue. However, daddy issues are a thing, and when you tell yourself for most of your dating life that you never "get the guy" (because you didn't get the first guy, a.k.a your father), and then you get someone who seems to be "the guy," and you've judged all of your self-worth, for your entire life, on acceptance from the opposite sex, you say what you need to say and do what you need to do in order to make sure you not only "get the guy" but also keep the guy. Even if that means saying something you're not even sure you mean because dammit, it just feels good to be wanted, to be accepted, to finally be chosen. That night I made the most tips I'd ever made. I was on cloud nine and nothing could bring me down. Not even the curmudgeonly regular ex-marine who insisted I be his server and then made me remake his martini seven times because it wasn't "just right." Even that asshole got service with a smile that night.

After my shift was over, I drove straight to the CVS across the street from my house and bought Jeff an entire diabetes travel kit. He'd told me that he wasn't great about checking his blood sugar, and sometimes he would get a little lightheaded while out. I purchased a little pouch that could fit in his glove compartment and filled it with a small glucose meter, test strips, Band-Aids (just in case he cut himself in class), and a bag of Skittles. The pharmacist told me that they are a good, quick way to raise blood sugar in an emergency. This man said he loved me, and I believed I loved him. There was no way I was letting him go, and "saving him" was right in line with my typical pattern of behavior, so I was right on track to do what I always did—fall in love with someone I had absolutely no business falling in love with instead of falling in love with myself.

Some habits are hard to break.

A IS FOR ADIBA,
B IS FOR BABY,
AND C IS FOR THE
CONDOM I DID NOT USE

Jill Scott owes me twelve years of back child support.

I'm not kidding. If it wasn't for Jill Scott and her irreverent, sweet melodic voice pouring out of the speakers on my bedroom radio that hot-ass August afternoon, I would have never gotten pregnant. I mean, seriously. It's Texas. In the summer. In heat thicker than the sweat in Satan's ass crack. And here I was cervix deep with this man I'd known for about a month (oh, don't act like you've never done it), with Jilly from Philly singing:

> *You woo me, you court me, you tease me, you*
> > *please me*
> *You school me, give me some things to think about*
> *Ignite me, you invite me, you co-write me, you love*
> > *me, you like me*
> *You incite me to chorus*

Jeff incited me to chorus alright. I chorused in the melody of "don't stop" and he chimed right in with "Okay," and lo and behold, we made music. That man did not stop.[15] Who knew he would *actually* listen to me?! Neither one of us moved in the seconds immediately after the two most unforgiving words *ever* fell out of my mouth and landed on my uterus. With his sweat dripping into my eyes and threatening to blind me, I broke the silence.

"Wait. Did you . . . did you really not stop?"

"Aaaaah . . . no . . . I didn't stop." He scrunched up his face as if to say, *Duh—of course I didn't stop. Why would I stop?*

"Did you cum?"

"I did."

"YOU DID?" I stiff-armed him in an attempt to move him as far away from me as possible, completely ignoring the law of physics that says when someone is still inside you, running away is futile.

"YOU SAID 'DON'T STOP'!"

"But that didn't mean you were supposed to keep going! Goddamn it! Don't you know that's just a thing people say?"

For the record, I had no idea if that was true or not. I mean, I'd heard it said in movies before but no one I knew had actually ever admitted to saying it and meaning it. And if they *did* say it and meant it, their significant others knew better than to take that shit seriously. I knew this because out of all of my friends at that time, only two of them had babies. So yes, all the other dudes apparently knew better. All of them except for mine. I pushed him off me as fast as I could and ran to the bathroom. I'd read in Cosmo that if you went pee right after sex, you'd have a better chance of not acquiring a urinary tract infection. And though I was smart enough to know that babies and pee came out of two very separate, very different holes, I felt like a panicky seventeen-year-old who'd just had very good, very unprotected sex for the first time. I just knew that if I could pee out bacteria, I could certainly pee out the sperm currently invading my cervix like angry warlords.

---

15.   Which just proves we can't fucking win. We tell a man to stop, he doesn't listen. We tell a man "DON'T stop" and we end up pregnant.

I know, now, that sadly, this is not something you can do.

I think I even tried to shove toilet paper into my vagina in an attempt to soak up any potential illegitimate children wandering around in there. But in the end, I emerged from the bathroom only to see his half-smirking face staring at me from the middle of my own bed. I looked at the clock. It was almost 8:00 p.m. Fuck. All the nearby pharmacies were already closed.

"Everything's closed. I'll have to pick up Plan B in the morning," I said, chewing the inside of my bottom lip.

"I'll pay for it," he offered.

"Uh, yeah you will."

That night I went to sleep praying that instead of my ovaries being absorbent little sponges, they were actually jagged, impenetrable little morning stars, impaling any and all spermatoid that dared get close. But deep in my gut I already knew. I already knew that six to eight weeks from that very day I would be eyeball to pee stick with a very positive pregnancy test. How did I know, you ask?

Funny story.

When I was twenty-three years old, I dreamt that I had a baby, a little girl. In my dream, I saw myself holding her in the delivery room, shortly after pulling her out of me. Her handsome father (I couldn't see his face in my dream, but it was *my* dream so I'm saying he was handsome AF) leaned on the bed, half sidled up next to me, as we just stared at this little nugget of a human. As we stared in delight at this brand-new person, I realized that she had a thick, Jell-O-like film over her face, keeping me from seeing her features. As I pulled it back, I came face to face with the most beautiful little girl I had ever laid eyes on. And though I couldn't have known it then, nine years later I was going to come face to face with it again—it belonged to the man who hours earlier came inside of me. Yup. The little girl I dreamed about when I was twenty-three years old looked EXACTLY. LIKE. JEFF. So yeah, no matter how much I was secretly hoping my ovaries would randomly burst into flames like ants under a magnifying glass, I knew deep down inside they were damn near throwing open the doors and tossing the keys to the castle. The only thing I could do now was wait for her royal highness to take up residency. Well, that and throw some alligators in the pond—i.e. PLAN B.

*

Shortly after ingesting the manna from heaven, I mean Plan B, Hurricane Ike hit Houston, Texas. The newscasters were advising people to evacuate if they could because the city has a history of catastrophic, fatal flooding. I lived approximately forty-five minutes north of Houston, in Cypress, and was considered relatively safe from flooding, but not roof damage, broken windows, and general hurricane shenanigans. The night before Ike barreled his way into town, Jeff knocked on my door while his children sat in his car. He informed me that he and his kids were heading up to Austin, to shelter in place at his dad's house. Nervous, because there was a whole-ass hurricane about to ravage my town, but grateful because my man had come to rescue me, I turned to grab my overnight bag and throw some essentials in it. It was going to be my first time meeting his dad and I wanted to be as presentable as one could be during a natural disaster. That's when he stopped me.

"No, baby. *We're* going. Me and the kids."

"I'm sorry, what? What about me?"

"You'll be fine here. You're north enough that you shouldn't get more than just heavy rain."

"But what if we don't. What if it gets bad? I have nowhere to go. I don't have family here. It's just me. Why can't I go with you?"

"Baby, the kids haven't even met you yet, my dad doesn't know we're dating, this just wouldn't be the best time to meet everyone. *Not like this.*"

I stared at Jeff with tears in my eyes, heartbroken and terrified. I couldn't believe that the man I loved was really going to leave me to fend for myself while he fled in the middle of a damn hurricane. I briefly thought to myself *"This is what men do with girls like me— girls who are never going to be 'enough.'"* I told myself all sorts of stories about my self-worth in the ten seconds we stood in the doorway star-ing at each other. I told myself that I wasn't "good" enough to bring home, and not good enough to stay with. That I wasn't worthy enough to garner his protection and not quite enough of enough to be a prior-ity. These were also all the things I struggled with as a child, wondering why my father couldn't get his life together enough to come see about me, and why my stepfather chose drugs over being my dad. Never chosen. It was all too familiar; all too real. He leaned in to kiss me.

"I just wanted to come see you before I left and give you a kiss goodbye. Don't worry, babe. You'll be fine."

He hugged me, kissed me on the forehead, and ran back out to his waiting car. I took solace in the fact that as he looked at me before running back to his car, I could see tears in his eyes. Surely that accounted for something that maybe . . . possibly . . . sort of amounted to what he thought about me and my worthiness in his life. This was how I justified his leaving me during one of the most terrifying moments of my adult life. His tears fought back against my negative self-talk and I told myself (and willed myself to believe) that it was okay.

Y'all, it was *not* okay.

The air outside was thick and muggy and hot and filling my lungs with every inhale, which was increasing by the second because I was beginning to hyperventilate. I had never been in a natural disaster and I certainly didn't want to brave my first one alone. I took some deep, cleansing breaths while pacing my kitchen. I counted the tiles on the floor and the colors in my mosaic window. I ran my hands along the countertops, feeling their coolness beneath my fingertips—anything to make me not think about the impending doom I was sure was about to swallow me whole like one of the animals that didn't make it onto Noah's ark. One would not think that all of those things combined would work to slow my raging heartbeat and nervous bubbleguts, but glory be, glory be, that shit worked (no pun intended). I managed to calm myself down enough to call my neighbor, Rosie, and ask if I could stay in her guest room for the night. Without hesitation she agreed, and I carted my sad behind over to her house. I also carted over a few bags of Flamin' Hot Limon Cheetos, a cheesy bean and rice burrito from Taco Bell, two chalupas, a few containers of their creamy jalapeno sauce, and a large Mountain Dew. At the time, I couldn't seem to get enough Taco Bell.

I woke the next morning to discover that not only had I survived my first natural disaster, but my little four-bedroom, two-bathroom house had survived too. My beautiful redbrick front was now a small lake, which had seeped inside under the door threshold and created a small puddle just inside the front door, but everything else was fine. Jeff called to tell me that he and his kids were fine, but I was not at all interested. Still annoyed that he had left me in Houston to possibly die at the hands of a hurricane named Ike, I responded by asking him if he thought the restaurants would be open because I was hungry. This was my modus operandi when I was so irritated with someone they made my soul itch. He could have apologized and begged for forgiveness and I would have responded by asking him if he thought I should get a dog. Basically, there was no way I was going to cave and let him see just how hurt and bothered I was by his actions. I learned this behavior my freshman year of college—never let a man see just how hurt you are because then he knows he's got you—and he holds all the power—and I refused to give a man my power. Or at least the power I *thought* I had. I didn't really have any power. What I *did* have was a constant need for food to be in my mouth, hence me asking Jeff if he thought restaurants were open. It seemed like I was always hungry, but I justified it in my head by telling myself that I was simply relaxing my eating habits now that I had a man.

Ladies, you know how we do.

We eat right, workout, give up soda in favor of lemon-infused water so that the citric acid can mix with our stomach acid and burn the calories of the dressing-less salad we ate for lunch, all so we can get a man. Then we get the man, thank our gods in heaven that someone deemed us worthy of actually *having* a man, and immediately hit up the McDonald's drive-through to celebrate the fact that all of our disordered eating has finally paid off. No? You never did that? Just me? Cool, cool, cool.

As I was saying, I was always hungry those days, but as I drove through my soggy little neighborhood, I saw that nothing was open. Not Taco Bell, not Kroger, not even CVS. Which was unfortunate because my period was about to come and I needed some tampons. And that's when it hit me. My period. It wasn't *about* to come—it should have already come! I pulled out my planner, flipped to the previous month and began counting forward from the date of my *last* period. I was a solid twenty-eight-dayer. Every twenty-eight days, like clockwork, since age eleven, Aunt Flow would rear her wretched little head and wreak havoc in my life for four to six days, without fail. I sat behind the wheel of my car, counting underneath my breath.

"Twenty-eight, twenty-nine, thirty, thirty-one, thirty-two, thirty-three, thirty-four . . . thirty-five . . . thirty-six . . . thirty-seven . . . thirty-eight . . . ."

I got all the way to forty-two before I began the incessant chanting of "oh shit, oh shit, oh shit." I pulled into my driveway, ran inside the house and straight to my bathroom, snatched open one of the pregnancy tests I had stashed underneath my sink for emergencies[16], and peed the longest single stream of pee in the history of my life. I felt like a camel emptying out both of the water-filled humps on my back. Pee splashed up off the stick, got on my hand, splashed back up into me, but I didn't care. I had counted all the way to day forty-fucking-two. I would have gladly gotten pee in my eye if it meant that my test was going to be negative.

*

You know how they say man plans and God laughs? Well, in my case, God damn near fell off the throne, cackling.

---

16. Don't judge me. I don't know a single woman who has never kept "just in case" pregnancy tests stashed away. We've all been drunk and dumb or dumb and in love before.

Plan B did not work.

I shit you not.

Those two tiny pills may as well have been tic tacs because no sooner than I had placed the cap on my pee stick and shook my hand free of my own urine, did that damn thing light up pink like a goddamn 1980s fanny pack. I was pregnant.

Fuuuuuuuuuuuuuuuuuuuuuck.

Shit! What the ever-loving fuck?!

This wasn't supposed to happen. The plan for Plan B was that those two little pills were basically going to stand guard over my ovaries and prevent every single one of those little hellions from entering the castle. Instead, they played dead and my uterus was overthrown.

Honestly, though, I shouldn't have been so shocked by the news. That morning I'd woken up from a dream (yes, another dream. That's how God gets my attention because apparently I don't listen when I'm awake) that I had lost a tooth. In my dream, I was holding one of my molars between my thumb and index finger, just staring at it. I woke with a start, bolted upright in bed and said, aloud, to absolutely no one but myself, "I'm pregnant." Now, you might be wondering how in the hell did I infer that I was with child, from a dream that I lost a tooth. Well, I'm Puerto Rican, that's how. And we have all sorts of folk-lore and old wives' tales about the meaning behind random dreams. In my family, if you lose a tooth, dream of fish, or if Titi Mimi has a dream about you, you're pregnant. And every time, without fail, it rings true. So, when I woke up from a dream of me having lost a tooth, I automatically knew that the idea of me being a responsible adult was nothing more than an idea affording me a millisecond of comfort. But, inherently knowing something in your subconscious mind, and having proof of that something in your pee-soaked hand is two very, very, I cannot stress this enough, VERY different things.

Did I call my mom? Did I call my new baby daddy? Did I drink a fifth of gin? Sorry to disappoint but absolutely none of the above happened. Not one bit of it. What did happen was I ran into my living room screaming while simultaneously laughing hysterically until that laughter devolved into huge, chest-heaving sobs, accompanied by random bursts of screaming. The kind of sobs that come from your gut, and you make an ugly face and snot makes its way into your mouth, but you don't care because your life is falling apart. Yes, *that* kind of cry. I didn't want to be pregnant. I wasn't ready to be pregnant. I wasn't supposed to be pregnant. And more than any of that, I wasn't married so I *couldn't* be pregnant! Yeah, I said it. At the time I was pretty religious (but obviously not *that* religious because PREGNANT). I attended church every Sunday and taught Sunday school to small children. How exactly was I going to tell the First Lady (a.k.a Pastor's wife for those of you who don't go to a Black church) that I couldn't teach the children because I was with child myself? Could I make a joke out of it and claim I was the second coming of Mary? Being pregnant (and unmarried) is not something you just casually offer up when Pastor asks if anyone has "a good word to share with the congregation," and I wasn't exactly interested in going up during altar call for the elders to "lay hands on me." So this was my dilemma: How do I tell Jeff, how do I tell my *almost a minister* mother, and how do I handle my church?

Let me start by telling you that telling the woman who starts every day with a daily devotional and a scripture reading was far easier and a million times less humiliating than telling Jeff and my church. I called Jeff and asked him to meet me at Fuddrucker's because I had news. I also had my girlfriend Pam with me for moral support. Ladies, make note: if you have to take a friend with you to tell your baby daddy that you're carrying his child, you probably shouldn't be carrying his child. But I digress; the conversation went a little like this:

"Hey. Thanks for meeting me."

"No problem, babe. What's up?"

I stared down at my burger like it was going to sprout wings and fly away.

"Um . . . I really don't know how to say this, so I guess I'll just say it. Uuuuummm . . . I'm prebjfsknant."

"What?"

This time I said it louder and not with marbles in my mouth.

"I'M PREGNANT."

And thus began the most awkward and uncomfortable silence ever to exist in the history of awkward and uncomfortable silences. He stared at me, I stared at my burger (which was now cold and sad-looking), and Pam stared at her phone. The three of us sat there, not moving, probably not breathing, and definitely not making eye contact for what felt like an eternity. In reality it was more like two minutes. Finally, Jeff broke the silence, doing the thing that dudes always do when they're shocked their penis actually did what it's supposed to do, which is shoot out sperm that creates tiny humans.

"Huh. You sure?"

"What?"

"Are you sure you're pregnant? You took a test?"

"No, I licked my thumb and stuck it in the air. YES, I TOOK A TEST!"

"But I thought you took Plan B?"

"I DID TAKE PLAN B! YOU WATCHED ME TAKE IT IN THE CLINIC PARKING LOT WITH MY DIET COKE!"

Now, y'all, I need to pause here. Just . . . let's pause because I can't in good faith, and certainly not in the name of sweet Black Baby Jesus, go one step further without sharing some very pertinent information with you that surely would have come in handy had it been written in BIG-ASS, BOLD-ASS LETTERS ON THE GODDAMN BOX OF PLAN B ELEVEN YEARS AGO!

Come close, friends. Y'all ready for this?

Plan B doesn't work if you weigh more than 155 pounds.[17]

Did you get that?

I'll say it one more time in case your brain just short-circuited like mine did when I found this information out ELEVEN YEARS AFTER I had my child.

PLAN. B. DOES. NOT. WORK. IF. YOU. WEIGH. MORE. THAN. 155. POUNDS.

---

17. Y'all think I'm playing. I. AM. NOT. Read this article from Healthline magazine and thank me later. https://www.healthline.com/health/healthy-sex/plan-b#weight-limit

Ain't that some shit? Who in the . . . what in the . . . HOW IN THE HOLY HELL DO THEY NOT ADVERTISE THIS RIGHT ON THE FUCKING BOX???

Well, okay maybe I'm being a bit dramatic here. It's not that it doesn't work, per se, it's just *less effective* if you're over 155 pounds or have a BMI over 30. Less effective? What does that even mean? Less effective is what you say when you want to tell someone that their hair gel won't work as well if it is applied to dry hair. Or that their tires won't stop as well in the rain if they're balding. Less effective is *not* what you say to someone when the possible outcome is A WHOLE-ASS BABY! Also, how is that even a thing that you don't plaster all over the goddamn box? Or announce in a commercial? I feel like this whole brand-new-to-me information could be (and probably should be) a skit on *Saturday Night Live*! Big girl goes to Walgreens to plan for a sexy night in. Big girl arrives at the cash register with two bottles of wine, a can of whipped cream, a blindfold, and a box of Plan B. As she's checking out the cashier picks up the box and looks at her. Big girl sheepishly grins and says, "You know, for just in case," and the cashier takes one look at her and says, "Uh-uh, honey. This won't work for you. Take this and I'll see you in nine months with newborn diapers and a pacifier at the register. Sis, you need to just go on ahead and double up on those Trojan Max."

I promise you, if I was said Big Girl, I would be thanking God on high for making me visibly fat so that I could be spared a pregnancy I might not be ready for. *But since that didn't happen* . . . I'm sharing this brand-new-to-me information with YOU. Big girls, don't do it. Don't fuck around[18], say "don't stop," and then think Plan B will save your ass because it will not. Use a condom (or two), use VCF or some other kind of spermicide, but do not, I repeat DO NOT rely on Plan B if you accidentally slip and fall on an unsheathed penis.

You're welcome. Carry on.

Pam remained glued to her phone, not even daring to blink.

---

18.   All puns and no puns intended.

Honestly, I think she was afraid to even move—the tension was pound cake thick. Jeff and I remained locked in a death stare, and then finally, with a sharp inhale, Jeff spoke.

"Okay. So, what do you want to do? I'll support your decision."

"Neither abortion nor adoption are for me, so I'm keeping it."

Another sharp inhale.

"Well, Okay, then. We're having a baby."

Jeff looked down at the table, and I could hear him mumble the words "we're having a baby" under his breath.

"Are you mad?"

Pause.

Pam, if you're reading this, looking back I wish you would have knocked me right upside my head for asking that question. "Are you mad?" Who the fuck cares if he was mad? It was too late to be mad. And even if he was—so? It's not like him being butthurt was going to change my mind. Ladies, don't follow my piss poor example. It doesn't matter one damn bit if homeboy is pissed. He'll live, and you'll still be pregnant.

Continue.

"Huh? What? Am I mad? Oh! Nah, baby, I'm not mad. We're gonna be fine. Just fine. Juuuuuuust fine! Okay. Was that it? Was that all you wanted to tell me?"

"Um . . . yes?"

"Okay! Well, thanks for letting me know. I gotta run. I'll call you tonight. Love you."

And just like that, he was up out of his seat and practically sprinting for the door. I watched his back as he hurriedly made his way out of Fuddrucker's and silently wondered to myself if this was a foretelling of the rest of my life. I turned back to my burger, still sitting in the basket, cold and untouched, and looked up at Pam, who had now taken her eyes out of her phone and was staring at the doors of the restaurant, mouth wide open, eyes glazed over.

"What just happened, Pam?" I asked.

No, seriously. What the fuck had just happened? This is not how it was supposed to go. I was a grown-ass woman attempting to live my best rom-com life, not Molly Ringwald in an after-school special. Jeff was supposed to take my hands, look sweetly into my eyes, and assure me that he loved me, and was going to be there for me every step of the way. He was supposed to cry tears of joy to assuage my tears of gut-wrenching fear, touch my belly and say, "Hi, baby! I'm your daddy!" I was supposed to regain my calm, and feel safe and loved and sure about the unsteady, unsure road that lay ahead. Instead, I felt like I wanted to vomit and was living my teenage nightmare of being pregnant before I had any business being pregnant. No one in that restaurant gave a rat's ass about me or had any idea that my Black rom-com fantasy had just turned into the nightmare on Highway 6. I stared at Pam in utter disbelief, waiting for her to assure me that what seemed like had just happened, in fact, hadn't really happened at all.

"Your baby daddy just left after you told him you're having his baby."

Thanks, Pam.

I'M PREGNANT,
JEFF'S DRUNK,
AND I HAVE MANGE

Picking up my burger, I took a bite and as suspected, it was cold, dry, and decidedly tasteless, even though I asked for just about every condiment they had to be slathered on the patty. I was slowly and methodically chewing the hunk of meat in my mouth when I turned my attention back to Pam.

"This burger tastes like Hurricane Ike smells: rotten. I hate it. I hate this place. I hate this. Fuck, Pam. What am I gonna do?"

And in her most sincere voice, with her sweet, sympathetic doe eyes, Pam grabbed my hand and said "You're gonna have a beautiful little baby, mama. And you're gonna be okay. Also . . . you gonna eat that burger? 'Cause I'm starving!"

Later that night, because I guess the universe had decided it wasn't quite done with me yet, Jeff called me, quite drunk, and exclaimed with absolute confidence that we were going to be just fine. We discussed how to tell his children, the rest of his family, and my mother. None of these were easy tasks. I mean, do you really want the first time you meet your boyfriend's children to *also* be the moment you tell them you're pregnant? Not ideal, but alas, that's exactly what happened. I met him and his two children at our local grocery store and proceeded to rock their world as we perused the produce section.

"Lola, Frankie, this is my girlfriend Adiba, and uh . . . you're going to have a new little sister or brother."

"Hi! Nice to meet you! Yep, I'm pregnant and right now the baby is about the size of this here grape!"

And then I gingerly tossed the grape into my mouth while his son and daughter looked on in shock and horror.

Okay, I'm kidding. It didn't *quite* go like that, but it felt about as awkward. Jeff introduced me, told them I was pregnant, and then I watched the slow smiles creep across their faces as they asked me question after question. What did I do for work? Did I have other children? Had I been married before? Where did I live? Did I have a house or an apartment? Did I want a boy or a girl? Just a barrage of curiosities as we walked the aisles of HEB—Jeff walking behind us, relieved, I can only imagine, that it had not turned into a full-on assault on his character. At least that's how I remember it. I remember his daughter, Lola, being so cute but also just as sassy as he'd said! Her adorably chubby little face held eyes that knew more and understood more than she should have known at nine years old, and a mouth that betrayed her feelings when she let it fly. Lola could give side-eye like a pro. It was something I admired and abhorred at the same time—not quite confident enough to express her deepest feelings but confident enough to tell you where to go and how to get there, and offer you bus fare to help you along the way—all with just a look. I remember telling Jeff that she was going to give me a run for my money.

Frankie, on the other hand, had bright beaming eyes, a sweet smile, and seemed to be very excited about the whole thing. I don't remember everything we talked about but I do remember that he asked more questions than his sister. And honestly, for a twelve-year-old to ask questions at all is pretty impressive. I also remember that he watched intently as I pulled out cash to pay for the groceries, and he commented that I must be rich. I found this to be a really odd statement for a child I'd *just met* to make, especially with his father standing right there, but

I simply explained to him that I was not rich, I simply worked two jobs to make ends meet. I'll never know what went through his head after that conversation, but I do know that he and his sister spent that night at my house and the next morning my money was missing. If this was the beginning of the road to family life, I was in for one long uphill climb. This was not how I imagined the merging of families would begin.

I also didn't imagine that I'd have to ask my godmother to fly to Texas to bear witness/protect me when I told my mother I was pregnant. But I was quickly learning that in regard to this pregnancy, even the simplest things were going to be bizarre. Now, you're probably wondering why I needed to have my godmother in the room as backup. Well, here's what you need to know about my mom—she's Puerto Rican, has a mean backhand, her *chancleta* game is strong, and at the time, she was on her way to becoming an ordained minister. Like, a full-fledged, sit on the pulpit, wear the purple robes and lead the church in prayer on Mission Sundays minister. At the time, she was very conservative in her views, knew nothing about Jeff other than his name, and her stock response to everything was "give it to God." Got a hangnail? Give it to God. Got bad credit? Give it to God. Boyfriend gave you herpes? Give it to God. Found yourself accidentally knocked up by someone you barely know? Give it to God.[19] This woman, my mother, also raised me with the understanding that babies are to be made when two people love each other, ideally within the confines of marriage. It was husband, wife, *then* baby, because THE BIBLE said so. So, you can only imagine the level of fear and anxiety that was coursing through my veins as I contemplated just how, exactly, I was going to tell her that I had literally gone against the one tenet she made sure I was well versed in, and was about to make her the only minister in the pulpit with an unmarried, knocked-up child.

In hindsight, I was probably giving this moment way too much power, but at the moment all I knew was I needed backup in case

---

19. For the record, this is still her response to EVERYTHING.

the *chancleta* came out, and I needed to do it in a public place—to help ensure that the *chancleta*, in fact, did not come out. I flew my godmother into Houston and then convinced my mom to let me fly *her* in so that she could meet Jeff in person. But I didn't tell her that my godmother, who is also her best friend, was going to be there. Sneaky? Yes, but sneaky with a purpose. See, in my mind, if she was so surprised and shocked by seeing her best friend, *and* if Jeff made a good impression on her, *and* if I told her I was pregnant in *public*, she'd be too overwhelmed to let me have it. So, in true Adiba fashion, I chose a restaurant to share the news—this time it was Wingstop. Nothing says, "Mom I'm pregnant and this man is the father," like lemon pepper wings and seasoned fries. I remember the smell of the frying grease making me incredibly nauseous, and the sight of chicken meat causing my stomach to lurch, but we'd come too far down this road. It was too late to back out now. When we got to our table, I purposely sat diagonal from her because it's harder to slap someone you have to reach diagonally for. Everyone made conversation while I quietly vomited in my mouth, and then, without warning, everyone got very quiet. It was my time to sweat and bay-beeeeee . . . I was sweating like Jay-Z stuck in that elevator with Solange *and* his wife.[20] There was no getting out of this one. I had gotten my mother a card that said something about something, but in the card, I had included a picture of my first sonogram. I slid the envelope across the table to her, inched my chair a little closer to the edge of the table so that if I had to suddenly get up and run, there'd be nothing in my way, and then held my breath. It felt like an eternity as she opened and then read the card, and then stared at the grainy black-and-white photo of what looked more like a kewpie doll floating in space than a baby. My godmother and I exchanged glances, I bit my lip, and then it happened.

"Oh my God! Oh my God! Is this . . . you're pregnant?"

"Aaaaaah, yeah, Ma. Yeah, I am."

Mom pushed her chair back and jumped up.

---

20. No shade, Bey and Jay! I LOVE YOOUUU!

"Oh my God! I'm gonna be a grandma! I'm gonna be a grandma! Oh my God. Thank you, thank you, thank you!"

This woman, this tiny terror, a.k.a my mom, ran around to my side of the table, threw her arms around my neck, and gave me the biggest hug I think we've ever shared in my life—and to this day. I stared at my godmother, bewildered, as I robotically moved my arms to hug her back. Who was this woman and what had she done with my mother? This was beyond what I was expecting *and* well beyond what I had prepared for. When she finally sat back down, I asked her if she was upset with me, and her response was one I will never forget.

"What have I always told you, Adiba? A child is a gift from God—a blessing. I could never be mad that he saw fit to bless you with a child, and me with a grandchild. This is a blessing. Just give it to God."

And there she was. My minister mom, telling me to give this tiny human, and all that was going to come with it, to God. At that moment, my mother was not my minister, she was not my teacher, she was not the woman trying to steer me this way or that. She was just my mom, doing what moms do—reassuring me that I was going to be alright. Regardless of what was going to come my way, I was covered.

Maybe Jeff was right. Maybe everything *was* going to be "just fine."

Maybe.

Wrong.

Everything was not just fine.

Not in the slightest.

About two weeks after my mother left, I began to feel pain in my left side. Not down by my uterus, but on the side of my stomach. It started as a dull ache—kind of like I had pulled an oblique muscle six weeks prior and it was still healing. Over a period of three days, that dull ache became a hot punch in the ribs anytime I tried to sit upright, walk upright, or go to the bathroom. I hadn't had a bowel movement in over a week, and even peeing hurt. Walking from the living room to the hall bathroom, maybe fifty feet, required me to lean against the wall for support. Not just due to the pain, but also lightheadedness. Driving in my car required a pillow behind my back because settling into the seat would send undulating waves of deep pain up and down the left side of my abdomen. I had never been more than five weeks pregnant before, so I didn't know that this wasn't a normal part of pregnancy. I had heard that some women experience constipation, and I think that little *What to Expect When You're Expecting* book mentioned it, but nothing and no one had gone into detail about what it should and should not feel like.

One morning as I drove to work with my trusty pillow propping me up straight like a brand-new driver, I sneezed and thought my life was ending. Pain shot through me like a jolt and tears came to my eyes. I also felt my underwear get a little wet, but again, I'd heard that babies basically turn your bladder into a La-Z-Boy recliner while you're pregnant, so I figured my baby was just getting a head start. My baby was *not* getting a head start. My baby was trying to make a speedy exit. Upon arriving at the school I worked at, I went straight to the bathroom. I hadn't brought spare underwear with me, and I couldn't run around in wet panties all day, so I did what I learned to do in junior high when I'd get my period at school and I wasn't allowed to wear tampons yet.[21] I took about ten squares of toilet paper and folded them until they made a rectangle small enough to fit on the crotch of my underwear. Then I lifted my skirt and pulled my underwear down, ready to make do with my very clever, very homemade maxi pad. However, what I was forced to make do with was blood on the crotch of my panties. Big splotches of rusty brown blood dotted the white fabric of my underwear. I used the makeshift pad to wipe myself and the blood was there too. Not allowing me to look away from it, not allowing me to unsee it.

I would like to say that I cried, that I went into panic mode, that I screamed for help, but I didn't. I felt the tears work their way up into my throat, trying to escape, but I swallowed them back down, made another makeshift pad for my underwear, pulled them up, readjusted my clothing, and went to my office to tell my supervisor that I needed

---

21. Because my mom wholeheartedly believed that if I did, I'd be losing my virginity. Gotta love that good old fear mongering church upbringing, huh?

to go home. She could tell that I was upset because I couldn't look her in the eye, but I very calmly packed my bag and said "I need to leave. I've started to bleed and I need to go home." Mrs. Lewis, my supervisor, a warm and kind Black woman who just loved the children we worked with, got quiet and said "Okay, baby. You go home and go home safely. I'll be prayin' for you and that little one." On the way home I called Jeff to let him know what was happening. He insisted on leaving work and coming home but I insisted he stay. I told him that if I was losing the baby, him being home with me wasn't going to stop it. He decided to stay at work. I called my ob-gyn and told her what I had been feeling and the blood that had shown up on my underwear and I'll never forget her response. She let out a deep sigh and said:

"Well, because of your fibroids we knew this might happen. There's nothing we can do to stop it so I suggest you just stay home from work tomorrow and through the weekend, and just let it happen. But call me if anything changes—like if the bleeding stops or the color changes."

I don't remember her saying I'm sorry this is happening or anything like that, but I do remember that I didn't cry the whole way home. I drove home in silence, I sat in my silent house, and just . . . sat. For a long time. Eventually I called my mom, best friend, godmother, and Jeff's aunt Alexis to let them know what was happening. My mom, coming through like the minister she is told me to "Give it to God," and this time I listened. I prayed. I prayed and prayed and prayed and went on to Facebook and asked my friends to pray or light candles or send the good juju, whatever is they did when they needed a miracle, I asked folks to do it. My friend's mother, who had never met me, started a prayer circle with her church group. Friends of friends of friends messaged me to tell me they were praying for this tiny human to hold on inside of me. That night the bleeding stopped. The prayers had worked. Until they didn't.

Operating on the side of caution, I decided to stay home the next day. Yes, the bleeding had stopped and I woke up to clean underwear, but I felt like I should not tempt fate. *Just take it easy this weekend*, I told myself. And that's exactly what I did. I made myself some breakfast and then plopped my still pregnant behind on the couch to take in my daily faves—the *Today Show*, and the show I loved to hate, the *Rachael Ray Show*. Everything was going along swimmingly and the pain in my left side had begun to subside substantially. I was feeling like a weight had been lifted off my shoulders—until I went to the bathroom and realized that that weight had been replaced by a boulder. There it was. Small dots on my panties. Except this time the spots were fire engine red. I closed my eyes and simply said "Okay." That was it. There was nothing more I could say. My doctor warned this could happen, and it was happening, so, "Okay."

I called Jeff and told him that this time I needed him to come home, and then I called the doctor's office who told me to come in at 1:30 p.m.—she had an opening. The nurse on the phone seemed rather nonchalant about it so I was pretty nonchalant about it too. We knew what this meant—my baby was saying its final farewell (with flair, I suppose), and we just needed to make sure nothing else was going on. We arrived at the doctor's office in what felt like record time and then just waited in the lobby for the nurse to call us back. However, while waiting I got the sudden urge to urinate and asked if I could use the restroom. This is where things get . . . interesting.

There was a restroom at the other end of the lobby, but they let me use the one behind the door, where the patient rooms are, just in case the doctor called me in while I was in the bathroom. I walked into the bathroom and saw my doctor in the hall. Dr. Thornton, a tall, heavyset Black woman, was not someone I would ever refer to as "warm and fuzzy." She was one of those doctors who you were never really sure if she liked you because she didn't smile much—not even when she was showing you your baby in a sonogram for the first time. Her deep-set, piercing black eyes could see you as much as they could look straight through you. She didn't wear make-up, or jewelry except for maybe a small pair of hoop earrings every now and again—and this was fitting of her. She was a no-frills, cut through the bullshit, tell-it-like-it-is kind of doctor. I didn't love her bedside manner, but I appreciated it because I always knew she was going to keep it real with me—no sugar coating. She was finishing up and would be right with me. I walked into the bathroom and forgot to lock the door (because I had to pee so bad). I pulled down my jeans, sat down, and immediately let out the most blood curdling, guttural scream I'd ever heard come from my body in my entire life. I'd never heard that sound come from me before, and I've never heard it again. My legs were covered in blood. It looked like someone had sliced open my femoral artery. You couldn't see the crotch of my jeans because it was covered in a literal puddle of blood. And then something large fell out of me. I screamed and cried as nurses burst into the bathroom. Someone called for backup. Someone called for my doctor. Another someone called for Jeff. A lot of what happened next is a blur. I'm not sure how, but somehow I made it into the patient room across the hall. Somehow, someone got me out of my pants and bloody underwear and into a gown. Somehow, someone got me onto the doctor's table. I'm not sure who or how because I barely remember having legs at that moment. Honestly, I barely remember having thoughts at that moment. I saw blood, I felt something leave me, I heard the plop as it hit the water, and then I heard my own voice leave my body. I laid on that table and stared at the ceiling, my tears forming soggy marshes on the tissue paper beneath my head. I tried to count the holes in the tile and thought back to days spent in Mrs. Heck's third-grade class, throwing pencils up into the air to see if they would stick in the ceiling tile. I whispered the words "I'm sorry" over and over again. To my dead baby. To Jeff. To myself. The doctor wasn't in the room, and it was just us—my whispers and Jeff's comforting "shushing" filling the still air with melancholia. It felt like an eternity before she slowly slinked in, placing a jar with my dead baby in it on the counter behind me. As she came around to where I could see her, she grabbed my hand, and this time, she apologized. She informed me that the nurses had collected the fetus from the toilet bowl and it would have to be sent to the lab for testing, which was the standard operating procedure. As she used wet-nap after wet-nap to clean up the blood that had dried onto my legs, she continued to explain that she would need to scope me to make sure everything had come out, and if not, she'd schedule a D&C for the following day. I said okay and continued my incessant apologizing to my unborn child. The room was so quiet, so goddamn quiet, as she slid the camera scope into my vagina. I squeezed Jeff's hand because I was at a point where I just wanted, no, *needed* it all to stop.

And then we heard it.

Bum . . . bum-bum . . . bum-bum . . . bum-bum . . .

I looked at Jeff, who looked at me with as much bewilderment, and then my ob-gyn turned the monitor toward us and exclaimed, in a voice that echoed our own silent shock "Well, damn! I'm not sure what happened or what is in that jar, but here's your baby! Look! Right here! There's the heartbeat!"

And there she was. This tiny little baby, floating around in my belly as if nothing had happened. Like we weren't all just screaming like banshees five minutes beforehand. I questioned Dr. Thornton over and over again if she was sure that that was my baby on the screen, and she repeatedly assured me it was. Jeff, a man I'd never seen cry, sobbed. Me, though, I laid on the table, still bewildered. I asked Dr. Thornton if my baby was still in my belly, then what fell out of me—what was in that jar on the counter behind me? She told me she didn't know—it could be a fibroid; it could be a twin that was noncompatible with life. That's a strange place to be, you know—stuck between gratitude and deep sorrow. Something, that could possibly have been my child, was sitting in a jar, fifteen feet from me, and the next day would be tossed in the garbage because they were incompatible with life. Simultaneously, I had life inside of me. Deep mourning, deep joy. The loss is unfathomable and while I don't think about it every day, there are times when I see a beautiful little brown boy that my heart feels a little bit heavier, the blood in my body feels a little bit thicker. It's like my body remembers, and perhaps, just perhaps, at those moments, their little soul is moving through me again.

*

Not one to dwell on the negative (or perhaps not one to confront pain head-on, potato, po*tah*to), I carried on with my pregnancy, grateful for the little one that hung on. Dr. Thornton put me on bed rest for the remaining four weeks of my first trimester, and I did nothing more than sit on the couch, lay in bed, and take a shower—which is difficult for a busy body like me. I couldn't do eight thousand target runs a week—stocking up on things that I wouldn't need for another seven months, couldn't visit with Jeff's family for birthdays and BBQs and such, I was miserable. But I suppose it was for the better because pregnancy did NOT look good on me. I'm not kidding. You know how most women go through pregnancy and they look like they're about to enter a beauty pageant and wipe the floor with all the other women? Yeah, that was not me. I was the mophead that was being used to wipe said floor. I'm not kidding.

My hair did the complete fucking opposite of what it was supposed to do. Instead of growing down to my ass crack, it fell out in bunny-size chunks. My skin did the complete fucking opposite of what *it* was supposed to do too. Instead of bathing itself in the glow of fetal hormones, it literally burned itself from the inside out. Yes, that's right. My skin decided it was a great idea to treat the miracle human growing inside of me like a goddamn foreign object and basically gave me the equivalent of what looked like a chemical burn around my mouth, in the crease of my chin, under my eyes, and on my forehead. If Freddy Krueger was a pregnant woman, I was her.

And then there were the spots.

In addition to balding and burning, I was also apparently turning into a damn jungle cat because I broke out in cheetah-like spots all across my chest and neck. Yes, y'all. I'm not kidding. Spots. Oh! And because my body, much like myself, doesn't know how to do anything low-key, it went for the jugular: my teeth. Did you just audibly gasp? Because I sure as fuck did when my tooth fell out in my second trimester! Yeah! That happened! This small person renting my uterus on a month-to-month basis wouldn't be content with making me look like a drug-addled cheetah with mange until they went for the only thing I had left—my smile. I had started to notice that I would wake up with a crazy toothache every morning, and then as soon as I had a glass of milk, it would go away. Being the smart woman that I am, I put two and two together and figured that this baby was most likely sapping every ounce of calcium my body had. I knew women could become anemic during pregnancy (as I was), so it only made sense that we could also experience a calcium deficiency. I tried everything I could to naturally up my calcium intake—milk, cheese, calcium chews, but this baby was determined and one day while enjoying my nightly bowl of Cap'n Crunch with Crunch Berries, I bit down into a berry that didn't feel like the other ones. I spit the entire contents of my mouth into my hand and lo and behold, this little asshole had stolen my tooth. My whole fuckin' tooth.

Hold up. I just realized something. The same tooth I lost in my cereal bowl is the same tooth that fell out in my dream the morning I found out I was pregnant. Damn, y'all. God has a really, really fucked up sense of humor.

DEAR GOD, THERE ARE OTHER WAYS TO MAKE YOUR POINT

It's one thing to lose a baby. It's another thing to lose one baby, yet still have another one resting easy in your belly. As I said earlier, deep mourning and deep joy, both served on the same plate at the same time with one fork for me to ingest. The whole thing was, and still is very much a blur. One minute I was screaming bloody murder in the doctor's office bathroom after feeling something heavy fall out of me and splash into the toilet, and five minutes later I was breathing a sigh of relief because my baby was still inside of me. But . . . my baby *wasn't* still inside of me. One of them was in a jar on a counter, fifteen feet behind me.

Now, in full transparency, I also had fibroids, so there was a question of could it have been one of those. Fibroids run in my family, and truly, they run in many Black families. Fibroids afflict Black and Latin women disproportionately[22], and so I wasn't fully willing to rule out the possibility that *that* could have been what I'd just lost. I don't remember Dr. Thornton ever coming back to me with a definitive answer as

22. https://www.healthline.com/health/womens-health/black-women-and-heavy-periods

to what it was or was not, but I also know that a mother knows. My symptoms were not compatible with spontaneous uterine fibroid eruption. So, if it wasn't a fibroid, and it wasn't the baby that was still in my belly, that only leaves me with one option—another baby that never became my baby. Also, if I really think about it . . . that day . . . that moment . . . I think I just didn't want to know. The whole experience was so traumatic—not just physically but also emotionally, mentally, and spiritually. I think there was this innate sense in my body that I was at capacity in every way, and I simply did not have it in me to hold deep gratitude and soul-crushing grief on the same plane, at that moment. It would have been the end of me—or at least the end of me as I knew myself to be.

I didn't talk about this to anybody. What was I going to say— "I passed what I'm pretty sure was a baby—not THE baby—but A baby, nonetheless. But don't worry, the baby we've all been gushing over is still in there so it's cool, it's cool, it's cool. No need to freak out?" No! I *was* freaking out—on the inside. And that little baby that never came to be, deserved to be freaked out over. Loudly. He (I say "he" because during this moment in my life, this is how I thought about the baby inside of me)[23] deserved every tear I didn't shed for him, every wail I didn't let escape from my throat. I was so angry—at my body, at my doctor, at God. Why the fuck did my body think it was okay to just make decisions on my behalf? Why didn't my doctor catch wind that there was another baby in there? Why did God decide to . . . be God? But in the same breath that I questioned God, I thanked him. Weird? Fucked up? Ridiculous? I know . . . trust me, I know. As time went on I often wondered how I was holding just as much joy as I was sorrow—the dichotomy between the two is at once too simplistic to be questioned and yet so complex, it begs to be questioned.

23. Since 2008/09, I have come to to appreciate the nuances of gender expression and identity. In writing this memoir, it was important to me to be authentic to the moment in my life and represent the moment as I lived it. Were this happening today, I would be using non-heteronormative language and they/them pronouns to write about a miscarried child.

The God I had come to know was supposed to be a just and merciful god. An awesome god. Or at least that's what they taught in Sunday school. Even the songs we sang said so:

> *Our God, is an awesome god*
> *He reigns from heaven above*
> *With wisdom, power, and love*
> *Our God is an awesome god!*

I was taught that if you loved the Lord, accepted Christ into your heart as your personal savior, put all of your faith and trust in him, and leaned on Him, not your own understanding, in the end things would be okay because God takes care of his children. But . . . how was this taking care of his children?

How was taking my baby awesome, just, and showing of any sort of mercy? Was I supposed to be grateful that now I'd only have to worry about providing for one baby and not two? Was I supposed to be glad that I didn't know about baby #2 beforehand because at least this way the grief wasn't so intense? But then, also, the grief *wasn't* so intense. It wasn't all-consuming and overwhelming and keeping me curled in a ball in my bed all day and all night. I still had another human to grow. On doctor's orders, I had to keep my stress levels down and my butt (mostly) in one place. So, what did I do? I ignored the thoughts that plagued my mind at night when I tried to fall asleep. I cursed God in the morning, right after I finished thanking him for allowing me to see another day. I ate canned pineapple every day until my lips and tongue blistered from the citric acid. Then when the blisters healed, I did it again because focusing on that pain was thirty times easier than reliving the pain of loss on a daily basis.

My mom had always taught me that life was what I made it. She practically drilled the damn phrase into my head. Whenever anything happened and I had to figure out how to handle a situation, she would just look at me and say, *"Pues,* Abuela would always say *'tu vida es lo que haces.'" Pero si es verdad,* what was I supposed to do with *this*? I didn't *make* this baby appear in my belly. Well . . . okay . . . I kinda-sorta did, but that's beside the point. I didn't make him appear just for him to disappear before I even knew he was there. I didn't make the landscape of my uterus so toxic that his tiny unformed self had enough intelligence in his like, eight meager cells to say, "Fuck this—I'm out."

I. Did. Not. Do. This.

So what, then, in the entire fuck was I supposed to do with it—'it' being the mishmash of emotions I felt at any given moment in time. Another thing my mother loved to say whenever something bad happened was that everything happened for a reason and that it was all God's plan, so not to worry.

Let me tell you something. If you want to get popped in the mouth, punched in the throat, or drop-kicked from here to next week, mess around and tell a woman who just lost a baby that everything happens for a reason and that God wanted this for her. G'head. Do it. I dare you. Do it and then send me an email with a photo attached of you missing ALL your front teeth because I *promise* you, that's what'll happen. That has got to be the most wicked thing one can say when your body has just betrayed you in one of the cruelest and inhumane ways possible. Yes, inhumane. If you miscarry the way most women miscarry, you literally have to just sit and let your baby die inside of you.

Let me say that again.

You have to sit . . . and let your baby DIE . . . inside of you.

You know how sometimes people will say "you had *one job*"? Well for a mom, when she's pregnant, her *one job* is to protect her and her baby for ten fucking months and then deliver a happy, healthy bundle of joy. If having a baby was to be compared to running a race, it's like hearing the shotgun, take off running, and then tripping and breaking your ankle ten steps in. Except I didn't break *both* of my ankles so I was able to hobble to the finish line. Yaaaaay. Go. Me.

So no, people do not think about that when they say those acid-dipped niceties in an attempt to empathize with you. And if you were raised like I was raised, you simply nod your head and quietly say "I know," because you're never, ever, EVER supposed to question the hand of God. Especially publicly. But my God, did I ever have so many questions. I often imagined myself face to face with God, going toe to toe with him. I imagined the conversation going something like this:

"Adiba."

"GOD."

"How can I help you, my child?" He rolls his eyes, clearly exasperated with me.

"Well, you can start by helping me understand why you thought it was cool to take *my* child back. I meeeeaaaaan . . . you have like eight trillion little baby souls just hanging out, waiting for their number to come up. My little guy's number came up and what—you got greedy? You became number dyslexic and called the wrong one up? Like—who in the hell do you think are just taking gifts back?"

God heaves a big sigh. "I think I'm God. And he wasn't ready."

"Says who? You?"

"Well . . . yes, actually."

I attempt to stare down God. "Well, fuck you, then, God! You're not mighty! You're just mean! Mean and cruel and selfish and you don't give one goddamn about your so-called 'children.' You just want what you want—fuck how it makes us feel! You're not a father at all! No father would claim to love his child only to kill his grandchild!"[24]

Now, before you get all self-righteous and indignant with me for cursing at God, (a) this was my imaginary conversation with God; (b) I was in the throes of grief and if you for one second thought I needed to be "respectful" at that moment, you don't know grief AND you should probably check yourself before you wreck yourself; and (c) even when I'm not pissed to high-hell with the big guy (yes, it happens), I talk to him like he's the homie because that's the kind of God relationship that feels authentic for me. God knows exactly who I am and how I do. We good.

---

24.   Good Christian ladies, please don't come for my neck, and please don't stop reading here. (a) The good book says thou shall not judge; and (b) I am a human being describing my very human feelings and experiences. Allow me the grace to experience this with me.

But like I said, this was my imagination. In reality, all I could do was have very one-sided scream-cry prayer sessions with a figure I wasn't so sure I still believed in because Mom said, "Give it to God." As far as I was concerned, I didn't want to "give it to God." The greedy bastard had already taken it away.

*

I've always had a . . . different . . . relationship with God and "the church." One of my earliest memories of God and saints and the likes thereof was spending summer afternoons at my Titi Ana's house, and seeing a bust of bloody Jesus wearing a crown of thorns, and looking as forlorn as the day is long. You were supposed to touch it upon leaving her house, as you offered the family blessings and prayer. I never did. It freaked me out. I mean, what seven-year-old wants to touch a bloody statue—Jesus or not? I used to think that as soon as I touched it Jesus was going to come to life and announce all of my seven-year-old sins to the family. Everyone would then know that I secretly daydreamed about my cousin, Carlitos. I wasn't touching Jesus. Titi Ana's house was full of statues of saints, and she had turned her hall closet into an *ofrenda*, complete with candles in little red cups, and incense and small bowls of water. She had a prayer for everything, and Lord help you if you used God's name in vain in her house. The paradox of all of this? This same woman, my Titi Ana, whom I loved with my entire heart, would gather all of my tias in the kitchen when Hector, the Puerto Rican tarot reader from down the hall, would come over. One by one they'd each have their fortunes told or cards and palms read. And then touch bloody Jesus on the way out, after offering up the signatory *"A Dios Te Bendiga!"*(translation: "May God bless you!"). Hector was at the house when I returned to Titi's house after her son's funeral. My uncle Willie had been murdered, and my mother took me to the funeral. I remember thinking it was so unfair that Willie died because he left behind my cousin Lisa. Lisa was two years younger than me and didn't go to her father's funeral. I remember thinking she should have gotten to see her dad one last time, and when I got back to the apartment, all of my cousins were asking me what it was like, what did Willie look like? I think Lisa heard me describing her dad, and I got in trouble for running my mouth. But in my mind, God would have wanted her to be there to say goodbye, but also, God wouldn't have taken him away in the first place. I didn't know who to be madder at that night—myself, God, or my tias and mom for scolding me. This was my first clear experience with God—he got me in trouble.

When I was eight, the white pastors at the church we attended tried to have Child Protective Services remove me from my mother's home, in the name of "doing the Lord's work," because we were living in a boarding house. According to them, that was no way for a young child to live, and they were going to do something about it. Were they right? Is a boarding house an ideal way for a child to grow up? Nope, it's not. But what is more important—having a roof over your head or having a certain *kind* of roof over your head? I'm not even going to go into the deep historical ties to slavery, the slave trade, and the separation of families this action held. However, the fact that these white pastors felt completely comfortable separating a Black girl-child from her Latin, Black-passing parent, and had the audacity to justify it with "because God said so"? Wheeeeew, child! You have no idea how much I wanted to knock the mess out of those pastors—to this day I can still imagine their faces running into my fists! Like, N-word, show me just where God said you should separate children and parents, and why you get to be the arbiter of this separation? This was my second experience with God—manipulation.

And the list goes on and on of instances I've had in various churches growing up that really made me question the whole idea of church, and definitely had me questioning God's work if these folks were his followers and carrying out his word on a daily basis. If these were supposedly the best of the best Christians, he needed to go back to the drawing board and maybe start with stick figures. The basics—starting with "thou shall not judge," because judgment is exactly what I found when I showed up at my home church in Richmond, Texas, a little more round and a little less married than when I'd left. Now, to understand all that I'm about to get into, I have to explain the hierarchy of the traditional Black Baptist church to you. First and foremost, you have Pastor and Pastor's wife, i.e. First Lady. Then you have the church mothers (the oldest ladies in the church who have basically been there since the damn thing was erected), assistant pastors, and the deacons. After that you have the choir director, who depending on how the pastor runs the church, may think they are actually next in line after First Lady. Rest assured, they are not. Lastly, there are the ushers. They are literally the gatekeepers. They stand between you and communion. You and Missionary Sunday. You and the opportunity to catch the Holy Ghost during the choir director's showy and extended version of Hezekiah Walker's "Grateful." Mess around and get to church at 11:15 a.m. and you can rest assured you'll be watching Pastor through the little windows in the doors—from the lobby.

In my experience, the ushers and the church mothers are also the carrier pigeons of the church. Yeah, I said it. Fight me. If you need to get a note to Sister Alston on the left side of the church, fifth row, three people in, you hand it to the usher and you best believe Sister Alston will make eye contact with you halfway through service and give you the "I got you, sis" nod. They know who's dating who, whose great uncle just passed to the other side, and who was "in the family way" before anyone else does. And just like carrier pigeons, it's only a matter of time before other folks know too. I was no exception. I hadn't been to church since the day I found out I was pregnant. Having grown up in a fairly religious home (don't take the Lord's name in vain, first comes marriage then comes baby, pray before every meal, etc.), I had a fair amount of shame around getting knocked up by a man I'd only known for maaaybeee two months. Feeling like I'd disappointed God, my mother, and yes, even myself (because I knew better, but Jill Scott will get you EVERY TIME), it took everything in me to pull on those ridiculously unflattering maternity pants, grab my bible and waddle my ever-widening behind into church that Sunday morning. Greeted by the ushers, I watched as their eyes went from my face to my much rounder-than-before belly, and listened as their voices rose three octaves and became so filled with saccharine I damn near got a cavity.

"Oh my word! Look who it is!" said Pigeon 1.

"Sister Adiba! We haven't see you in so loooong!" said Pigeon 2.

I shifted my weight uncomfortably. "Yes, ladies, it's been a while."

"It certainly has been!" Pigeon 1 replied, glancing at my belly.

"Well, it looks like you've been pretty busy growing a new little one!" Pigeon 2 continued.

The tongue-in-cheekness of this comment was not lost on me.

"Oh! Yes, yes I have been. This is some work! I'm going to go to my seat—my feet are screaming. Bye, ladies!"

By the time I'd waddled myself to my usual seat on the second pew two people in, the pigeons had carried out their work. George, the choir director and someone I used to chat with on the regular, sat down on the pew in front of me, draped his arm over the back of it, and turned to look at . . . my belly. I looked at the top of George's head.

"Miss Adiba."

"Hi, George!"

George finally looked up at me.

"So," he said, popping his tongue, "a little birdie told me that you have a little one on the way."

Internally, I lit myself on fire. Externally, I stayed cool as Badu.

"Oh? A little birdie, huh?"

George allowed his eyes to travel back down to my belly.

"Yes, ma'am. And from the looks of it, they were right! Congratulations, honey. Who's the daddy? And how come I haven't met him?"

Y'all.

When I tell you I wanted to read George from Sunday to Sunday, loudly? Whew, chile! Who did this busybody choir director think he was, questioning why he hadn't met the father of my unborn child? This man took six months to get my name right—he wasn't entitled to a damn thing. No sir, not you, George. But I was in the House of the Lord, so reading George for filth was out of the question. But never forget. I am a Scorpio. We live for the sting.

I looked at George square in his nosey-ass face.

"George, did I ever tell you about the pet bird I had that I intentionally fed raw rice to, because it talked too much?"

And just like that, George up and walked back to the choir stand. I pulled myself up out of my pew, squeezed through the numerous groups of people talking and glancing at my belly as I passed them, rubbing belly to belly, and walked out of the church. Fighting back tears and swallowing down the lump in my throat as hard as I could, I pushed past the pigeons as they called behind me, and quickly waddled to my car. Once there, it was all I could do to keep from screaming "I'M SORRY" at the top of my lungs. The tears rolled down my face, hot and heavy and dripping brown foundation onto my tan pants. Two years prior, when I began attending that church, I felt it was much too big for me, having come from a teeny, tiny church in Mesa, Arizona. It was kind of crazy that within five short months, it could instantly feel like I had gotten too big for it. Again, I was at a crossroads with God. I had come to his house seeking solace, and what I found was poorly hidden judgment. Now, I'm sure someone reading this is saying, "Sis, God wasn't judging you—people were," and while that's true, at that moment they were one and the same, and there was no longer room for me in the house.

God might as well have just changed the locks.

MY BABY REVEAL TRUMPS YOUR GENDER REVEAL

"Why is she white?"

"I'm sorry, what did you say?"

"Why is she white?" I said emphasizing each word.

Those are literally the first words that came out of my mouth as they pulled my daughter out of my belly and held her pruned-up body over the curtain for me to get my first glimpse.

"Adiba, all babies are born white. They get their coloring as time goes on," my OB-GYN explained to me through poorly hidden chuckles.

Her words simply did not register.

To give you some context, I am the exact same color as a Hershey's milk chocolate bar, and her father was only one, *maybe* two shades lighter than me. The tiny human that was pulled from me? That child was lily-white. So I immediately turned to her father, looked him in the eye, and swore up and down that I had not cheated on him. Like the doctor, he too chuckled. Oh, the irony. The truth behind that chuckle wouldn't hit me for another seven months.

But we'll get into that later. Right now, I'm telling you about the first moments of my life with my daughter.

Truthfully, the day I became a mother is kind of a blur. I remember my doctor being surprised that she was so tiny (only 5lb 13oz) since I looked like I had ingested a deflated beach ball and then slowly inflated it with each breath that I'd taken over nine months. And I remember whispering the words "please cry, please cry," to both my tiny human *and* myself.

I had experienced what felt like damn near every possible trauma during my pregnancy—three months of bedrest, the loss of her twin, losing my job, preeclampsia, and the news that my neighbor had died by suicide, leaving a wife and two young children behind. The mere fact that *I* had survived all of that was a miracle. The fact that *she* survived it warranted a teeny tiny purple heart—and a cry—if only to prove that she'd made it, against the odds.

I needed to cry as a sort of proof that I was going to be a great mom. I mean, wasn't I supposed to be feeling all sorts of happiness and profoundness, manifesting itself into a puddle of tears?

But, really, I was terrified, so I just kept praying. *Please cry, please cry, please cry.*

The room was eerily silent—it felt like everyone else was waiting for her to cry too. And then, finally, there it was. A wail that pierced the air, and subsequently the hearts of everyone in that delivery room.

Everyone's except mine.

I lay there, my body cut open and strapped to the operating table like Jesus on the cross, and I had no idea who I was or, more specifically, who I was supposed to become.

I had no understanding of how this teeny tiny human, who couldn't even see colors, would make me into a full-fledged adult who pays bills on time, stares down neurologists, and Milly-Rocks through IEP (Individual Education Plan) meetings. They say having a kid changes everything. I'd add: especially when that kid has a disability.[25]

---

25.   In hindsight, those first few minutes of my kid's life are so authentic to who we are (now), Miss Emory and I, individually and to each other. Me, mostly confused about what the hell is happening around me but participating fully in an exercise of "I'm okay, you're okay," and Emory, doing what she damn well pleases when she's damn well good and ready.

*

A tall man with a fluff of dark hair on his head squeak-walked into my hospital room and my first thought was, this can't be good. His hair was so fluffy it looked like he perpetually walked around being followed by a rain cloud, like Joe Btfsplk from the *Li'l Abner* comic strip. Hair like that can't bring good news.

"Hi, Mrs. Webster. I'm the pediatrician on duty today."

"Nelson."

"Ma'am?"

"Nelson. I'm Ms. Nelson, not Mrs. Webster. My daughter has her father's last name, but we're not married."

I'm sure Jeff was less than thrilled with my response—his heavy sigh filling up the room, and serving as evidence of his disapproval. But I didn't care. As far as I was concerned, he was half the reason I was even in this situation.

"Oh. Okay. Well like I said, I'm the pediatrician on duty today, and I've seen your daughter this morning. We had to—"

"Is she still white?"

"Ma'am?"

"Emory—my daughter. When they took her out of me, she was really white, but they assured me she would get her color. I'm wondering if that has happened yet."

I'm sure you're thinking, "Why the hell is this girl so fixated on this poor baby's skin color?" Well, for one, I had absolutely no idea two brown people could produce a white baby (without there being albinism in the family). And secondly, it was basically the only thing I could wrap my head around at the moment.

This older white male doctor looked simultaneously perplexed and annoyed. "Is she still white . . . yes, ma'am. Your daughter is still white and will be for quite some time. It can sometimes take months for their color to come in. But I want to talk to you about her—"

"What was her Apgar score?"

Y'all. I was like the interrupting cow in those jokes second graders like to tell. I couldn't let this man finish his sentence for the life of me.

"Her Apgar score? How do you know about Apgar scores?"

"I studied child development in college, on my way to earning my bachelor of Social Work."

"Oh. Okay. Well then, you'll be happy to know that we did it twice and she scored an eight, and then a nine. She's doing great. However, she has something called Erb's palsy. Are you familiar with that, Mrs. Webster?"

"Nelson."

"Oh yes, I'm sorry. Have you heard of Erb's palsy before, Ms. Nelson? Did they study that in your classes?"

I swear he asked that last question with a hint of smugness in his voice, as if to say, "Since you know so much, let's see if you know this."

"No. I have never heard of Erb's palsy—only cerebral palsy. Is it like that?"

"Oh no, no Mrs. We—Nelson. Erb's palsy is nothing like cerebral palsy except that they share a last name. Basically, her left arm doesn't function. It is completely limp. We are sending you home with this list of exercises to do with her on a daily basis to help her gain use, strength, and mobility of her arm."

All I could think was, *Ain't this some shit?* I mean, I wasn't even supposed to have *gotten* pregnant. I wasn't! I took Plan B and that shit failed. And then I lost her twin in the bloodiest of bathroom scenes, took extra care of myself because *this* kid had to make it, only for this doctor to essentially shrug his shoulders at me and say, "You get what you get and you don't throw a fit." Sorry not sorry, but I wanted to throw a fit. I wanted to throw the biggest goddamn fit this hospital had ever seen. I wanted them to 5150 my ass because how in the hell was I expected to do exercises to strengthen the arm of a baby I wasn't supposed to have, didn't even know, and wasn't even sure I could love? I felt like I was on one of those game shows from the 1950s where the host informs you that you've won a brand new toaster, instead of the whole kitchen remodel you thought you were getting, and the camera zooms in on your face so the audience can see your disappointment masquerading as happy contentment. I understood the words that were coming out of his mouth, but they weren't quite computing.

Was this doctor really telling me that in addition to not fucking up my tiny human, I had to also fix her? Right out of the gate? Jesus H. Christ. What kind of fresh hell is this?[26]

I tuned back in.

"For how long will we have to do said exercises? Will her arm eventually work?"

"Well, you'll do them until you can't do them anymore."

I think this is where I gave him "the Adiba." That's what my best friend calls the look I give when someone says something that is completely ridiculous, or so out of pocket that I want to claw their face off. I raise one eyebrow. Just one.

"Excuse me? Until I can't do them anymore? What does that even mean?"

"Well, Mrs. We—"

"Nelson." I snap back at him through clenched teeth.

"Ms. Nelson, it means that by the time your daughter is four or five months old, she will have all of the mobility she will ever have in that arm. Then what you have is just what you have, so you don't have to do the exercises anymore. But don't worry—she'll be fine. Any other questions?"

My brain raced. Any other questions? A million, in fact, like: Who raised you? Didn't your mama teach you better? Don't you have home training? You don't deliver news that someone's baby isn't perfect like you're explaining why a shoe doesn't fit! I've seen waiters have more compassion in explaining why the kitchen can't cook my steak to medium correctly! And why the hell is it so hard for you to remember my last name?

---

26. Reader, you can judge me if you want to. But what you're getting here is the pure, unadulterated, unfiltered thoughts of a new mom who up until nine months prior to this moment had reconciled herself to being everyone's cool Aunt 'Diba. So yeah, I think a healthy dose of shock and awe are apropos for this moment. Continue.

However, what came out of my mouth was kind and pleasant and thankful (because *I* have home training). "No other questions, thank you. When will they bring her to me?"

"Shortly."

And with that, the pediatrician with the dark cloud of bad news hair turned on his heels and squeak-walked out of my room.

I never saw him again.

I laid in my bed, somewhat in a stupor. On one hand it sounded like I had just been told that my daughter had a disability, but on the other hand, it sounded like the doctor didn't think it was a *big* disability, that I shouldn't worry about it too much.

I didn't realize there was a "sliding scale" of disability. My mom had been a special education teacher when I was a kid, but that was in the '80s when mainstreaming (preinclusion) was the hot new thing, and most of her students had pretty severe disabilities and behaviors. So, when the pediatrician was so cavalier about this Erb's palsy thing, it just didn't make sense. In my mind disability meant big and laboring and intense, and Miss Emory was teeny and tiny. And though I would soon find out how intense she could be, at that moment she was just a delicate little thing.

They brought her to me, wrapped up like a tiny burrito. I knew I was supposed to do something with this child. I was supposed to ooh and aah and proclaim to any and everyone that was in my room that this was the happiest moment of my life, and spew out all those things that new moms say in diaper commercials. But I had just gotten news that my kid had a disability—that, granted, may or may not correct itself—and was white.

I was scared. I was in shock. Hormones were coursing through my body like a damn dumpster fire. How do people do this, I wondered? How did my mom do this?

Sweet baby Jesus in the manger.

I was a mother.

I was a mother and I didn't want to be. I hadn't planned this. I was a mother and I didn't know *how* to be. I mean, as a child and family social worker I had coached hundreds of new moms on how to bond with their baby, and the importance of skin-to-skin contact, and how it aids with baby's self-regulation, but for me personally? I had never done any of those things—I was just telling moms to do what my studies told me worked. But did I *really* know how to establish a bond with a baby? Heck no! What was I supposed to do with this small person?

I stared at her in her clear, plastic bassinet for a long time. They kept saying she belonged to me. We even had matching bracelets saying so, but she didn't *feel* like mine. For fuck's sake, she was white! I didn't feel like I was her mother. And what's worse—I didn't feel bad about feeling detached. I felt . . . indifferent. You could have told me they had fruity pebbles on the hospital lunch menu and that would have elicited more excitement than everyone squealing and squawking about me being a new mom.

I didn't know this person, yet I was expected to instantly love her? I'm sorry, but no. I don't work that way.

In hindsight, my feelings in this moment are difficult for me to wrap my head around. I loved growing this child. I did. Everything about being pregnant, even the really difficult parts, I loved. I made sure to eat (mostly) healthy foods—no fast foods, no sushi, no lunch meats, and only half a cup of coffee every other day. I took my prenatal pills religiously and added iron when the ob-gyn told me I was testing anemic. My only vice was strawberry Fanta and Captain Crunch with Crunch Berries. I did yoga. I played music through headphones and placed them on my belly. I read bedtime stories to her. I. Loved. This. Baby. So that love *should have* continued after I delivered her, but it didn't.

So, when the witch of a lactation specialist came in and tried to coax my child to drink from my non-filling breasts, it should have come as no surprise that this white baby wouldn't latch on. Fitting, ain't it? It was almost as if this tiny human sensed that I wasn't really feeling her and was just like, "Well, fuck you, then! I didn't wanna drink from your raggedy-ass titty anyway!"

And so it was. After about fifteen minutes of Broom-Hilda the Lactation Witch positioning this child in twenty-nine thousand ways to prompt latching, manhandling my breasts with her stubby, cold fingers, putting a nipple condom, a.k.a latch guard, over my areola to get the kid to suckle from the plastic teat of indifference, we gave up and stuck a bottle in her mouth. My kid drank some infant formula (judge yaself), and I stared blankly at the television. I watched *The Price is Right* and secretly wondered what the price would be for a new baby.

I've never admitted that thought until now. But here it is. Living outside the dark corners of my mind, on the page, in perpetuity. It was a fleeting thought. Like when you briefly wonder what your mail person would look like naked and then you're like, "Ew! Fuck! What the hell was that?" and you shake your head to rid yourself of the thought. It was that kind of thought. But it was there.

I didn't hold her much after that feeding. I didn't dress her to come home. I didn't put her in her car seat. I let everyone else do all the things because I simply couldn't. I couldn't make my hands and fingers move to the choreography of "doting mother," and I couldn't make the receptors in my brain seek out and latch on to the new mom endorphins that were supposedly racing through my body. Instead, I did what I do when I find myself in a crowd of people I don't know. I hung back in the cut, waiting to see how this small person was going to . . . be . . . so I could decide if I liked her or not, if I wanted to spend time with her or not. Detached is putting it nicely. I did not know this person and wasn't sure that I wanted to. I knew that I was *supposed* to, but I just couldn't.

On paper I was a MINO—Mother in Name Only.

In my heart, I was lost.

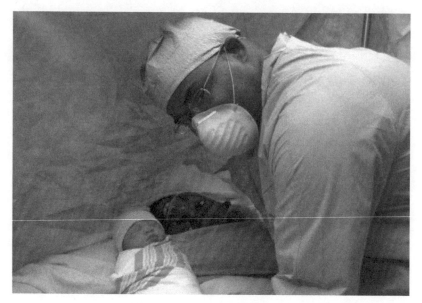

Two very brown parents, and their very white baby

DOES THIS BABY MAKE ME LOOK SAD?

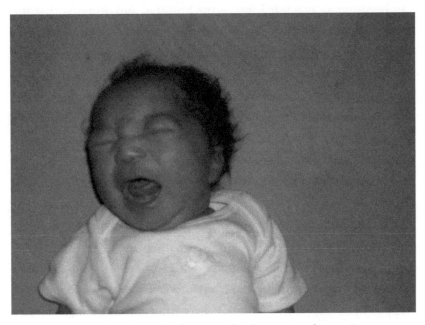

First day home. Is she a tiny bird, or a tiny human?

This.

This screaming baby is who I brought home from the hospital. This photo was taken within thirty minutes of us being home, and her sentiments mimicked mine to a T. She was screaming her face off like a damn banshee, and I was doing the EXACT SAME THING—on the inside. It felt like there were tiny razor-sharp minions trying to claw their way out of my skin and carry me away.

Almost like they were reconfiguring the cells in my brain so that I could see my child but not fully comprehend what it was I was looking at, or what I was supposed to do with it. I wanted to be anywhere but there. In hindsight, that is probably why I took this picture. I was so detached from this tiny human that the notion of mothering was as foreign to me as cleaning and disemboweling fresh fish. Not a thing I knew how to do, nor a thing I wanted to do, and if there was a way I could get out of doing it, I was going to try. I remember looking at Emory screaming at the top of her lungs, laying on our couch next to a mountain of laundry that had not been put away while I was in the hospital, and thinking that she looked like one of those baby birds who squawk relentlessly after they are born, waiting for the mama bird to come vomit into their mouths. It was at that moment that I nicknamed her "Birdie." This small human, squawking and squawking, waiting for me to put her to my bare chest and coo in her ear that it was all going to be okay, and not to worry because she was home now. But I did not do that. Instead, I grabbed my camera to document the pure disdain this child had for her new environment. Unbeknownst to me this was also, inadvertently, the very first documentation of the detachment I felt for the person that was literally attached to my insides just four short days ago.

I looked at this child, screaming on my couch, snapped a photo, and walked into the kitchen to chat with my neighbor who had just popped in to meet the new baby. I don't know if they thought it weird or mean or cruel that I didn't comfort my newborn, but I figured she was fine because Jeff was nearby. In hindsight, it *was* weird, it *was* mean, and yes, it *was* cruel.

Over the next two months, my imagination became so vivid and so gruesome that I refused to hold my child. My imagination led me down dark and twisted alleyways. Alleyways I'm embarrassed to admit to. I saw myself feeding my baby limb by limb to large packs of rabid dogs. I imagined dropping her on the hardwood floor, shattering her into a million little pieces, sending blood spraying up onto the walls, into my hair, onto my tongue. My imagination convinced me that I would surely kill my child any chance I got. Soon my imagination was joined by a sadness so deep and so foreign to the cells of my body that the only thing that felt familiar to my limbs was the light blue robe and slippers I wore every morning for the ten months of my pregnancy. My body rejected T-shirts and leggings and bras and underwear. Everything made me itch. Everything made me want to crawl out of my skin. For days on end I insisted on wearing the beautiful, mesh, over-the-bellybutton underwear the nurses send you home with after giving birth. When I had run through all the pairs, I called the hospital and asked where and how I could get more.

One night, approximately two weeks postpartum, I swore my body had finally rejected itself. I woke up to feed a very hungry Emory, and midway through nursing her I felt like I was going to drown her in my vomit. I held her close to me as I stumbled down the hall to my bedroom, halfway tossed her onto the bed, and ran to the toilet. I hovered over the cold toilet as sweat rolled down my temples, down the tip of my nose, and drip-dropped into the toilet and onto the floor, creating a small puddle of myself around me. My heart was racing and my head was pounding. I laid on the floor and wondered if *I* would burst into a million pieces and mingle my blood with my sweat, and maybe congeal with Jeff's tears when he found me. The tile was cold. I was hot. I was begging God to either take me or save me. And then I vomited again and fell asleep. On the floor, in a pile my own vomit, dreaming of a life I didn't know. I do not know how long I laid there, but I woke to Jeff peeling me up off the floor, as I tried to convince him to call 911. He refused to call, convinced it was something I ate, but I knew better. Something was very wrong, but I didn't know what *it* was. I didn't have a name for it. In the mornings it turned my mouth into a foreign entity on my face, my tongue a stranger in a strange land. The only taste that felt familiar on my tongue was coffee, which I drank every morning, in the same spot, at the same time, crying the same tears, every morning. Everyone in the house was buzzing around me—Jeff was playing with Emory, his other children were watching television, everyone was coming in and out of the kitchen for cereal, juice, and they would look in my general direction, but I didn't so much as shift to the left or right. I simply sat and tried to stave off the screams threatening to erupt from my throat at any given moment. Jeff asked me questions or began conversations with me, and I stared at him blankly, knowing that he was speaking (because his lips were moving), but not understanding the words coming out of his mouth. It was like listening to the teacher in the Peanuts cartoons: "Womp womp, womp-womp-womp, womp."

Jeff tried to involve me in caring for our daughter, but I simply couldn't bring myself to do much of it. It didn't help that I was failing miserably at breastfeeding. Apparently, I had flat nipples. Broom-Hilda, the Lactation Witch at the hospital, sent me home with nipple shields to help Emory latch on. If you're not familiar with what those are, I will tell you. They are these small, round, flat-ish plastic discs that you place on top of the areola, and supposedly your baby sucks *that* into their mouth, which in turn is supposed to suck your nipple up and into the little plastic cone that has formed in your child's mouth. When this does not happen, what they *actually* do is succeed in making you feel like an incompetent piece of shit mother who is destined to send your child into lifelong therapy because you're messing up key parts of growth and development that are formed from the mother/child skin-to-skin bond that everyone tells you about. This bond was not happening. Breastfeeding was not happening. Nothing, absolutely nothing, was coming out of my nipples, no matter how many different ways I positioned that damn disk or my child. Emory gulped down air bubble after air bubble, which if you know anything about babies and air, led to extreme gas in her belly, which led to, you guessed it, screaming. Lots and lots of loud, violent screaming. I say violent because in her frustration of hunger paired with pain, she would physically push her body away from mine when I would attempt to breastfeed her.

She had one good arm, and with it she pushed as hard as she possibly could to get away from the woman who was making every meal a nightmare. The physical rejection only added to the emotional dissonance I was already feeling. I felt hopeless. I wondered if her physical rejection of me was in some way her response to my own physical rejection of her. Did she know I was struggling? Was this her way of "paying me back"? Was she taking the position of "Well, if you don't want anything to do with me, I don't want anything to do with you either"? These things, as irrational and nonsensical as they were, popped into my brain time and time again, serving to keep me in the downward spiral of shame and despair, and a sadness I'd never known.

I wish I could say it ended there. That I miraculously snapped myself out of it, pulled myself together, and got on with the act of mothering, but that is not how my story goes. It wasn't just two weeks of feeling "down in the dumps" or having the "new mommy blues." This was a constant, everyday yoke around my neck. At my two-week check-up, Dr. Thornton handed me the Edinburgh Postnatal Depression Scale (EPDS) assessment, instructed me to answer the questions to the best of my ability, and left the room. I looked at this form with its ten questions and slowly began to answer them, having no idea what any of the questions and answers meant in the grander scheme of things. Questions like:

1. I have been able to laugh and see the funny side of things.
   - As much as I always could
   - Not quite so much now
   - Definitely not so much now
   - Not at all
2. I have been anxious or worried for no good reason.
   - No, not at all
   - Hardly ever
   - Yes, sometimes
   - Yes, very often

And eight more questions about how I felt on a day-to-day basis during the previous week. The highest you can score on the assessment is thirty points. The rubric states that "mothers who score above a thirteen are likely to be suffering from a depressive illness of varying severity."[27] Dr. Thornton walked back into the room and I quietly handed her back the form, not looking up from my fingers fumbling with each other in my lap. I figured if I focused on my hands, I would not have to make eye contact with her and run the risk of bursting into tears right there in her office. After a few moments I could feel her eyes on me.

"Adiba, how are you feeling today?"

"Do you mean, like, am I hungry, oooor . . . " my voice trailed off.

"Emotionally—how are you feeling?"

I still couldn't look at Dr. Thornton, but I did open my mouth to speak. Except no sound came out. I closed my mouth, swallowed. Swallowed again, and then opened my mouth to speak again, and that's when I felt that familiar tug at the corners of my lips. The tug that told me my heart was about to betray me. I quickly covered my mouth and felt the hot tears weaving trails of fire down my cheeks.

"Adiba, the highest you can score on this assessment is thirty. You scored a twenty-five."

There was nothing I could say to that. I had no response. I couldn't tell her that I wasn't sad because the proof that I was actually *more* than just sad was right there, in black and white. All I could do was sob, and gulp for air. This woman, Dr. Thornton, who was typically so stoic and rather brash suddenly softened and put her arm around my shoulders as my chest heaved up and down, heavy with an invisible pain I could not name.

"Do you want me to get Jeff?"

I managed to squeak out a barely audible "No."

"Okay. Do you want to talk to someone about what's going on?"

---

27.   Quoted directly from the Edinburg Postnatal Depression Scale (https://www.fresno.ucsf.edu/pediatrics/downloads/edinburghscale.pdf)

Again, I whispered, "No."

At this point she crossed the room, folded her arms across her chest as she leaned on the desk, and just watched me. You know how little kids cry when they've gotten scolded, and they can't catch their breath and it sounds like they're hyperventilating and then all of a sudden they'll let out a very weird sounding moan, of sorts; before starting the entire charade all over again? That was me. She hadn't mentioned my daughter. She hadn't mentioned my traumatic pregnancy or the fact that my child was born white and with a bum arm. She had simply asked me how I was feeling. And this was my answer.

I'm feeling about like THIS.

"Adiba, you are in the throes of postpartum depression. Many women experience this after giving birth—it's due to the body's sudden drop in hormones after delivering a baby. Some women's bodies can readjust and get back to normal and they are fine. Other women's bodies struggle, and their brain alters a bit, causing shifts in mood, energy, and overall wellness. But there's help available. If you are not willing to talk to someone about how you are feeling, would you like to try some medication?"

I looked at her and wondered why she wasn't asking me exactly *what* I had been feeling the previous week. Why hadn't she asked me what thoughts I'd been having, what was making me cry, how did I feel about being a new mother? Jeff didn't ask me these questions either. Two people on the planet now knew that I was "in the weeds," yet neither one of them bothered to ask me what was keeping me there. Jeff perhaps didn't know what to ask, or what to do with the information if I told him. But Dr. Thornton—wasn't that part of her job? Wouldn't that have been a proper follow-up? In hindsight, I am truly dismayed that not just a woman, but a fellow Black woman, left me out there. We hear testimonies so often these days about Black women not being believed by medical professionals, and read the studies that show that the mortality rate for Black pregnant women is two to three times as high as that of white women[28]—it hurts my heart knowing that one of my own didn't check on me—like *really* check on me and push me a bit harder, ask me more questions, but I digress.

"No, Dr. Thornton. I do not want to try medication. I don't know how my body will respond to that so I'd rather not."

"And you don't want a referral to a therapist?"

"No. I don't. Postpartum depression passes after some time, right?"

Clearly exasperated with me, she puffed out her cheeks and let out a slow, heavy sigh.

"Sometimes. But sometimes not without assistance."

"And how long does it typically take to pass, if it should pass on its own?"

"There's really no way to tell, Adiba. Some women get back to feeling like themselves in a few weeks, some women take months, and for some, it spirals into postpartum psychosis if left untreated."

I wiped away the teardrops that were gathering like a beard on my chin, sniffled, and finally looked right at Dr. Thornton, half chuckling.

"I highly doubt I'll slip into postpartum psychosis. I'm not *that* bad. Thanks for the information but I think I'll just let my body do its thing. I'll be fine in no time—I'm sure of it," I quipped as I hopped off the examination table and turned to leave. I was done. Done with this conversation, done with these feelings, just *done*. I met Jeff and Emory in the waiting room. Emory was asleep in her carrier, and I just stared at her, waiting to feel something come alive inside of me. What I felt was the sudden urge to knock the carrier out of Jeff's hands and walk away. I immediately turned my attention to Jeff.

"Everything go okay?" he asked.

"Yep! Everything is fine."

"You sure?"

"I'm sure."

---

28. Stat taken from the Centers for Disease Control website (https://www.cdc.gov/reproductivehealth/maternal-mortality/disparities-pregnancy-related-deaths/infographic.html)

Truth is, I was NOT sure. I wasn't sure of anything. And as fate would have it, I wasn't going to be sure of anything for quite some time.

Four weeks into motherhood. I do not recognize this woman at all.

I woke up Saturday morning and just stared at the ceiling. It was the day that Jeff was going to be returning to work, and I was going to be home alone with Emory for the first time. She was three weeks old and up to that point someone had always been around—my godmother had come to visit, Jeff's kids were at the house, he was home, so I was able to skate by, not having to do much by way of actual physical care of my child by myself. I didn't have to bathe her because . . . drowning. I fed her from the safety of the couch because . . . dropping and shattering. I mean—don't get me wrong. I tried to do the typical mom things like tummy time and reading to her, however, Jeff put the kibosh on my bedtime reading routine when he caught me reading Edgar Allen Poe's "The Pit and the Pendulum" to our week-old daughter. The writer in me justified it as a way to expose her to the rhythm found in the cadence of beautifully constructed sentences. He quickly informed me that she could find the same thing in *Brown Bear, Brown Bear,* and hoisted her off my lap and into her bassinet. He couldn't say I didn't try. However, I had managed to play it mostly safe, not doing much, up to that day. But Saturday was upon us—there was no escaping it. I laid there and just stared at the ceiling, trying not to move a muscle, not even to breathe. I could hear her stirring in her bassinet at the foot of the bed, and I was fairly sure that if she heard me or saw me, she'd want me, and then I'd actually have to mother. Jeff was still asleep, knocked out cold, and I secretly resented him for not only still sleeping, but for actually not stopping when I'd said "don't stop" eleven months ago, and for not being more observant and proactive about how not okay I obviously was. I wondered how on earth he thought it was okay to leave his newborn child with a woman who wouldn't even cut her baby's fingernails for fear that she'd cut the whole tip of her finger off, and had literally tried to argue him down to keep him from doing it. But we had bills to pay, mouths to feed, and a mortgage to cover so I had to pull on my big girl mesh panties, and mother.

Ugh.

I sat up in bed like it was the morning after my twenty-first birthday. I was wobbly, couldn't see straight, and could literally feel my insides shift. Thanks, C-section. I stared at Emory's profile through the netting of her bassinet. One little baby nose, an ear, eyelashes that could already land her a contract with L'Oréal Paris, and a head full of curls. Her perfect little lips puckered and retracted over and over, and I knew she was hungry. *Welp, I guess I'm gonna start this mothering thing today, whether I want to or not,* I thought to myself as I got up off the bed and slipped into the blue robe. Sliding into my matching slippers, I shuffled over to the bassinet to stare at the baby people continuously said was mine. With as much indifference as I offered her, she offered it right back to me, staring at me, blankly. Both of us assessing each other, imagining what the day had in store for us. I wondered if she had an imagination at that young age, and knew that if she did, she was most likely imagining a world where someone else was her mom. The look on her face said it all. "Ugh. God. It's you. Fuck this up and it's a wrap, chick." And I knew it too. I had one job. One job: Don't kill the baby. That was it—make it through the day with both of us in one piece, mostly sane and fully fed and hydrated. I sucked my teeth, huffed, and kept shuffling to the bathroom and I swear on sweet baby Jesus in the manger I heard that child suck her teeth right back. Served me right.

Brushing my teeth and washing my face was part of my daily routine, but looking in the mirror, not so much. I knew I had been handling the most basic of my daily living activities—taking a shower, brushing my teeth, wiping front to back. But it was then when I finally looked at my reflection in the mirror that I caught a glimpse of the hot mess I'd become. The circles under my eyes were dark—goth girl dark. My hair, which I had recently cut because pregnancy had me looking like I had mange, was once again matted in the back, and liter-ally running away from my face in every goddamn direction. Did you know hair could do that? Hair can do that. Hair can literally say, "Ah, hell nah, bitch—we out," and try to make a mad dash for it. My skin was dry and ashy—the kind of ashy where if your grandma caught you outside like that, she would come out and grease you down in front of all of your friends—top to bottom—and dare you to say something about it. You could catch the best Wi-Fi in Houston just off the lines in my forehead. I. Was. A. Sight. If Beyoncé said pretty hurts, I was telling you that new motherhood was a full-frontal lobotomy with no anes-thesia. But this is what my kid was getting. I couldn't be bothered with cuteness when I was busy trying to not lose my shit minute to minute.

Swaddling Miss Emory and wrapping her into my robe, I held her against my body and shuffled us both along the carpeted pathway to the living room, placing her in the safest place in the house—the round, vibrating, bouncing chair that all babies love. Though I *wanted* to duct tape her to the dang thing (this way there was absolutely no way she could roll out—even though she was only weeks old and not even lifting her head on her own yet), I secured the straps around her little swaddled self, moved that chair to the very edge of the living room, where the carpet met the tile of the kitchen, and left her there while I made my coffee; while I made my toast; while I made her bottle. She watched me silently, probably making sure I didn't lace her milk with anything, and I moved silently. There was no cooing, no humming, no singing, only the shuff-shuff-shuffling of my blue slippers on the tile floor. Jeff emerged from the back of the house dressed and ready for work and immediately began doting on Emory. Something arose in me watching their love affair. It was a vaguely familiar feeling, but I recognized it. It was jealousy. I was jealous of the way Emory looked at him, the way he seemed to know exactly how to parent, the fact that he had absolutely zero fears when it came to holding our child. She smiled at him, slept on him, curled into him. She . . . well . . . we, had a marked disdain for each other, clumsily trying to figure each other out, and negotiating our relationship to one another on a daily basis.

I had to drive Jeff to work that morning and on top of panicking about having to put on clothes that I was pretty sure were not going to fit, I was almost in hysterics at the thought of having to drive my child home, alone, in Houston traffic. Getting there was easy because Jeff drove, but as soon as I sat in the driver's seat, I felt the walls of the car closing in. I saw the bloody car crash in my mind. I squeezed my eyes shut as tight as I could and tried to breathe my way into a regular heartbeat. After what felt like an eternity (but was probably mere seconds), I was able to begin driving, but my child wouldn't be my child if she wasn't going to make me face ALL the fears at one time. Ten minutes into the thirty-minute drive home, Emory began whimpering in her car seat. I immediately launched into prayer, begging God to keep her calm until we got home and I could get her back into the holy chair of good vibrations. But as usual, God was ignoring me, and this child catapulted herself into a full-on fit on I-45. She wailed at the top of her lungs the whole way home. And you know what? I wailed too. I didn't know what the hell else to do, and nothing I was trying with my one free hand was working. Not shaking her foot, rubbing her leg, extra-reaching to hold her pacifier in her mouth while steering with the other hand—nothing. Not even the trick of stopping the car two car lengths behind the car in front of you at a stoplight and then inching forward while applying the brakes every couple of seconds. I thought for sure that would lull her to sleep. Nope. But it *did* piss her off even more—so there was that. By the time we got home my nerves were shot and it was all I could do to not punt her into that damn vibrating chair. I put her down without bothering to strap her in and ran to the hall bathroom. I was sweating bullets, my heart was racing, the tears were flowing, but dammit, we were home, alive, and up to that point, I was succeeding at doing the basics of my job—keeping us both alive. Nobody said anything about keeping us both happy—we were just focusing on ALIVE. Anything else was a perk.

I would like to tell you that that was the last meltdown of the day and we went on to have the most perfect mommy-daughter day ever because my postpartum depression miraculously disappeared. That would be a lie of epic proportions. What happened later that day is hands down one of the most frightening, heartbreaking, and truly unfamiliar experiences of my motherhood journey. Remembering it, I don't even know the woman I'm about to tell you about. I'd never met her before that day. But apparently, she lived deep inside of me and just needed an opportunity to introduce herself.

It was around 6:00 p.m. and Emory had just woken up from her last nap of the day, screaming bloody murder at the top of her pint-size lungs. She was hungry and had no qualms about letting me know. I got up from the couch and walked into her room, already feeling the anxiety rise in my chest. In my head I was trying to talk myself down out of the tree I was climbing, en route to the highest limb I could find.

I wanted to get as far away from my child as I could. In reality I was quietly swaddling Emory as fast as I could so I could place her in her favorite chair and start making her bottle. I needed the screaming to stop as fast as possible. As I attempted to fold the bottom of her blanket up and over her feet, I noticed that my hands were shaking, and in my mind, I was getting higher and higher in that tree, closer and closer to that far out limb. I managed to get her swaddled pretty tightly, perhaps a little more tightly than need be, and got her to her chair but she wouldn't stop screaming. She was getting louder and louder by the second and the limb was getting closer and closer—that far out limb was now within reach. This tiny baby, who probably felt like I was starving her, scrunched up her face and screamed and wailed the most piercing scream I had ever heard. Every breath and wail felt like an indictment of each of my failures as a new mother. I felt the hot tears pour out of my eyes, and that's when I grabbed the limb.

I bent down and picked Emory up out of her vibrating chair and held her at arm's length. She was still screaming in my face, but I refused to hold her close to me; to comfort her. Instead, I held her at eye level, and screamed back at her.

"What? What do you want? Why won't you stop screaming? Stop it! Goddamn it, just stop! What is wrong with you?! Stop it!"

In my mind I felt that far-out tree limb I had grabbed onto begin to splinter. In reality, I felt my grip on my screaming daughter's swaddled body tighten, and in a brief moment of clarity I knew exactly what was about to happen if that limb broke; if I didn't put her back in her chair, immediately. I was about to shake my baby. I saw her head in my mind snapping back and forth on her tiny neck. Of all the horrific images that had paraded themselves across my frontal lobe since the minute we left the hospital, *this* image scared me the most—because it was real. It could *actually* happen. I could *actually* shake and potentially kill my child. I put her back in her chair before that limb gave way completely. I think I scared the shit out of myself. I was a child and family social worker with a background in child development. I knew all too well what happened when parents shook their babies, and

I knew that at that very moment, I was definitely not in my right mind. I was too high up in that tree, too far out on that limb, and I needed to climb back down as fast as I could. I may have been in the middle of a complete mental breakdown, but I knew that regardless of the thoughts I was having, I could not hurt my daughter. I stared at her, still screaming in her chair, still hungry, and walked past her into the farthest corner of the kitchen. I leaned into that corner, slid to the floor, screamed at the top of my lungs, and pulled at my hair, tears flowing uncontrollably from both of us. I cried and screamed and cursed God for what felt like an hour. I felt so ill-equipped for this so-called gift he had given me. Everyone had always told me I was going to be such a good mother, and I had always seen myself with four or five children, but here I was faced with one and I couldn't even handle our first day alone. I was terrified. I was devastated. I felt lost and alone and truly out of my element, as well as my mind. I didn't know a single person who had ever experienced postpartum depression, and the only things I'd ever seen about it was in Lifetime movies where white women killed their babies in bathtubs. This wasn't a Black woman thing. This wasn't a Puerto Rican woman thing. And if it was, we sure didn't talk about it—ever. Not to each other at least. I had managed to climb down out of the tree, but there was no one to tell about how high up I'd gone or what I'd seen.

I can't tell you how I managed to pull myself together because I honestly do not remember. I don't remember eventually feeding Emory, putting her to bed, or even Jeff coming home. I don't remember taking myself to bed, and I'm pretty sure I didn't tell Jeff about the events of the evening because the shame hung around my neck like a damn ox yoke. I also never told my doctor about that night. Instead, I prayed to God. Yes, the entity that I was beyond livid with and wasn't even sure I still believed in—that guy. I prayed that he would take it all away—the shame, the fright, the thoughts of harming my child, the jealousy I felt about the relationship she was forming with Jeff, the overwhelming never-ending sadness—all of it, just take it away, a little more each day.

For the next four weeks I tried my hardest to connect with her, to no avail. She still preferred to be read to by Jeff, still preferred to sleep on his chest, still curled her body into his first thing in the morning when he would bring her into our bed and lay her between us. I often felt like this was her way of paying me back for that night in the kitchen. I had abandoned her in her time of need and she knew it, and so not only had no further use for me but didn't trust me and didn't like me. But I pressed on. I was her mom and we had to have a relationship—a good one. She had to know me, had to love me. Because as the days went on that tree that had once been so huge, with far-reaching limbs, was looking more and more like a small shrub. The limbs could not support even the slightest bit of heavy and that was fine because my thoughts were becoming lighter and lighter every day.

Then, finally, there was no weight.

I found myself wanting to play with her more, wanting to hold her more, feel her heartbeat against my heartbeat more. I remembered being in the early stages of pregnancy and feeling her move right under the ribs on my left side, getting as close as she could to my heart. I held on to that feeling.

I finally worked up the nerve to give Emory a bath (by myself) when she was just about seven weeks old. It took me that long to rid myself of the thoughts that I might intentionally drown her in the tub, and though I definitely had some anxiety about it, I did it. I made up a silly song for her while she splashed the water with her feet. I washed her hair, watched her swat at the bubbles, and finally felt the tiniest inkling of "this is motherhood." The morning was starting off on the right foot, and I was feeling fairly light as I wrapped her in her towel and laid her on my bed. What happened next will forever live in my memory as the exact moment the weight disappeared. I laid her on my bed, leaned over her, and made a silly face.

She laughed.

My child, who had once held me in such disdain (as far as I believed), now looked at me, her mama, and laughed. And then she took her little hand and touched my face and smiled.

"Oh my gosh! You smiled at me! You think I'm funny!"

And like a kid with a new toy, I made that same silly face, just to watch her laugh and smile at me, over and over again. We had turned the corner. My child knew me, and for that moment, if *only* for that moment, she liked me. I grabbed the camera and snapped a picture. I never wanted to forget the moment my daughter forgave me for not being able to be her mom for her first two months of life. I needed to cement it in history as proof that we'd survived what seemed, at that point, to be the unthinkable. I dried her off, lotioned her up, dressed her, and proudly marched her into the kitchen (yes, the tile floor kitchen) to proclaim to Jeff that our daughter had smiled at me. His response: "Of course she smiled at you—you're her mother."

Yes, he was right. After almost two months of a deep and painful fog, and one deeply disturbing encounter with tree limbs, I was *finally* her mother.

The day the weight lifted, and I was finally her mother.

*Author's Note: I have shared some pretty intense feelings regarding my child in the earliest stages of her life, and you may be feeling some sort of way about it. You may be judging me. You may be ready to put this book down and write me off. But before you do that—ask yourself if you've ever asked any of your girlfriends what they went through *emotionally* after their babies were born. Odds are that you haven't. And there's nothing wrong with that, and everything wrong with that. As women, we are told that there is a laundry list of things we are never supposed to talk about, much less talk about out loud. How many women have taken their grief, their joy, their shame to the grave with them? I'm talking about it because nobody asked me, but my emotions around my early days as a mom are as real today as they were in 2009. The shame is still there. The embarrassment courses through my veins when I look at Emory today and wonder how I felt anything less than love for this child who literally makes me feel like I might explode when I see her, who I try to squeeze all the air out of when I hug her, and this child who tries with all her might to return the favor. So yes, I am sharing the ugliness of my motherhood story because there might just be a mom in the middle of her own ugly who needs to know that there is beauty on the other side.

I also want to state that in no way, shape, or form am I suggesting that the way I handled my postpartum depression be ANYONE's way of coping with clinical depression, or ANY mental health issues they are encountering. What I did was irresponsible, unsafe, and the complete OPPOSITE of healthy coping. I *should* have gone to see a therapist. I *should* have taken a prescription for antidepressants. Prayer and prayer alone is not the answer. I know this now.

WHOSE TRAUMA
IS IT ANYWAY?

"It's always something."

That is basically the motto of every special needs parent out there. There's always *something* in ourselves that we have to face, something going on with our children that we have to deal with, some new insurance agent we have to fight with—it's always *something*. It doesn't stop. When Emory was ten months old it was the comforting shock of her diagnosis. Comforting because Jeff and I finally had answers and our suspicions were confirmed, but shocking because, woah. Hello, major life change!

On this particular morning, eleven years after her initial diagnosis, the "something" I was contending with was Emory's menstrual cycle doubling as my own personal romp through Traumaland. This morning I found myself once again having to administer Emory's rescue medication (Diazepam) because her seizures were not stopping. While we have them mostly under control, once a month Aunt Flo rolls around and completely fucks our shit up. For most of us she just brings her usual bag of shenanigans—bloating, cramps, back pain, diarrhea, and a healthy dose of "I hate everything about everyone and you all should just die." But for my kiddo she pulls out the heavy artillery—all of that *plus* hormones that are raging so intensely her brain literally short circuits and throws her into a multiple seizure land. How's that for Shark Week?

A lot of blood, sweat, and tears goes into administering this rescue medication. First, because I'm not some maniacal demon mom, I let Emory know that I have to give her the rescue medication to get her seizures to stop. This leads to resounding screams of "No!" filling the room with the terrified and mad as hell shrills of an eleven-year-old girl. Then I have to prepare the medication, which means I remove the cap, open the packet of petroleum jelly, and insert the tip of the syringe into the foil numerous times until the entire length of the tip is covered in jelly. Emory watches this entire process, growing ever louder with each pass of the tip into the jelly. Next up, removal of shorts and panties, while trying to make sure period blood does not leak onto the freshly laundered sheets. And this is where trauma enters the room, and I ask myself throughout the entire ordeal—whose trauma is it anyway?

The last step of this process involves me attempting to pin my daughter down to the bed while simultaneously rolling her onto her side and bending one leg so as to give me a better grasp on her butt cheek. Then I have to pull on said butt cheek until her anus is exposed and gently insert the lubed-up syringe into her rectum. All the while she is screaming bloody murder and proverbially fighting for her life. She is fighting like mad to free her legs from my grasp, to twist her body out from under the weight of my elbow pressing into her, holding her in place. She is staring at me and screaming, burning my face into her memory as "the woman who claimed to love her but then did this." She's reaching her little hand out, trying desperately to grab my hair, my shirt, my glasses—anything that will succeed in making me stop. And then it's over, and she lays there, mouth agape, no sound coming out, tears streaming down her face, and I, the violator of the day, pulls her panties and shorts back on, pulls the blanket up over her shoulders, and whispers in her ear, "I'm so, so sorry, Emory. Mommy is so very sorry, but I have to do it in order to make the seizures stop." She won't look at me. She literally turns her entire face away from me, and it is the most painful, gut-wrenching, traumatic experience of this ordeal, by far and bar none. It harkens back to every violation I endured at the hands of men I didn't want touching me, but who did anyway—hands snaking up under my shirt, under my bra, into my shorts. And to one boy in particular who pinned me to the ground when I was fifteen and attempted to slide his hands into my shorts to "cop a feel." He was much larger than me, much stronger than me, and had I not threatened to scream so loud all of our friends in the next room would come bursting in, I firmly believe he would have raped me.

At that moment, with my daughter, I felt all of that fear and anxiety and deep visceral pain come rushing back to me, pushing its way through my body and settling behind my eyes, pushing and pushing until I found myself sobbing as I kissed the back of my daughter's head, told her I loved her, was sorry, and left the room. Though I know it is nowhere near the same, I can't fight the feeling that I am now the violator, and my child, though eleven, is experiencing the pain of fifteen-year-old me. I felt like that boy was trying to take my life with his violence, and yet here I am, trying desperately to *save* her life with mine. I retreated from her bedroom to let her settle into the five- to seven-hour slumber Diazepam always delivers, sat on my patio, and with a shaky hand, lifted a cigarette to my lips. *Really*, I thought to myself. *Whose trauma is it anyway? This is a horrible thing to relive in the most heinous of ways possible. How do I offer comfort in the midst of my own rising anxiety? Did I do it right—the comforting? Will she forgive me? Does she know I love her? Why wasn't this in the manual?*

No one mentioned all the ways trauma can rush in on May 14, 2009, the day Emory came into this world, nor did anyone mention it on April 1, 2010, the day I received her official diagnosis. Between two months and ten months of age, WebMD had basically assured me my baby was dying. Eleven years later, it may as well be me. Reliving my own trauma while traumatizing my child is threatening to be the end of, well, both of us.

*

It started on the day she was born, with the arm that refused to arm—a.k.a Erb's palsy. That was the first indication that something was different about Emory. I had never heard of or even seen Erb's palsy. At least not that I knew of, but there it was, staring back at me in the form of a tiny human. I briefly wondered how this would affect the rest of her life. I say briefly because as quickly as I pictured difficulty, she managed to work her one good arm out of her swaddle blanket and was gnawing on her hand as if to say, "Bitch, do you even know who I am? Like one arm is gonna stop me—one arm ain't shit. I gets what I wants." Eleven years later I'd like to report that yes, she pretty much gets what she wants. She has got cute on lock—but with a mere six hours of life under her belt, I had no way of knowing. I stared at Emory in pure shock and disbelief. Disbelief that I was a mother. Disbelief that I was a mother to a child with a disability. And disbelief that this so-called disabled child managed to work her way out of the infant equivalent of a strait-jacket. Who had I *actually* given birth to and what was I *really* in for? I truly had no idea, and I was not in any way, shape, or form prepared to find out. Between my mind trying to come to terms that my body grew a whole-ass human and I was supposed to love it right off the bat, and my body trying to convert itself back to human form after looking like a deranged cheetah for nine goddamn months, I essentially forgot every damn thing I learned in all of my child development classes in college. Every textbook, *everything,* went right out the window and I was left with nothing but intuition. I guess one could say that new moth-erhood is where I honed that gift, but let me tell you, I am *sure* . . . I mean absolutely *sure* there are other ways to hone your intuitive skills than by way of your nondeveloping baby. For instance, you could see a psychic. You could learn to read tarot. You could meditate. You could study up on your chakras. Hell, you could even call Miss Cleo *and* Dionne's Psychic Friends Network! Any of these things would be more favorable than honing your intuition skills on the misshapen back and malformed arm of an infant.

Right around the time my mind had come to terms with the fact that yes, I'd made a human, and yes, I did love her (so, approximately two months after she was born), I started to notice that Emory wasn't doing things that my friends' babies were doing. We went for a play-date with my girlfriend and her new baby (who was just a few months older than Emory), and I remember my friend asking me if she could pick her head up yet. I said no and made a joke about how her dad probably jacked up her arm *and* her neck during our second trimester sexcapades,[29] but I made a mental note to refresh my baby milestone memory when I got home. She was two months old—I was pretty sure she was supposed to be doing more than pooping, crying, and being irresistibly cute. When I got home, I did what all new moms do when their kid so much as sneezes—I went straight to WebMD. New moms, don't do this. It will have you re-upping your Xanax prescription faster than you can pump out wine-laced breastmilk, but in short, these are some of the milestones my child was supposed to reach by two months of age: cooing, giggling, excitement when you reenter a room, smiling when I speak to her, holding her head up, being a squirmy baby when on her back, kicking her legs when being changed, holding onto toys for short bursts of time, grabbing my finger when I touch the palm of her hand . . . and the list goes on and on . . . and my girl was doing none of these. Not a damn one. Well, I take that back, she *was* starting to smile and laugh at me when I talked to her. But everything else—nah. Outwardly I did not freak out. I'm the mom. I hold down the fort. If mom *loses* her shit, everything *goes* to shit, so on the surface I was coasting along, making bottles and changing diapers like I had stock in Desitin. Internally, I had the world's longest and ever-growing list of questions and observations to share with our pediatrician at Emory's upcoming two-month check-up. I needed to know what was going on because

---

29. Oh don't "ew" me—if you've had a kid you know damn well that second-trimester sex is literally the best sex you will ever have in your entire life. If second-trimester sex didn't lead right into the third trimester and birth, I bet we'd all be pregnant all the time *just* to have second trimester sex. DON'T LIE.

something was up. I knew it—moms always know. I just didn't know what that *something* was.

I wish I could say that all of my questions were answered and my fears laid to rest at that appointment, but nope. I walked away with more questions and a hell of a lot of frustration. There is nothing more belittling and wholly aggravating than a doctor who dismisses your concerns with a pat on the arm and an, "Oh, mom!" I'm not a violent woman, but I *am* a Scorpio. I'll sting the fuck out of your face when you least expect it and then just sit back and watch you wriggle and writhe in pain. Well, pretherapy Adiba would, and to be clear, I didn't start therapy until Emory was eight years old, so in my head, this pediatrician's face was swollen beyond recognition. I wanted to read her for filth (for my non-Black sisters who have never heard this term, it means I wanted to tell her off) and drag her mama, too, for not teaching her better. In hindsight, even with all the therapy I've had, I still wish I had done exactly that. I wish I had pushed and pushed and acted a damn fool in that office that day, and all the days and months following when this same pediatrician continued to essentially tell me I was worrying for nothing. If I told her Emory's posture was off and her back seemed crooked to me, she told me that all babies' backs are "a little wonky" after being curled up for nine months and that she'd straighten out. If I told her that Emory's hips seemed a little more rigid than they should have been, and she couldn't fully rotate her hips in their sockets, she'd counter with: "Oh, mom! Babies' bones are malleable—she'll be fine!" She really hit me with the okey-dokey when at Emory's nine-month appointment I told her that Emory wasn't rolling over, or getting onto all fours, or army crawling, or picking up Cheerios, or babbling up a storm. She replied, and I quote (placing her hand on my upper arm): "Oh, mom . . . all babies develop at their own rate. Stop worrying! She'll be fine!"

Y'all.

I'd had it.

This woman, who did I mention was also a new mom, had blown me off for the last goddamn time! I looked down at her hand on my arm and moved back to the wall because I did not trust myself to be within arm's length of this woman.

"Dr. Thuy, I have been coming to you since Emory was two weeks old. And from the time she was *eight weeks old* you've been dismissing every single concern I've brought up. I tell you she's not tolerating her formula you tell me to switch. I tell you *that's* not working, you tell me to switch again. It took four visits for you to finally dig deeper and realize she had GERD. You've never raised a single concern about the fact that her left arm has minimal functioning, nor have you offered any sort of intervention services so that we can work with a therapist to strengthen it. And no matter what I tell you about her development and missed milestones, you tell me not to worry, and that all babies develop at their own rates! Well, Dr. Thuy—she's not developing! There is no rate because it's not happening! It's not happening! There is something going on with her brain, and you're not listening! And Dr. Thuy, I am not leaving this office until you refer us to a specialist or a therapist or something! Emory is almost a year old—this is ridiculous!"

I was irate and I had every damn right to be. This bullshit of the medical profession not taking Black folks seriously had been happening to parents who look like me for *decades, if not centuries*. But I was not (and if we're being real, still am not) the one to play with when it comes to my child. Historically, and currently, Black folks are not believed when it comes to our own concerns about our health. We're not believed by the medical community when we rank our pain levels, and many medical devices and studies (older *and* more recent) are inaccurate because white folks have been used as the baseline of normalcy. Black folks have been mistreated from the moment we were loaded onto the slave ships. We learned quickly not to complain or fight back because that was certain death. So, we endured the horrors, atrocities, and unbelievable violence of the slave trade, slavery itself, and Jim Crow just so we could make it home to our families at the end of the day. This violence-induced endurance was seen as "high tolerance for pain." If we complained of poor health we were accused of laziness and trying to get out of working in the fields or in the Big House, and thus

the lie (I refuse to call it a myth—it was an outright lie) was perpetuated and passed down from generation to generation and doctor to
doctor. And what is the lie, you ask? Black folks don't feel pain, and
our health concerns are not real, but rather excuses to get out of work
or school. It is a vile, deeply racist belief that is still in effect today. As
a matter of fact, as recently as 2016, 50 percent of medical residents
surveyed by the National Academy of Science *emphatically* endorsed at
least one medical lie that had been perpetuated about Black patients,
and twelve percent endorsed some of the lies.[30]

In 2016.

Let that sink in.

I was struggling to get my daughter seen by a specialist in 2009 and
2010. Are you at all surprised that our pediatrician couldn't be bothered to explore my concerns about her development—or lack thereof?

I'm not sure if Dr. Thuy was startled by my outburst, or simply
realized she'd fucked up, but she immediately began filling out a form
for early intervention services and told me I'd receive a phone call from
a social worker in a week or so. She *also* made a referral to Shriner's
Children's Hospital—but not for her brain. Not for a neurologist to
take a look at my daughter and figure out why she's not developing or
meeting milestones. Nope. Not for that. Dr. Thuy referred us to Shriner's Children's Hospital for her left arm.

Jesus, Mary, and Joseph.

One month later Jeff and I arrived at Shriner's Children's Hospital,
and I was immediately taken aback by the vastness of the lobby. It felt
huge and overwhelming. There were children (with their parents) in
wheelchairs, on crutches, or with burns scattered throughout. Chairs
lined the walls. We took a seat. Emory was as calm and relaxed as she
could be in her car carrier, and we waited for someone to call our
names while I filled out registration paperwork. I filled in Emory's

---

30. "Racial bias in pain assessment and treatment recommendations, and
false beliefs about biological differences between blacks and whites"—Kelly M.
Hoffman, Sophie Trawalter, Jordan R. Axt, and M. Norman Oliverb, https://www.
ncbi.nlm.nih.gov/pmc/articles/PMC4843483/

name, address, date of birth and then paused at "reason for visit." Was I supposed to put the reason we were referred, or the *real* reason we were there? Since the blow-up in Dr. Thuy's office, I had continued to do my research on the interwebs and kept coming across the same two possible outcomes—cerebral palsy and something called schizencephaly. I'd never heard of the latter but was familiar with the former from my mom's days as a special education teacher, my cousin with CP, and my summer as a camp counselor for kids and adults with disabilities. Each one of the symptoms listed for both of these disorders were things I was seeing in Emory, and I was fairly sure these were what we were dealing with. But I was no doctor—I needed THEM to say it. I put "Erb's palsy" in the reason for visit box, and decided I would explain my concerns and findings to the pediatric orthopedist when she arrived. It felt like a million hours passed between the time we sat down in the lobby and the time we were taken upstairs and into a patient room, but in reality it was more like fifteen minutes. Fifteen short minutes was all that lay between life as we knew it and life as it was going to be.

Jeff and I waited in the doctor's office, neither one of us speaking our thoughts into the air, instead allowing them to fill our brains. I focused my attention on Emory, making silly faces at her and doing everything I could to make her laugh. She had recently reached the milestone where she got excited whenever I walked into the room, and though she was about seven months late in reaching it, we reveled in hour-long games of peek-a-boo. I was mid-peek when the doctor entered the room and I was immediately stunned when I turned around and saw her face. Could it be? Was it possible that the actress, Carla Gugino, star of *Spy Kids*, *American Gangster*, and *Watchmen*, was moonlighting as a children's orthopedic specialist at Shriner's Hospital of Houston? Um, no. That wasn't possible. This was a real doctor, not a Hollywood celebrity who played one on TV. And I had to remember why we were there— my daughter's brain—not selfies with a woman who could very well be a Hollywood stunt double.[31] She breezed in and offered her hand.

---

31.   Yes. I KNOW it's beyond weird that at such a pivotal time in my daughter's

"Hi! I'm Dr. G and I understand we have Miss Emory here today! Let me see this girl—ugh! Gosh! Look at this beauty—Mom, she's just gorgeous! You're just gorgeous—do you know that? Just a beauty!"

Dr. G, a.k.a, secret celebrity, gushed over Emory, and Emory, true to form, smiled and cooed at her, trying to touch her face with her tiny baby hands. Looking at Emory, you would have zero indication that something was amiss. She was as beautiful as the day was long, cuddly, and had just the sweetest disposition. Everyone fell in love with her as soon as they laid eyes on her. We couldn't run the simplest of errands, or even go out to dinner as a family, without someone stopping us to ooh and aah over how beautiful she was. There was something about Emory . . . but there was also something going on with Emory. In the appointment I did most of the talking, explaining to Dr. G that even though Dr. Thuy had referred us to Shriner's to have the Erb's palsy in her left arm assessed, there were other issues I was concerned about that had me convinced that perhaps what was going on with her arm, in conjunction with these other things, was more of a neurological issue and not an orthopedic issue. I explained to her that I accepted the orthopedic referral because I couldn't get our pediatrician to listen to my concerns about Emory's development, so I figured if I could just get in front of a specialist, *any* specialist, then I could plead my case and possibly get some help for my child.

I explained how Emory had missed numerous milestones and was very late getting to the party for others. I explained how even though she visually tracked toys and people very well, grabbing her toys, holding her bottle or utensils, or even holding our hands was a completely different story. I told Dr. G about all the research I'd done on the

---

life, I'm wondering if her doctor is a celebrity on the side. But my mind goes to weird places when I'm in extreme situations. One time, when I was twenty-one, my date and I were approached by a cop for being in the park after hours. The cop ran our IDs and it turned out there was a warrant out for my arrest (it turned out to be bogus—calm down), but when he went back to his car to investigate further, I pulled out my lipstick and began to calmly reapply it. My date, freaking out, looked at me in horror and asked me what the hell I was doing. My response: "Well, if I go to jail tonight I'll likely have to take a mugshot and I don't want to look busted in the photo!" Like I said—my mind goes to weird places when I'm in extreme situations. It's a thing.

interwebs and how WebMD had me convinced she was either dying or disabled—there was nothing in between the two according to that science. Dr. G listened intently, nodding her head at times, audibly agreeing with me at other times, and then said the words I'd waited months to hear.

"Well, Adiba, I definitely think you're onto something here. I agree with you—I'm not so sure this is strictly an orthopedic issue. I think there could be something neurological at play, but I'm not a neurologist. Let me step out and grab my colleague, Dr. Mancias. He's one of the best pediatric neurologists in Houston. Let's bring him in, he can take a look at Miss Emory, and then we can decide where to go from there. And I'll fill him in on everything you've just shared with me so you don't have to repeat yourself. Be right back."

As she turned to exit the room, I turned to look at Jeff as if to say, "What just happened?" All he could do was let out a deep sigh as we stared at each other, cautiously. I think both of us instinctively knew what the final outcome was going to be, and we'd already silently agreed that it wouldn't change how we were raising her, but waiting for confirmation of our suspicions was brutal. Oddly, the suspicions were also the one thing that kind of kept us in place as a family unit. Though most days I was so angry with him for dragging me into his web of lies and infidelity, when it came to Emory's care, I was grateful to have him to lean on when the worry transformed itself to wild fear and brazen anxiety. I wasn't ready to be a single mother yet, and that day I was grateful to have the support of a partner. A few moments later, Dr. G. returned with a short, boisterous Hispanic man whom she introduced as Dr. Mancias. He was all smiles and full of energy, and as she had promised, Dr. G had already apprised him of our situation. He did exactly what Dr. G had done and walked straight over to Emory, immediately remarking on how beautiful of a baby she was, and how she was already stealing his heart with one glance. This wasn't the first time we'd heard this—she stole everyone's heart.

Dr. Mancias asked if we could take her out of her carrier and lay her on the office bed—he wanted to do some visual tracking exercises with her, and test her ability to cross midline with her hands. He wanted to see how well she sat up, if at all, and test her ability to get to all fours and crawl—all things I'd been begging our pediatrician to look into. We obliged him, and true to form, Emory tracked like a pro, batting her long, beautiful eyelashes at Dr. Mancias like she was trying to get a date for prom. She followed that man's face, pen, tie, and stuffed animal everywhere he moved them. But when it came time to test the other things, the delays were on full display. I told Dr. Mancias about my suspicions of cerebral palsy and schizencephaly and asked him what his best guess was. He couldn't tell me anything without doing an MRI, but he agreed, something was definitely going on neurolog-ically, and he was going to figure it out. He assured me that we were going to get answers, and scheduled an MRI for the following month. A thirty-day wait for answers was less than ideal, but if it meant we'd finally be on the road to some answers, I was willing to wait. In one day we had gotten a thousand steps closer to an answer than I'd been for the previous eight months—I could wait for another twenty-nine.

The day came for Emory to have her MRI and we arrived at Texas Children's Hospital a bundle of nerves. The nurses advised that they would have to do the procedure with general anesthesia, but we would be allowed to stay in the room while they put her under. They advised that it can be a scary experience for small children, and having the parents present can help keep the kiddos calm. What they *didn't* advise was the sheer terror the parents would experience watching their children essentially fight, for what they believed was their life, as the mask administering the anesthesia was placed over their mouths and noses. Emory was no different. Her eyes widened and she began to scream bloody murder—flailing her arm and legs in every direction as the bright lights shone overhead. The doctors and technicians buzzed around us, checking all the vitals and doing their best to distract her (while also doing their job) so she could calm down, and I could hear a symphony of beeps, high and low in tone, telling me my baby was still with us (even if it felt like we were killing her). At one point Jeff had to hop in to help the nurses hold her legs down. Jeff and I struggled to hold it together, to keep from drowning our child in our own tears, as our daughter stared at us in horror, wondering why we were betraying her in such a horrible fashion.

Then the anesthesiologist had a brilliant idea.

"Mom, do you have any special songs you sing to her that calm her down?"

Did I have any special songs? I was the queen of special songs! Singing made-up songs was something I'd done since Emory was two months old, and they always succeeded in making her laugh. I would take popular songs and change the words so they became funny little bops about her, and whatever we were doing at that moment. When she had a poop-filled diaper, Michael Jackson's super hit "I'm Bad" became "You Stink." If she had a pee diaper, the drive-in movie classic jingle "Let's All Go to the Movies" became "Don't Put Your Feet in Your Diaper." Well, I really needed her to laugh and so I turned to our favorite little made-up ditty. I started off low, and close to her ear . . . I needed her to hear me.

Who is the prettiest girl
In the whole widest world?
She makes my heart unfurl!
Eeeeeemory . . .
Sometimes you like to drool
But I love you like a fool!
You are just toooo cool!
Eeeeeeeemory . . .
You're growin' and changin'
Everyday . . .
Laughter and sunshine is
Comin' your way!
Growin' up is not so tough
Except for when you've had enough
I am all out of stuff
Eeeeeeemory . . .

Eeeeeeemory . . .
Eeeeeeemory . . .
THAT'S YOU!

By the time I got to the end of the song, not only had Emory fallen asleep, but the entire room full of doctors and nurses and anesthesiologists were humming the song along with me. After making sure Emory was out cold, one of the doctors turned to me.

"Hey, Mom—what song was that? I swear I've heard it before—we all know it . . . but we don't *know* it!"

I grinned, embarrassed by the admission I was about to make.

"It's the theme song to *Caillou*. I just changed the words."

The room erupted in laughter and choruses of "I knew it!"

Yes. I used the most annoying character to ever exist in all of children's programming, second only to Barney the dinosaur, to save the day. Caillou—the whiny, perpetual four-year-old who looks like a fresh Brazilian wax.[32] That kid saved the day. Who had I become?

I'd become a mother.

After the hellish start I'd had with this tiny human, and not being sure I was even ready to be her mom, at that moment I knew that I was uniquely designed to be her mom. Not anyone else's, but hers.

They assured us she was going to be just fine, advised us the procedure would take approximately thirty minutes, and that they would come find us in the waiting room when they were done. And with that they wheeled our girl out of the room, down the hall, through double doors and she was gone. Jeff and I looked at each other and simply collapsed into each other's arms, sobbing. I don't know if it was fear or relief or trauma over what we'd just physically experienced with our daughter. What I do know is that once again, I was relieved to be going through this moment with him. Regardless of how much I hated him, that day I loved him. I needed him.

---

32. WHAT? HE DOES! And *that* probably just cost me a deal with PBS Kids, but COME THROUGH NETFLIX—YA GIRL GOT A PITCH FOR YA!

Waiting for anything, in general, is tough. Waiting two weeks to get the results back of your infant daughter's brain scans so you can begin to figure out what the rest of her life (and yours) is going to look like is unbearable and may even teeter on the verge of intolerable cruelty. If patience is a virtue, I shall see you in purgatory because I don't have it. From the time we left the hospital after Emory's MRI, to the time we got the call to schedule our follow-up appointment with Dr. Mancias at Shriner's hospital, it felt like an entire year had passed. I answered every single "unknown caller" and "private number" call that came through, which if you know anything about anything, you know that the only people that do that are people with good credit and no overdue bills. I did not fit into either of those categories, but I was willing to take the risk of getting roped into a credit card settlement offer that I could not afford just so I didn't miss the call that had the potential to change all of our lives—forever. The car ride to Shriners Children's Hospital was quiet—the air was thick with uncertainty, fear, and hope simultaneously, and fervent silent prayer. That thickness walked into the hospital with us, rode the elevator with us, and pulled up a seat right next to us in the doctor's office as we waited for Dr. Mancias to arrive. It hung heavy in the air, like nimbostratus clouds, threatening to envelop everything, and weaving all of our feelings into one giant fucked up tapestry. Who knew where hope stopped and fear began? Neither one of us spoke to each other, only to Emory. Maybe we were trying to distract her, maybe we were trying to distract ourselves. Whatever it was, we were laser-focused on our child, so much so that I jumped with a start when Dr. Mancias finally joined us in the room, after seeing his previous patient.

"Hi, Adiba. Hi, Jeff."

"Hello, Dr. Mancias," we replied in unison.

"How are you two doing today? How is our beautiful girl?"

Again, in unison, and nervously: "Good! Good, Dr. Mancias."

"Oh, great! So, let's get to it. Ah . . . Adiba, what did you say you went to school for?"

"Ummm . . . I got my bachelor's in Social Work."

"Uh-huh. Um . . . Have you ever thought about going to medical school?"

"Um, no sir. Why?" I ask, perplexed.

"Well, mom, you might want to think about it because you were spot on. Your daughter has schizencephaly. The only thing you didn't diagnose is the fact that it's bilateral schizencephaly, meaning—"

"She has holes on both sides of her brain."

"Yes! Here—let's look at her MRI images so I can explain to you how the location of the holes are affecting her development!"

Dr. Mancias excitedly pulled out the black image films and turned on the light board, as Jeff and I stared at each other in what could only be described as a mixture of utter disbelief and sheer relief. I glanced down at Emory in her car carrier, who had her eyes fixed on Dr. Mancias, and slowly brought my eyes to the light board. Lit up for the entire room to see was my daughter's brain, and two black spots— on the upper right front/side portion of her brain, and a smaller black spot on the lower-left corner of her brain. I walked over to the light-board and touched them.

There they were.

The holes.

The culprits.

The answers.

One on the left, one on the right.

Dr. Mancias went on to explain that the location of the holes in Emory's brain (frontal lobe and lower temporal lobe) were likely going to affect her muscle development, motor skills, speech development, and most likely her cognitive development—but to what extent he did not know. She would likely need physical therapy, occupational therapy, and speech therapy for the rest of her life. He said she most likely would never walk. If she spoke at all, he said speech would be diffi-cult but that sometimes the brain will swap one ability for another if it deems one more necessary than another. He went on to talk about the brain's plasticity and how neurotransmitters were firing but not connecting one set of neurons to another set of neurons due to the holes, essentially never carrying messages to the other side of her brain. I looked over at Jeff. This man I'd spent every day with for the last eighteen months, I'd never seen him look so heavy. His shoulders slumped like he was carrying the heaviest boulder in existence on his back. He refused to make eye contact with me. Perhaps he feared that looking directly into my face would break him. He'd watched me struggle to love her and then become completely consumed with her. Acknowledging my pain might have burst the dam of emotions he was holding back. So he sat, staring ahead at the wall, jaw clenched, hands holding each other, shoulders heavy. Then there was me. At that moment, I needed his eyes, his face, his hands to reassure me that we were going to be okay—that Emory was going to be okay. A flood of emotions filled my mind. If there is a word for feeling sad, angry, utterly devastated, relieved, determined, and scared all at the same time, that's what I felt.

I did that thing that I think all parents do when they initially hear what could be deemed as devastating news about their child: I thought about all the things we *wouldn't* get to do. In an instant I saw it all ripped away from us. Goodbye dance class, cheerleading, and Saturdays at the roller rink. Peace out, prom. But then as quickly as I tuned out, I tuned back in and remembered who the fuck I am. I'm not a girl who quits and I'm certainly not a girl who doesn't try. Shit, I'll try most things at least once. I tried out for my high school cheerleading team with a pulled hamstring, against doctor's orders—and I made the squad. I blew out my knee in junior high and the doctor told me I should never take another dance class because I was going to keep blowing it out to the point of needing surgery. I gave myself a week and continued to dance until my sophomore year in college. Hell, I drank thirteen cosmopolitans, three shots, and a beer on a random Saturday night when I was twenty-one! When I tell you I don't quit, I don't quit. You tell me I can't do something, and I'll show you just how well I *can* do it, and dare you to tell me something else I can't do. It was at that moment I made up my mind that we were going to do all the things— all of them. Whatever that little girl wanted to do in life, we were going to figure out a way to do it. I wiped away the single tear that had rolled down my cheek and turned to speak directly to Dr. Mancias, who had stopped speaking and was silently watching me, as was Jeff.

"She's going to be just fine, Dr. Mancias. How soon can we start therapy?"

A slow smile crept across his face.

"She will be. She's got good parents, and parents make all the difference." He told us the nurse would get us set up with the specialty treatment clinic for kids with special and ongoing medical needs, called the Chosen Clinic. From there, they'll refer us to get Emory early interventions to add physical and speech therapy to her services.

He dismissed himself to get the paperwork started, explaining his nurse would be with us shortly. I turned and looked at Jeff, who was standing next to Emory, one hand on her carrier handle, one hand in his pocket. He finally made eye contact with me and held it.

"She's going to be just fine," he whispered.

I whispered back.

"She's going to be just fine."

There was a beat of silence and I let my eyes fall on my daughter, blissfully unaware of the fate Dr. Mancias had just tried to place on her.

"You're going to be just fine, Emory Yvonne. You're *our* girl. You came from *us*. You're going to be just fine."

Jeff and I drove home mostly in silence, save for the sound of Emory chewing on her fist in the back seat. I turned to look at my sweet girl and began to sing.

Who is the prettiest girl
In the whole widest world?
She makes my heart unfurl!
Eeeeeemory . . .

A smile crept across her face as she looked at me with her sparkling brown eyes and lashes fit for a Maybelline commercial. She stopped chewing her fist long enough to let out a giggle.

"You're gonna be just fine, baby girl . . . just fine."

This was a message for my girl as much as it was for me. We were going to be just fine. We had to be. I refused to accept any other option.

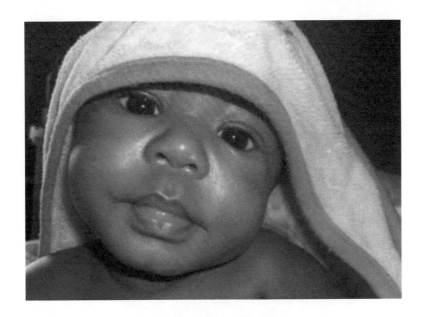

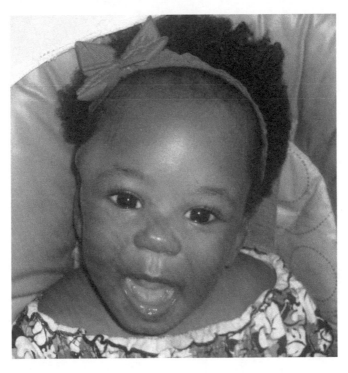

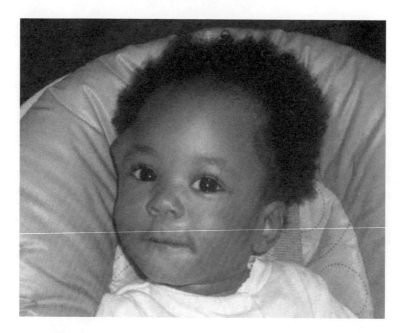

WE WERE NOT JUST FINE

Just five months before our baby girl's diagnosis I found out that Jeff was still married to Bunny. Ain't that some shit? That's not the kind of thing you just happen across while reading the morning paper. You happen across it at a funeral as I did. Even though the words Jeff's father said to me were confirmation of the thing I had felt deep in my gut but never allowed myself to acknowledge for over a year, I still couldn't bring myself to believe it. That night, as Jeff drove me and his children home from the funeral in Austin to Cypress (a two-plus hour car ride), I sat in the passenger seat with a plan. Using our mobile hotspot (thank God for Cricket Wireless), I scoured county marriage and divorce records on my laptop, but I worked hard to make it look like I was just surfing the web. I immediately found the marriage license that Jeff and Bunny filed with the court some years prior, but I spent the next two hours scouring county divorce records for 2006. Line by line, name by name—there was nothing. I looked up records for 2007. Nothing. I looked up records for 2005. Nothing. For two hours I endured confirmation after confirmation that I had been living a lie. That absolutely nothing was how I'd allowed myself to believe it was.

As the car sped down the highway, I vacillated between deeply fulfilling rage and a too-strong cocktail of shock and sadness. I wondered what he would do if I just opened the car door and let myself fall out of the car like I'd let myself fall into this completely fucked up situation. Would he pull the car over and fight back if I began to beat him with the computer on my lap? Rage will make you contemplate all sorts of things. Given just the right opportunity, any woman with rage bubbling up internally could easily become Lorena Bobbitt. Mix it with shame, guilt, sadness, and feelings of failure and you've got a Molotov cocktail waiting to happen. In that car, at that moment, I was the cocktail. I knew if I confronted him about it while he was driving, he would lie. That lie would inevitably ignite the napkin, and we'd all go up in flames. Every last one of us in that car would be as good as gone, so I waited.

I closed the laptop, stared out the window, and we drove home in silence.

"Are you okay?" Jeff asked me periodically.

"Yes," I'd say.

The children snored in the back seat. I envied the peace they had. Me, I had an enormous decision to make. Stay with Jeff and allow him to fix things with Bunny by finalizing his divorce so we could move forward with planning a wedding and raising Emory in a two-parent household, or should I say, "Fuck this shit," making the conscious decision to be a single parent? I was supposed to break the generational curse of having children with, or hell, even just being involved with married men. Living this way went against everything I believed in. Before I could decide, we were pulling into the driveway, and it was time to jostle the kids and get them in the house. I carried Emory's car seat in, went straight to her bedroom, quickly changed her into her pajamas, and laid her in bed. I managed to do all of this without waking her, and I thanked all my stars for that blessing. I didn't have the mental and emotional capacity to deal with a cranky, sleepy baby at that moment. I tiptoed out of her room to find Jeff in the hallway leaning against the wall. He was waiting for me. We made eye contact, and I quickly turned and walked toward the kitchen.

"Can we talk?" he called out to me.

"About what?" I asked flatly without bothering to turn and look at him.

Jeff followed me into the kitchen and was watching me pour myself a glass of water from the refrigerator door. I kept my back to him, not even wanting to breathe his air.

"About why you were so quiet in the car."

I cocked my head to the side and walked briskly past him toward the living room.

"You sure you want to talk about that?"

"Yeah. I'd like to know what the hell is going on. You haven't said two words to me all night. What's up?"

I turned around with one eyebrow raised and a smirk on my face. *Well*, I thought to myself, *here we go*.

"You're right. I haven't. But since you want to talk, let's talk."

I moved to the brown leather armchair that sat across from the couch and sat down. I didn't want to be anywhere near him.

"I'm going to start this off by telling you that I already know the truth, but I'm going to ask you a question anyway in the hopes that you'll be honest with me. It's in your best interest to just tell the truth from the jump because the more you lie to me the angrier I'm going to become. Cool?"

Jeff half chuckled. "Okay, cool."

The audacity of this man to chuckle like this was some sort of fucking game or joke. I managed to contain my rage and sip my water.

"This really isn't funny, Jeff. I'm going to give you three chances to tell me the truth. If you lie to me three times, you can leave tonight and go stay at your aunt's house."

I hadn't planned to say that. I wasn't ready to become a single mom that night, but the words just fell out of my mouth. Jeff's face fell into a serious disposition, and he clasped his hands and looked down at the floor.

"Okay . . ." he said.

My heart was racing. It felt like it was about to beat right out of my chest and take my tongue with it. I had to take several more swallows of water just to get the words out.

"Did you ever get a divorce from Bunny?"

"What? Yes! Adiba, what are you talking about? I told you I did!"

The heat was on in the house, but my hands went ice cold.

"Jeff, I told you. I already know the truth, so I'm going to ask you again."

My voice remained calm.

"Did you get a divorce from Bunny?"

Jeff, still adamant in his denial, wrung his hands and answered me with a smile on his face and a chuckle in his voice.

"Babe. I don't know why you're asking me this. I already told you yes!"

And now here we were. Chance number three.

"Goddamn it, Jeff! Your dad told me everything! Just fucking own it! Fess up! Tell me the fucking truth for once in this whole fucking relationship! DID YOU OR DID YOU NOT GET A DIVORCE FROM BUNNY? ARE YOU STILL FUCKING MARRIED? DID I HAVE A BABY WITH A MARRIED MAN?"

I was now practically yelling, and I didn't care. I didn't care if I woke the kids up, if the neighbors heard me, if I lost my voice—I didn't care. I just wanted the truth. I wanted to hear Jeff say it with his own voice.

Jeff sat back on the couch, a man defeated. He clasped his hands behind his head and let out a deep sigh, staring across the room at me. The tension in the air was thick like Louisiana Bayou mud, and I was not budging. Finally, Jeff spoke. His voice was low and measured.

"What did my father tell you?"

"What your father told me doesn't have shit to do with shit, Jeff. Answer the goddamn question."

"I need to know what he said, Adiba."

"No. You don't, Jeff. What you *need* to do is either answer the fucking question or start packing a bag. Those are your options."

I think Jeff could tell that I wasn't going to let up because all of a sudden he got up and started to walk toward our bedroom at the end of the hall. Then he turned around and came back, standing in front of the couch, staring at me. Sitting back down, he rubbed his hands over his face and over his goatee a few times, and then finally, after what seemed like an eternity, muttered the words that had been threatening to pull me down beneath the surface for quite some time.

"No. I never got a divorce from Bunny."

The rage in me overflowed and I erupted like a volcano that had been simmering for the last two and a half hours.

"You liar! You motherfucking liar! How could you? For over a year, Jeff! Over a year you've been lying to me! And you had the audacity to propose marriage to me when you already have a wife? What the fuck is wrong with you? Who does that?!"

He knew how proud I was to *finally* be breaking the curse of infidelity in my family, except I wasn't. He listened to my hopes and fears and lied to my face. The worst part about following in the same goddamn tradition of my grandmothers and mother is that I didn't even have a motherfucking say in the matter. I was done. I had nothing left to say and not a single tear to cry. I just stared at Jeff, sitting on the couch, no longer recognizing the woman sitting across from him. He opened his mouth to speak and no words came out. He tried several more times and I watched as his eyes began to fill with tears. I felt nothing. Finally, words.

"I'm sorry. I know it was wrong to lie to you. I should have told you from the beginning, but I'd never met a woman like you before, and then I fell in love with you, and then you were pregnant and it just never seemed like the right time. I was going to try and just get it done before we got married, so there wouldn't be any problems. I love you, Adiba, and I want to marry you. It's been over with Bunny for years. Basically since a week after we decided to try and work it out."

"You mean since a week after you begged her not to leave you?"

"Is that what my father told you?"

"Jeff, don't even try to talk your way through or out of this. I already told you—I know everything!"

"I'm not. I'm not. Listen, I love you. I want to marry you. I'll fix this, I promise. But it's late. Let's go to bed and we can talk about this in the morning."

He stood up, moved toward me, and held out his hand as if I was supposed to follow him to bed.

I stared at it, unflinching. The unmitigated gall of this man. I stood up too.

"Don't touch me. I'm going to bed. You can sleep out here. You know where the extra blankets and pillows are."

And with that, I pushed past his hand without even glancing up at his face, walked up the hallway toward our bedroom, stopping once to check on Emory, and then carried myself to our room and closed the door. Jeff said nothing as I walked away, nor did he knock on the door after I disappeared behind it. That night I cried myself to sleep. How had I gotten there, and where did I go from there. So many questions, not nearly enough answers.

*

I stayed. I wasn't ready to be a single parent, and I was determined to break the generational curses that seem to run rampant in my immediate family. We put a deposit on a location—the gorgeous Magnolia Hotel in downtown Houston. We placed a deposit with a string quartet to play at the reception and met with the head chef at our favorite restaurant to begin putting a dinner menu together. We designed a cake and picked out a color scheme, and I purchased my wedding dress from Alfred Angelo. I made an appointment to do a fitting with both of Jeff's aunts present, and my mother and aunt present via Skype. I was all the way in it. I trusted Jeff to do right by me and our daughter, and end things with Bunny for good, *before* our April 23 wedding date the following year. I trusted him. Let me say that again. I trusted him—the man that lied to me for over a year, let me have his baby, and then continued to lie to *his family* so that he could stay comfortable. And I had decided to trust him—or at least that's what I told myself.

Given the right circumstances, trust and fear can look the same. But I can't lie, it was definitely fear. I knew it then and I know it now. Things were going horribly wrong in our relationship. Aside from telling me the world's biggest lie, and in addition to taking care of a child I knew had some sort of a disability, Jeff's history of not taking care of himself, not staying on top of his diabetes, and not eating properly had finally caught up with him. One day I got a call from his manager while he was at work. Jeff had passed out while speaking with a customer, and landed on a glass dining room table, sending glass shattering, customers running, and screaming ambulances speeding down the highway. By the time I got to the hospital, Jeff was awake, but in ICU. His diabetes had moved from bad to fatal. While I visited Jeff in the hospital, he begged me, in front of his aunt Alexis, not to leave him. He knew we were on very thin ice, and he also knew I adored his aunt and would not want to humiliate him in front of her. I whispered to him that we could discuss when he got home but he wanted an answer right then and there. He told me he did not want to spend the night not knowing that I was with him. Ugh. I felt like the tiniest pebble being crushed between the rock and the hard place. Not wanting to cause a scene, I agreed to stay, and almost as soon as I said it I wanted to swallow my tongue. Not only did Jeff now have to be on dialysis, but his kidneys were so badly damaged by the years of abuse that he ended up being placed on a kidney transplant list. What. Was. I. Thinking?

Now, I could go into how Jeff must have been feeling at this news and do a deep dive into the sympathy I had for him at this moment, but this book isn't called *Loving through the Lies*, it's called *Ain't That A Mother*, and it's called that for a reason. I'm not the least bit ashamed to tell you that when I heard this news my very first thought was "You have *got* to be fucking kidding me," followed by "Ain't that a mothafucka," and lastly, "DAMN, DAMN, DAMN!"[33] All I could see was another person I was going to need to take care of, and to be honest, I wasn't

---

33.   Thank you, Florida Evans.

sure I had it in me. I was working full time, trying to figure out what was going on with my daughter's health, planning what was probably going to be the most ill-fated wedding in history, battling with Jeff's children who *still* hated me, and now I also had to care for Jeff. No. Just . . . NO.

Selfish as it may sound, I didn't want to add him to my list of responsibilities. That is hands down probably one of the cruelest thoughts I've had as an adult, but it was also a very clear sign that I was no longer in love with this man, and I had absolutely no business trying to marry him. Of course, I ignored that sign; and every sign before *and* after that because why break a bad habit? Why choose me when I'd spent a lifetime choosing men who didn't deserve me? Nah. Let me stick to what I know! I ignored us arguing every day, I ignored the general lack of motivation to help with anything in the house, I ignored the minimal amount of financial contribution he was making to our household of five, and the fact that every month our bank account was in the red (yes, I added him to my bank account. Dumb. I know.). It seemed like every time I turned around I was on the phone with the mortgage company, the car company, the light company, trying to negotiate an extension. I even ignored him almost getting arrested after picking me up from work one day. He'd made an illegal U-turn and when the officer asked for his license, we discovered that it was suspended. Jeff played it off like he didn't know, and I honestly think the only reason the officer didn't arrest him is because Jeff said he was rushing home to do his dialysis, and all the kids were in the car. So. Many. Signs. And I just . . . didn't want to see them. But this . . . I couldn't *not* see the constant stomach pains, the bloating, the moon pie face.

As it turned out, Jeff was a good candidate for at-home peritoneal dialysis. With me working full time, Jeff only working weekends, and us not being able to afford full-time childcare so Jeff could go to a dialysis center, this was the perfect option—the only option. A dialysis center was no place for a baby. We decided that his dialysis machine would be in our bedroom, and it would connect to the dialysis port in his belly. In the morning, after dropping me off at the park'n'ride bus stop and the older kids at school, Jeff came home and attached himself to (what seemed like) a one-hundred-foot tube and began his treatment. He played with Emory, fed her, watched television with her, and they napped. That was the daily routine. He paused treatment when it was time to pick the kids up from school and me from the park'n'ride, and one of us would make dinner while the big kids did their homework. Day in and day out, this was the routine.

I quickly began to hate it, and my resentment toward Jeff grew stronger and stronger with each passing day. Every time I had to take time off work to go to a doctor's appointment with him, I felt conflicted. I felt obligated to be there because (a) I was his fiancée, and (b) I didn't trust him to tell me the truth about what was going on with his health. Whenever we had to drive the two hours to Galveston to visit the transplant center for this appointment or that appointment, I resented him. This was around the time that I had been having to take time off work quite a bit to take Emory to the doctors at Shriners Hospital, and then the Chosen Clinic. It seemed like I was asking for time off every other week, and it did not go unnoticed. When the executive director calls you into their office to "see if things are okay because you've been out a lot," you know people are watching you—and not for good reason. Adding his appointments into my schedule of things I *had* to be present for did not bode well with my supervisor, and my attendance issue cost me a position I was perfectly suited for within the company. It felt like every day another nugget of resentment was being added to the already growing mountain.

One day I decided to take a look in the notebook Jeff was using to keep track of all of his numbers and levels at the start of each dialysis session. I noticed days were skipped, columns were skipped, and when I questioned him about it, I was told it was no big deal—the doctors weren't going to freak out over a day here or a column there. We argued about it, with me stressing the importance of accurate record-keeping, especially if he was going to be a candidate for kidney transplant surgery. This led to him screaming at me to mind my business, snatching the binder out of my hands, and filling in blank spots with random numbers. Made up blood pressures, phosphate levels, glucose readings. To add insult to injury, he also wasn't eating right. He knew how to cook delicious foods that were diabetes-friendly, but he refused. He continued to eat what he wanted and drink what and how much he wanted. He was a fan of tequila. For a while, there was nothing I could do about it—until one day I did do something.

After his umpteenth check-in appointment, I decided it was time. I may have been well over his shit but at the end of the day, he was still my daughter's father and I wanted him to be well. In hindsight maybe I should have kept my mouth shut because autonomy is a thing, but so is responsible parenting. While at the dialysis center, I pulled one of the nurses aside and told her that he was making numbers up, and not eating well, and that his moods were changing rapidly throughout the day. He was angrier and yelling a lot. Jeff had always had a bit of a temper, but it seemed that lately everything was a trigger, everything was bigger. If his son didn't want to put on his seatbelt, it became a shouting match and a physical altercation. They advised that sometimes this happened with dialysis patients because it is a big mental shift. They said that some patients fall into a deep depression because their life looks and feels completely different to them—almost unrecognizable, and nothing is within their control anymore. The doctor pulled Jeff into a separate room and spoke with him for about five minutes, and when they emerged, Jeff turned to me with a smile on his face and said 'I'm sorry for worrying you. I'll do better. Promise,' but I didn't believe it. And I was smart not to. As soon as we got outside Jeff let me have it as I was putting Emory into the car.

"You had absolutely no right to talk to them about me! That's my business! If I wanted the doctor to know I would have told him myself!"

I just stared at him in silence. The nerve of this asshole!

What went through my head was: "Here I am, busting my ass to keep a roof over our heads, keep everyone fed, diagnose my child, plan a wedding to your already married ass, AND trying to keep you alive, and you have the *audacity* to chastise me for letting your doctors know you're not doing well? Oh. Oh, hell no. This is some straight fuckery and I am not having it."

What came out of my mouth (while looking him right in the eyes) was: "You know, if you're so hell-bent on killing yourself I wish you'd just hurry up and do it instead of dragging us all along with you."

And there it was. Every argument, every frustration, every tear I'd cried—all bundled up in twenty-seven words. They lay suspended between us, erecting an impenetrable wall that I had no intention of removing. He just stared at me, his eyes filling with tears. And I stared back, steely-eyed. I felt absolutely nothing at that moment. In shock, he took a minute to collect himself. "How could you say something like that to me?"

"Because it's true," I blurted. "Everyone is more concerned about your health than you are and quite frankly, I'm sick of it. Either go die or get on board!"

I had reached the point of no turning back. I meant every word I'd said and I didn't give a rat's ass if it made him feel some sort of way. I was over it. I was over all of it. The lies, the arguing, the indifference to literally *everything,* all of it. I was done. We drove home in silence. We ate in silence. We fed Emory in silence. We went to bed. In silence.

My therapist (and Brené Brown) would tell you that my behavior outlined above was not exemplary and certainly did not lead with empathy, and they would not be wrong. I had reached the point where the crack in the foundation had just about become an all-out crevasse. Am I proud of how I handled it? Not necessarily. But I also know me, and even with the me I am today, three years of therapy and a little less Scorpio in my ways, I can't say I would respond any differently today. There comes a point in every woman's life when the bullshit reaches eye level and it's either go blind or clear that shit out. I had a child who I was pretty sure was going to be relying on me for much of her natural-born life, and it was crucially important to me that I not lose myself somewhere in the mix between parent, caregiver, and employee. I needed a partner. I could already feel myself becoming a shell of who I was and I knew that if I stood any chance at being a semisuccessful parent, I had to be whole and well. For that I needed support, and I wasn't getting it. Yes, he needed support too. I'm sure he was scared half to death about the turn his life had taken, but at the end of the day, I simply had no fucks left to give. And yes, I understood the optics of it then and I understand the optics of it now. I was essentially giving up on a very sick man, who needed me. And under different circumstances, you best believe I would have been more sympathetic, empathetic, and loving toward him. But one thing I learned from my first marriage was that no one can or should stay where they are no longer being served, and as far as I was concerned, I wasn't even really invited to the party to begin with. I was invited to the shit show—but definitely not the party. Everything that existed between us was based on a lie. Everything except for Emory—she was the only true and real thing we had. And it was beyond amazing that out of so much smoke and mirrors, a being as beautiful as she was created.

Days went by with us not speaking to each other, and I was okay with that. I had nothing left to say on the matter and I didn't care that he was furious with me. In the words of the greatest housewife to grace this planet, Ms. Nene Leakes: "I said what I said." Then one night I was going through the mail and all of a sudden, I had words. Oh, I had *so* many words! There was a letter addressed to Jeff, from the Travis County Police Department in Austin, Texas, and this letter stated that there was a warrant out for his arrest, and he owed approximately $5,000 in fines. They were giving him the option to pay the fines or face possible arrest should he be pulled over the next time he was in Austin. I stood in the kitchen, holding the letter in my hand as I stared at the back of his bald head while he watched television. The collar on my plain white T-shirt suddenly felt too tight, and I felt a throbbing headache coming on, right on my right temple. It was as if whatever vein that travels down the side of my head was trying, unsuccessfully, to burst free. I closed my eyes and willed myself to breathe at a slower than usual pace—one thing I did not have the capacity for was a panic attack. Inhale . . . two, three, four—exhale . . . two, three, four. I'm not a violent person but I *promise* you that at that very moment I just wanted to pop him one good time, right upside his head. You know, like how your mom would do if you came home with a failed test. It always felt like when she drew back that hand, it came back through with the strength of ten thousand hammers. Your mom didn't do that? No? Just mine? Cool, cool, cool. My point is, I was seeing red and if someone had said, "Go ahead and knock this man out—you'll be fine," my response would have been, "Say less." I continued my breathing exercise until I was sure I could speak without screaming my questions at the top of my lungs, and then prepared myself for the barrage of lies I was sure was about to come my way.

"Jeff, did you read this letter?"

"Which letter?" he asked with a deep sigh, not bothering to turn around.

"This blue one from Travis County Police Department."

"Oh. Yep."

"Did you see it says that there is a warrant out for your arrest and about five thousand dollars in fines?"

"Yep," he responded, still not bothering to look me in the face. I felt my breathing begin to quicken again, and I didn't bother trying to regulate it with yoga breaths this time.

"Did you know about this?"

"Yep. But it's no big deal. I'm not worried about it."

"Jeff, five thousand dollars is a big fucking deal!"

"It's just a scare tactic. They send them to everyone. Don't worry about it," he said.

"Jeff. Did you know you had these fines?" His nonchalant attitude was now fully under my skin. His refusal to turn around and face me forced me to cross the kitchen and stand directly in front of him, blocking his view of the television.

"Ugh. Yes, Adiba. I knew I had the fines," he replied, letting out a heavy sigh. This fool *still* refused to look me in the eye. He chose instead to look at my waist.

"And you never paid them?" I asked, studying his face, and then the blue sheet like it held the secrets of the Holy Grail.

"No, Adiba, I never paid them."

"What are the fines for?"

"Speeding, parking . . . dumb shit."

"And you never thought to—" he cut me off.

"GODDAMN IT, ADIBA! WILL YOU JUST QUIT BITCHIN' ABOUT IT? IT'S FINE! IT'S NOT A BIG DEAL! LEAVE IT ALONE ALREADY!"

Y'all.

You know those scenes in movies where one girl gets a little too slick in the mouth with another girl, and the one girl starts silently taking off her jewelry—hoops first? You know exactly what's coming next. Someone is about to get their ass *whooped*. Well, I felt *all* that beat-down energy rise up in my body and it took every ounce of strength I had not to respond with: "WHO THE ACTUAL FUCK DO YOU THINK YOU'RE TALKING TO? HAVE YOU LOST YOUR GODDAMN MIND?" But Emory was sitting right next to him on the couch, and she began to cry when he raised his voice. This infuriated me more than his blatant disregard for these fines and the warrant, and more than him yelling at me. The one thing I swore I would never expose my child to was me being disrespected. I refused to let her see me be treated any which way. I probably hadn't been very successful since up to that point she'd seen me do the lion's share of the work in the house with little to no help from her father. That wasn't respect either. But this? This was a whole different level of disrespect and I was not going to tolerate it. I picked her up and held her to my chest, shushing in her ear and bouncing and rocking her until she calmed down.

"It's okay, honey. Mommy's okay. I'm okay. You're okay. Daddy's just upset . . . shhhhhh . . . shhhhhh . . . it's okay."

When she finally calmed down, I placed her in her activity chair and met Jeff in the kitchen, where he had now moved to, and was rummaging through the refrigerator. Once again, I found myself staring at the back of his head. GOD, I wanted to pop him just one good time! I spoke in a hushed tone, so as not to alarm Emory again.

"First of all, Jeff, don't you ever in your life speak to me in that tone or with those words in front of our daughter again. Ever. I am the mother of your child and soon to be your wife, but if you keep this up, you can kiss that goodbye."

He refused to turn around, still standing in front of the refrigerator, now just eating directly from it.

"Secondly, Jeff, you're not driving my car anymore. It's too much of a risk. I can't have you out here, driving around town with Emory in the car, and you have a suspended license and now *a warrant* for your arrest. We *just* got her diagnosis, Jeff! If you get pulled over and arrested with her in the car and I'm at work, do you know what happens to Emory? She goes to Child Protective Services until I can pick her up, Jeff. CHILD. PROTECTIVE. SERVICES. I'm a social worker, Jeff. For children and FA-MI-LIEEEEESSS, JEFF. There are so many things wrong with that picture, Jeff. So. Many Things. There is no way in hell *my* child is going into CPS custody. Absolutely not. So, no. You cannot drive my car anymore. You can get a ride to work on Fridays and I'll pick you up in the evening, and I'll drive myself to and from the park'n'ride for work in the mornings. On weekends I'll take you and I'll pick you up, but you absolutely are *not* driving my car again until the fines are paid and the warrant is removed! Period."

We stood there in silence for the better part of a minute—me staring at the back of his head, him staring into the fridge. Then, without warning, Jeff slammed the refrigerator door closed, turned around, stared right at me, and walked by without so much as a whisper. Once again, the rest of the night was spent in silence, but I absolutely meant what I said. I could not take the risk that my daughter—a little Black girl, disabled, and nonverbal, might end up in Texas state custody. The same state that was the last in the union to inform slaves they were free until two and a half years after the fact. The same state that just eleven years prior saw James Byrd Jr.[34], a disabled Black man, tortured, dragged behind a truck, decapitated, and his headless body dumped in front of a Black church? Hell no was I going to risk my child going into

---

34. "Black Man Dragged To Death" by Sue Ann Pressly, *https://www. washingtonpost.com/wp-srv/national/longterm/jasper/charges061098.htm*

a state system with that history, or risk her being placed with people who could inflict such heinous violence. Over my dead body.

*

Morning came and the silence remained just as heavy in the air as it did the night before. Neither of us spoke as we stood in front of the bathroom mirror and brushed our teeth, nor as we moved around each other as we got dressed. We both spoke to Emory and showered her with our usual morning affections, but to each other, no. If one of us needed something near the other, we silently waited for the other person to move out of the way, and then carried on with our business. You would have needed a chainsaw to cut through the tension between us. When it was time to leave the house to take Jeff to work, I picked up my keys, my purse, and Emory and headed toward the door.

"What are you doing?" Jeff questioned me as if I was doing something completely foreign to him.

"Putting Em in the car. C'mon, let's go. You're gonna be late."

He paused, and then as if he had deemed the situation copasetic, followed me out the door. I snapped Emory's car seat into the base and quickly hopped into the driver's seat. Jeff jogged to the car and caught the driver's side door just before I closed it. He was glaring at me.

"What are you doing, Adiba?"

"I'm driving you to work, Jeff. Like I said I would. Now c'mon. Let's go."

"Get out of the car."

"No, Jeff. You get *in* the car so we can leave."

"Adiba, get out of the driver's seat, give me the keys and get on the passenger side. I'm driving."

He was still holding on to the top of the door.

"No, Jeff. You're *not* driving. I meant what I said last night. You're not driving my car anymore. You're not."

Jeff was becoming more and more enraged. His eyes were already very dark brown, but they looked as if they'd turned completely black.

He clenched his fists and jaw and began to speak to me through clenched teeth, but I wasn't backing down. I wasn't afraid of him.

"I don't have time for this, Adiba. Get out of the car!" he said, this time raising his voice.

I looked in the rearview mirror and up and down the block to see if any of my neighbors had come out into their front yards. They hadn't and somehow, I managed to remain completely calm. In hindsight, I think that was a survival technique. If I could stay calm while he was becoming irate, I could remain in control of the situation, and with Emory in the backseat, it was imperative that I remained in control of the situation.

"No, Jeff. You get *in* the car," I said sticking the key in the ignition and starting the car. I attempted to pull the driver's side door closed, but Jeff tightened his grip on the door frame right as I tried to close it.

"Jeff, let go of the door." I pulled the handle and it didn't budge.

"Adiba, get out of the car."

"No, Jeff. I'm not getting out. I'm taking you to work. Now let go of the door and get in so we can go."

"I'll let go when you get out of the car."

"Oh my God, Jeff. Are you serious?" I didn't expect him to be, and I was edging closer and closer to complete and utter annoyance.

"Dead serious. Get out. You're not driving me to work."

I wielded all my strength to close the door a few more times, and each time I failed. I was fed up, and finally I made a move. I shifted the gear in the Toyota Corolla into reverse. I wanted to just leave him standing there in the driveway. If he wasn't going to get in the car so I could take him to work, he could find his own way to work. The car jerked and rolled backward down the driveway a bit. Jeff, still gripping the door handle, lost balance and he fell onto his side, landing just underneath the bottom edge of the door and sandwiching him between the door and the ground. He let out a yell, and I slammed on the brakes.

"Oh my God, Jeff! Are you okay?" I said. I was in shock. I couldn't believe this was happening. "Don't move! I need to move the car forward so the door isn't on you!"

Frantically, I maneuvered the car until he was able to wriggle his body out from beneath it. He laid on his side for about thirty seconds, screaming that I was purposely trying to run him over.

"Jeff, I'm not trying to run you over! You fell because you didn't let go of the door! Now don't move. Let me pull forward so the door isn't on you."

He continued to yell until the door was no longer touching him. He sat up in the driveway and just stared at me. He honestly looked like he wanted to kill me, and now I was scared. I whispered to him.

"Jeff, I'm sorry. I didn't mean for that to happen. But I really need you to get in the car so we can go."

"Shut the fuck up," he replied as he rose to his feet.

I quickly closed my door and he just stared at me through the window as he made his way around the front of the car to the passenger side. He got in and slammed the door so hard I was surprised the window didn't shatter. I glanced at Emory in the rearview mirror and we made eye contact. She was startled, her eyes wide. I cooed to her in a high-pitched, sing-song voice—I needed her to be okay.

"Hey, mama! You're good. It's okay. We're just gonna take Daddy to work. It's okay."

I could see her body visibly settle as she slowly smiled at me. I inhaled as I smiled back.

"Yeeeees . . . there's mama's beautiful girl! I see you, mama!"

I needed to keep her happy and smiling. I needed this to not be the moment her memories of a happy childhood were shattered. I needed to somehow remain in control of this situation, and so far, I had been doing an alright job of that.

"Thank you for getting in the car, Jeff."

"Shut the fuck up and drive."

"Jeff, I've already told you not to speak to me that way in front of Emory."

He said nothing, but I looked over at him as I slowly backed out of the driveway and I could see his chest heaving up and down. I had seen him angry before, but never like this. I didn't know this Jeff. We had been in heated arguments before, but he'd never cursed at me. He'd never full-on *yelled* at me. I mean, sure he'd raised his voice—but yelled? Never. This was now twice in two days that he did both. I no longer knew what to expect from him, but I decided the best thing I could do was just drive him to work and hope that he cooled down along the way.

Sadly, that just wasn't in the cards.

It was Sunday morning, and Sunday morning in Houston means church traffic and the Bloody Mary Brunch crowd. On some streets police were directing traffic so that people could safely pull into and out of church parking lots. That should tell you how bad Sunday mornings in Houston can be. It was 9:00 a.m. and the roads were already packed. We drove along in silence for about two miles, and then Jeff grabbed the steering wheel and pulled the car to the right. We came within inches of hitting the car next to us before I could steer us back into our lane.

"Jeff! What are you doing? Stop it! You're gonna get us in an accident."

He said nothing as he stared ahead out the front window and jerked the steering wheel to the right again.

"JEFF, STOP IT! WE HAVE EMORY IN THE CAR WITH US! STOP IT!"

No sooner than I corrected the car back into our lane of traffic, Jeff grabbed the steering wheel again, this time forcing us into the lane next to us. Thank God the cars behind us decided to stay back a short distance, or else we definitely would have had an accident. Now I was the one yelling, convinced he was trying to kill us all.

"WHAT? WHAT IS IT, JEFF? WHAT DO YOU WANT?"

He calmly stated (through clenched teeth): "I want to go to Starbucks and get a goddamned Frappuccino. Is that okay with you?"

"A Frappuccino, Jeff? A Frappuccino? You almost killed us all for a fucking milkshake? Go. Get your fucking milkshake."

I pulled the car up to the Starbucks, put it in park, and immediately turned around to check on Emory. She was very alert, and it dawned on me that she hadn't made a sound the entire time. Not at the house, not in the car, not just now when I'd raised my voice and her father was jerking the car right and left. She remained completely silent. I knew the silence of terrified children all too well—it was a silence that lived within me too. My eyes filled with tears as I assured her, again, that everything was fine. That mommy was okay and daddy was just getting a coffee, but we were all okay. I told her after we dropped her daddy off at work, she and I would spend the day playing with her toys, and maybe see Titi Mere and Titi Rosie and Baby Tristan in the afternoon. She remained silent, alert, watching me. She grabbed ahold of my finger with her right hand as I touched her cheek. I swear her big brown eyes just saw right through me and straight into my soul. I wrapped my hand around her teeny tiny hand and told her I loved her before I turned back around in the seat. Jeff got in the car a moment later and said one word to me.

"Drive."

I could not have predicted, in a million years, what happened next.

SHIT NOBODY
TALKS ABOUT

We continued down the road in silence. I diverted my eyes to the rear-view mirror, constantly checking on Emory. In an instant yet out of the blue, Jeff turned to me, put his nose within three inches of the side of my face, and screamed at the top of his lungs.

"You bitch! You fucking bitch! You tried to kill me!" he screamed close enough to my face that I could feel his breath. "Is that what you wanted? Huh? You want me dead?" His next words cut even deeper. "I hate you! I fucking hate you! Get out of the goddamn car!"

I was terrified, but somehow, over all of his yelling and physical intimidation, I heard it. I heard Emory's wailing in the backseat. I looked in the rearview mirror and her mouth was wide open. So wide open. And a sound I'd never heard from her was escaping her tiny body. She wasn't crying, she was screaming. Screaming so much and so loud she could barely catch her own breath. My heart shattered into a million pieces—what was I doing to my baby? I was supposed to remain in control of the situation. She wasn't supposed to know this life. She was never supposed to experience this level of fear—especially not as a baby. Me going through it at one year of age was enough—this was not another generational curse that needed to continue.

I made the split-second decision to pull into the closest parking lot I could find, a Walgreens. I stopped the car with Jeff still screaming at me and told him he had to get out. I wasn't taking him any further. He could call a cab or a friend, but I was done. He took one look at me and reached over and snatched the keys out of the ignition. Like something out of a movie, I threw my body over the center console (still strapped into my seatbelt, mind you) and reached for his hand that had my keys in them. I got a hold of the keys with a few fingers and pulled. He pulled them back and yelled at me to let go.

"No! *You* let go, Jeff! You let go!"

Emory was still screaming, and Jeff was stronger than I was. He pried my fingers from around my keyring, opened the car door, and took off running through the Walgreens parking lot, toward the back of the store.

Crying and heaving so hard I could barely catch my breath, I thought, *what is happening? How was this even my life?* The only thing I knew to do was to call the police and then call Jeff's aunt Alexis— the closest thing I had to my own family in Texas. I told her what had happened and she asked me not to call the police. I told her I already had, and I could hear the disappointment in her voice. Now, I love Aunt Alexis with my whole heart, but I was so hurt that she would ask me not to do that when I was clearly in fear for my and my daughter's life. However, that was her nephew. The oldest child of her favorite sister, who died too young. Jeff drove her crazy with his antics and bully behavior, but he was her favorite. I could understand why she didn't want me to have him sent to jail. What I couldn't understand is why she was okay with the fact that he had just tried to kill us all, moments earlier.

The police showed up shortly thereafter. The female officer (a white woman with blond hair, pulled back into a bun) stayed with me while her colleague walked the parking lot to look for Jeff. I sat in my car with all of the doors open. It was June 5 and the Texas heat was already being disrespectful.

"Are you okay, ma'am?"

"I'm okay."

I was not okay. Not in the slightest. Panicked and in shock, yes. Okay? Definitely not.

"What about your daughter? Is she okay?"

"Actually, let me take her out—she's pretty scared."

"Did he hurt you, ma'am?"

"No, just scared me."

"Has he hurt you in the past, ma'am?"

"No."

"Did he hurt your daughter? Or has he in the past?"

"No, ma'am. He would never."

"Do you feel like you're in imminent danger?"

"Ma'am?"

"Like, urgent danger . . ." she said, ready to explain the full dictionary definition.

"No, I know what imminent means . . . I just . . ." my voice trailed off as I watched the other officer emerge from behind the building with Jeff—my keys in hand. I began to shake.

"Ma'am, does he have any weapons on him, that you know of?"

"Um, yes. He has a silver-and-black pocketknife in his pants pocket. He uses it for work."

"Do you fear he'll use it to hurt you?" We stood in the Walgreens parking lot in the summer heat with several seconds of silence between us.

"Ma'am?" I just stared at her blankly, Emory in my arms and tears rolling down my cheeks cooling down her head in the most unfortunate way.

As Jeff and the other officer got closer to the car my shaking became more visible. The female officer stood close to me and spoke in a low tone.

"Ma'am, do you want us to arrest him today? We can arrest him for reckless endangerment of a child and domestic disturbance in a public setting."

I stared at Jeff. He was hot and sweaty and scowling at me from across the roof of the car. I kept hearing his aunt's voice in my head, asking me to not call the police.

"Um . . . no. No. Don't arrest him. I just . . . I just need to get him to work."

"Okay, would you like us to follow you?"

"Yes, ma'am. Please do that."

"Okay. You go ahead and put your daughter back in the car. I'll take his knife and put it in your trunk so that it is not on him while you drive. We'll follow you there, and once there he can retrieve the knife from your trunk since you say he needs it for work. Okay?"

"Okay."

I put Emory in her car seat and got back into the car, not daring to even breathe in Jeff's direction. I just wanted to get him to work and get home. I kept my eyes focused on the road in front of me, and periodically checked my rearview mirror to make sure the police were still behind us. This was the absolute last straw. While I answered all of the questions the officer was asking me, I had also made up my mind. I was done. I was 100 percent, all the way, no turning back, done. And that was when I made the very conscious decision to become a single mom. I had no other choice. I felt that our lives, mine and Emory's, literally depended on it. While Jeff was at work, I changed every single lock on every window and door in my house. This was the straw that not only broke the camel's back but ground it into a powder so fine glitter was jealous.

*

Later that afternoon, while Emory slept in her crib, I quietly packed and moved all of Jeff's belongings, including his dialysis machine, into the garage. The garage door didn't lock so he could come and get his things anytime he wanted, but I felt safe in my home behind my locked doors and windows. I could no longer live with a man I did not love, did not trust, and was quite literally afraid to be around. That morning, he could have killed us all, and he acted with complete disregard for his daughter. I couldn't do it. I simply could not do it. I was not going to raise my daughter in a home where she had to learn survival techniques as a toddler. Childhood was for playing and laughing and being silly, not hiding under tables until the fear subsided as I did. As I sat on the edge of my bed and typed out a lengthy text to Jeff explaining that the actions of the morning were stopping right then and there, tears streamed down my face. I sobbed deep and heavy tears as I told him that I loved him once, but didn't anymore, and couldn't ever again. My chest burned as I let him know that he would always be Emory's father, but he couldn't be her father in our home, that he had to go, that he was no longer welcome. I ended the text with these words:

> *I'll always love you for giving me Emory, but my heart and my home are no longer open to you. Your things are in the garage, and you can get them tonight, but you cannot stay. Goodbye, Jeff.*

And with that, I laid on my bed and screamed a scream that came from deep in my gut—leftover hurts from every fight, every tear, every lie, every frustration I'd endured during our relationship. It was filled with the remnants of a relationship that had rotted to its core. This was not what I had set out for our lives to be. When Jeff and I first got together we talked about living our best life in France, with him cooking and learning from culinary greats by day, and us savoring French wines and testing out new recipes by night. Was it a realistic dream? Of course not! I hardly knew the man when I found out I was carrying his baby—but I thought I did. And I always believed in the fairy tale—or at least I always *wanted* the fairy tale. But you know what? The song is not true. Fairy tales don't come true—not even if you're young at heart. Not if both hearts aren't honest—and I don't believe his heart ever was. Jeff's heart was 100 percent devoted to our daughter, but there was never going to be any room in there for me. Also, there was something I never paid attention to about fairy tales. They never showed you what life was like *after* the fair maiden got her "prince." All we knew was that he rescued her from some unfortunate situation and then they lived happily ever after. The end. They never showed you *how* they got to the happily ever after, or what that happily ever after even looked like. Was there screaming and yelling and warrants for arrest? Is that what happened once Cinderella went back to the castle? Did Snow White pop out of the kitchen and hit her up with, "Sorry, boo, that's *my* man." No, couldn't be. If anything, my life had turned into the cautionary tale *before* the fairy tale actually began.

How did I get here, I wondered to myself. How did *we* get here? What was I doing to my daughter? Could I actually make it on my own? I had also just lost my job because, well, you guessed it, too much time away from work to care for Emory and Jeff. (Turns out employers really expect you to show up for work—even if your entire world is crumbling down around your feet. Who knew?) I had no job, no job on the horizon, a stack of bills, a child with a pretty intense disability, and I was consciously deciding to walk away from not only the little bit of financial support I did have but also the only parental support I had. I had a child who relied on me for literally *everything*, and I could not be a good mother for her if I couldn't keep her, much less myself, safe. I was once again faced with the same question I had when I found out Jeff was still married: Should I stay or should I go? If I go there will be trouble, but if I stay there will be double. I'd find a way to handle the trouble if I left, but I wasn't certain we'd survive the trouble if I stayed. I had only one choice—leave the fairy tale that never was and go.

I laid on that bed and cried until, eventually, I fell asleep. I was exhausted from the morning and afternoon as a whole, and I had no idea what lie ahead for the evening. I awoke with a start, hearing Emory crying in her room. I jumped from the bed and ran down the hall to check on her, fear racing through my body. The morning's events had traumatized me to the extent that I felt like every cell in my body was on pins and needles. I was hyper-aware of every sound the house made, every set of headlights that drove by, every voice that walked by my house—all of it made me jump and made my stomach turn. After settling Emory in her high chair for dinner, I checked my phone to see if Jeff had responded. He had—with one sentence:

I'll be by after work to pick up my clothes.

I looked at the time—it was 8:30 p.m. His store closed in thirty minutes meaning I had just about an hour before he arrived. Instantly I felt sick to my stomach and ran to the hall bathroom to vomit. Hovering over the toilet with sweat dripping from my temples, I knew I wasn't ready to face him again. I was terrified, not knowing if we would argue again, if he would try to hurt me (he had his knife on him), or if he would just go peacefully. Whatever it was going to be, it was going to be—I couldn't hide in the bathroom because despite whatever I was feeling, I still had to be a mom. There was still a little girl in the kitchen who needed me to feed her and bathe her and sing her to sleep and make her world right. As I shuffled back toward the kitchen, I remember thinking to myself that this is the part of motherhood that nobody tells you about. The part where you have to put your feelings and your fears and your own emotions on the back burner sometimes, simply to make it to the next day. Parenting waits for nobody, and it sure as hell doesn't give a damn if your life is melting away like it's been hit with napalm.

I was still feeding Emory when I heard the knock at my front door. I looked at my phone and he was right on time—it was 9:30 p.m. on the dot. I opened the door to find Jeff looking, well, tired. And solemn. He looked like a man defeated, and for a moment I felt immense sadness for him, for us, for all the things we were *supposed* to be. He looked at me with tears in his eyes and for a moment we just stood there, staring at each other, neither of us saying a word. One of us had to make the first move.

"Hi," I said, softly.

"Hi," he replied. "Can I come in?"

"Ummmm," I shifted back and forth from foot to foot.

"Look, I'm not gonna hurt you, Adiba. I need to get my clothes out of the garage, and I'd like to see Emory before I go."

"Um. Well . . . okay."

I stepped aside to let him in and as soon as Emory laid eyes on him, she went wild with excitement, flailing her arms and flashing her big, gummy grin from ear to ear. She's such a daddy's girl, and their bond was so special to watch. It broke my heart to see her nuzzle into him and know that this was going to be the last time that was going to be happening for a while. She squealed and giggled as he tickled her and kissed her face over and over, his goatee tickling her cheeks, his tears staining *his* cheeks. It took every ounce of strength I had to hold myself together as I watched them. I couldn't recall a pain this deep in my adult life. Actually, I couldn't recall a pain this deep as a child either. This was fresh, new pain that left me feeling as though all seven layers of my skin had been peeled back, and I was just raw for all the world to see. At that moment, the pain became my second skin. But again, I felt like I had no other choice. I knew what abusive relationships looked like—up close. I did not need to stick around to see what happened next.

He moved to the couch with Emory, and I was still standing by the door, too scared to move. I didn't want him there any longer and was becoming increasingly nervous with him still being there. While fundamentally I understood that he was just trying to get in as much time with Emory as he could since it might be a while before he saw her again, he had essentially terrorized us that morning and this was not the time to get comfortable.

"Okay, Jeff, you need to go."

"I'm trying to spend time with my daughter."

"Jeff, you need to go."

"Just five more minutes, Adiba. Please. Just five more minutes."

"Jeff, I'm sorry. You have to go. You *have* to. Please."

By this point I choked back tears, pleading with him to leave my home. After a few more seconds of whispering into Emory's ear, he stood up and brought her to me. I held her so close to my body as Jeff retrieved a bag of clothes from the garage. In that instant the memories of my mother and father getting into a tug of war *with my body* when

I was about the same age that Emory was came rushing back to me. I didn't know if that's what Jeff had in mind but I'd be damned if history was going to repeat itself with my child. Jeff came back into the house and over to me and Emory as we waited for him by the front door. He leaned over to give Emory a kiss on the top of her head, and then looked at me with tears rolling down his cheeks.

"I'm so sorry, Adiba. I'm sorry for everything. I never meant to hurt you. Can you please, *please* forgive me? I'll get the divorce, I'll do better. Please."

My words came out stifled, and through tears.

"No, Jeff. I can't. I can't. This morning was just too much. I can't do it anymore. I can't. I'm sorry. I'm sorry. You have to go."

I opened the door with one hand, still holding Emory close to my body with the other. I followed Jeff as he walked out onto the porch, and down the walkway to the sidewalk. We stopped at the end of my driveway and Jeff turned to me one more time.

"You know, I loved you the minute I laid eyes on you. I loved you then and I love you now. I'll always love you, Adiba. Always. I'm sorry I hurt you. But I won't anymore. I won't. Make sure Emory knows her daddy loved her so much. So, so much. And make sure you tell her that I loved you too."

I stared at him, both of us crying. Something about the way he was speaking sounded off to me.

"What do you mean *loved* her so much, Jeff? What are you talking about?"

And with that, Jeff leaned over, kissed me on my forehead, and turned to walk down the street. I called after him, still crying.

"Jeff! What do you mean? What do you mean you loved her so much? What are you saying? Jeff!"

But he just continued to walk, never turning back around. I stood at the end of my driveway for what felt like an eternity, watching him walk down the street until I couldn't see him anymore. I didn't want to let my mind go to the dark place it was heading because I knew exactly what he meant. I was a trained social worker—I knew how to spot suicide talk a mile away, but I didn't want to believe that Jeff would do that. He was thirty-five and had three young children to raise. I told myself he was just being dramatic and emotionally manipulative. That it was a ploy to make me feel bad for ending our relationship. He wasn't going to kill himself. I went back inside and was in the middle of placing Emory in her high chair when I received a text from Jeff. He apologized for all the hurt he'd caused and said he felt everyone would be better off without him. I could see the words on the screen but my brain could not comprehend what I was reading. What was he saying? That he *was* going to kill himself? What? No! How? What was happening? My pulse quickened and my vision got blurry. Is this what it felt like to pass out? I grabbed the corner of the dining room table to steady myself, and no sooner than I did that, my phone began to ring. First it was Jeff's aunt Alexis, then his aunt Erica, then Bunny. Apparently Jeff had sent everyone the same message, and they were all calling me, asking me what had happened and if I knew where Jeff was. All I could tell them was that I had ended things with him and I didn't know where he was. That was the truth. I told them I would try calling, and I'd let them know if I got a hold of him. The most difficult of all the phone calls was hearing his children crying in the background as I spoke with Bunny. It broke my heart. We were not close (for obvious reasons), but at that moment Bunny and I were in the same situation. Two women, attached to the same man, who in that very moment, seemed to be leaving his children behind.

I looked at Emory and wondered how I would explain this day to her when she grew up. How was this day going to end? What would I say? Would she understand? Would she forgive him? Would she forgive me for leaving?[35]

It was almost eleven o'clock at night, and I still couldn't get a hold of Jeff. Part of me wanted to go out to look for him. The father of my child was missing after he sent a suicide note, but I was conflicted. I

35.   For the record, I still haven't told her about this day, or the full unabridged story about what went down between her father and I, causing me to end things with him.

was deeply hurt and angry with him. But I also understood that this moment boiled down to choices we'd each made. Did I have to have unprotected sex with him? No. But did he have to give me his number, lie to me and tell me he was divorced, and ask me out on a date? Also, no. And I could go back and forth with the *he didn't have to*'s and the *I didn't have to*'s all day, but in the end, it just boiled down to choices. He lied and I accepted the date. My gut told me otherwise and I chose to ignore it. He got caught and I chose to stay. Choices. So while yes, I was deeply hurt and angry, there was also a part of me that felt like, "Well, Adiba, you got yourself into this situation. The responsible thing to do would be to look for him." But also, at that moment, I just didn't want to. I felt like I was done. I had given him so much—I didn't owe him anything else. No more of my time, my energy. No more inconveniencing myself for him. I was done.[36] But then there was Emory, staring at me with her giant brown eyes, and long, curly eyelashes. She got those from Jeff. She was the spitting image of her father. How could I look this little girl in the face one day and tell her that I didn't at least *try* to look for her father after he told me he was going to kill himself.

I loaded Emory into the car and drove through my small suburban neighborhood. Every house looked the same, every yard the same, and there was no sign of Jeff. I exited the neighborhood and drove up and down the main road closest to my home—FM 529. This road does not have any streetlights. It is an open pasture on one side and a thick forest on the other until eventually it becomes a thick forest on both sides. This road always scared the hell out of me and I vowed never to go down it at night. It looked like a place where either Klan rallies were held or where people go to bury a body—which is precisely why I was driving down that road. Yes, I knew that when people decide to take their own life, they tend to do it in a place where they will be found, but Jeff looked so sad and ashamed earlier that evening, I thought he

36. And to his children and family who may be reading this, I am sorry. I know that is incredibly difficult to read. I know this. All I ask is that you try to understand the complexity of my emotions and the situation at that time.

might have just walked off into the woods to think . . . or to take his own life. I went as far as I could before I turned the car around, too scared to drive any farther in. As I drove back up the road toward my home, my cousin called to check on me after seeing my Facebook post asking for anyone who had seen Jeff to call me immediately. I was explaining the sordid events of the day to her and I could feel that my anxiety was on level ten. I had a pounding headache, I was nauseous, and I couldn't stop my hands from shaking. I needed a cigarette to calm my nerves. As I pulled up to the intersection at the corner of Fry Road and FM 529, I noticed that the Walgreens to my left was already closed, but the CVS across the street was open. The same CVS that I had purchased a diabetes travel kit for Jeff to keep in his car when we first started dating when I was hell-bent on saving his life.

Rather than turn left onto Fry Road to go home, I decided to go through the light and pull into the side entrance of the CVS parking lot.

"Oh my God. oh my god!"

"Dede, what's wrong? What's happening?"

"Oh fuck, Quiana—I gotta go! I found Jeff!"

I'm not even sure I brought my car to a full stop before I jumped out of the car screaming for someone, anyone, to help me. Jeff, still in his work clothes (a button-down shirt and slacks), sat on the ground with his back propped up against the building, unconscious and half slumped over with his legs extended in front of him. His duffle bag of clothes was to the right of him. To the left of him, a half-empty water bottle. In between his legs, five empty pill bottles—three months of blood pressure medication and two bottles of sleeping pills. I shook him. I screamed his name. I slapped his face. Someone asked me if I needed help and I yelled at them to call 911. I called 911. I looked up at my car.

Emory.

She was sitting in her car seat, watching all of this. Her giant brown eyes with their long curly eyelashes. Jeff's eyes, taking in the scene, staring back at me. My God. What had I done?

You know how in movies, when a bad car accident happens and

the main character happens to drive by and realizes it's their partner in the demolished vehicle, they slow the entire scene down and everyone sounds like a Beatles record playing at one-quarter speed? Well, they do that because it's real. One minute felt like one hour before the paramedics, fire department and police all arrived. The officer, a short Asian woman with a round, broad face, asked me the normal questions—his name, age, health history—and it sounded like she was speaking with a mouth full of cotton after a dentist appointment. It was all just mush, but somehow I answered her. And then she asked *the* question.

"Ma'am, what is your relation to him?"

"What?"

"Your relation? How do you know this man?"

I stared at her blankly—the tears continuing to run at a marked pace down my cheeks.

"I . . . I . . . I was his fiancée, but . . . but . . ." I struggled to get the words out. "But tonight I . . ."

"Okay . . . okay. I understand. You don't have to explain. We're going to log this as a suicide attempt, but here is the station address, phone number, and police report number. You can come down to the station next week to get a copy of the report, should you need it."

I looked at her and opened my mouth to say thank you and nothing but dust escaped. All I could do was stand in front of her and cry.

"Ma'am, they're about to transport him to the hospital. You can follow the ambulance and we'll follow you, so you don't inadvertently get pulled over for speeding."

"O-o-okay," I mumbled as I got back in my car and prepared to follow the ambulance and fire truck out of the CVS parking lot. As we pulled into the road it dawned on me that the only time I'd ever been in caravans was for funerals. Was this a precursor of things to come? Was I going to have to bury my daughter's father? Was the curse of the daddyless daughter following me too? My mind was going in every different direction possible. I was hyperventilating and screaming and crying and my daughter was in the back seat, quietly bearing witness to all of this. I called my best friend, Faith.

"Hey!" she said, laughing as she answered.

"I think he's dead!" I replied, scream-crying into the phone.

"What?"

"Jeff! I think he's dead!"

"What! Hold on. I'm at this event with Robert, let me get to a quieter place . . . okay, now *what* are you saying?"

"Jeff!! I think he's dead! He tried to kill himself tonight and it's my fault because I called off the engagement and told him to leave and he took a bunch of pills and I'm following the ambulance to the hospital but he barely has a pulse! He might die, Faith! He might die!"

I was now full-on screaming into the phone, no longer able to control any part of my emotions. It was a miracle Faith was able to understand my words because in my head I sounded like Mushmouth from Fat Albert. But Faith—my best friend, my BFSLDITWW—did what best friends do.

"Okay. Okay. Do you need me to come out there?"

"No? Yes? I dunno."

"Okay. Get to the hospital and find out the situation and let me know, but dammit, Adiba, you hear me and you hear me good." She was now crying. "It is *not* your fault that Jeff tried to kill himself. Don't you dare tell yourself that, and don't you dare let anyone else try and convince you of that. You did what you needed to do to make sure you and your baby girl could live a safe and happy life, and that *wasn't* going to be with him. He lied to you, he essentially stole from you and put you *and* your daughter's lives at risk *more* than once. You did what any mother would do! And Jeff responded in the only way Jeff knew how to. This is *not* your fault. You remember that. And I swear to God, Adiba, if anyone tries to tell you differently, you send them straight to me. You don't deal with that shit. You focus on being a mom to that sweet girl of yours, do you hear me? *Do you hear me?*"

"Yes," I said, still in tears.

"Okay. I love you. Find out what's going on and either call or text me when you can. I don't care what time it is. I'll have my ringer on and right next to me. You call me. Got it?"

"Yeah."

"I love you."

"I love you, too. Thank you."

"Bye, honey."

"Bye."

*

I hate hospital waiting rooms. They always fill me with anxiety—the television that is always playing some god-awful news station, poised to tell you all the evils of the world. Everyone sitting around wearing their optimism like a badge of honor—distracting themselves with cell phones or magazines, but damn near giving themselves whiplash every time a doctor or nurse steps out of the double doors marked "hospital personnel only."

I was no different. I texted Jeff's family to let them know which hospital we were at, and one by one, a different family member showed up. Aunt Alexis, Aunt Erica . . . I think his cousin Mark came too. There was praying and crying, and cuddling Emory, but for the most part, we all stayed very quiet, not saying much to each other. When the doctor finally came out and asked who Jeff's next of kin was, I raised my hand, and he asked if I could follow him into a small meeting room. I asked Aunt Alexis to come with me and left Emory playing with Jeff's aunt Erica, and her cousins. The only thing I remember about this doctor is that he was a tall white man with sympathetic eyes. He started in very slowly.

"Folks, we're not sure how, but somehow Jeff is still alive. Any other person who took the number of pills he took would have either had a massive heart attack, a brain bleed, or a stroke—each of which would have killed them. We have checked for all of these and so far none have happened. This doesn't mean he is out of the woods. He has done further damage to his kidneys, and we're monitoring the rest of his organs—specifically his pancreas and liver. We will also continue to watch for swelling on the brain. His blood pressure is dangerously low, and I'm sorry to tell you this but I can't guarantee you he'll make it through the night."

Then he turned around, pulled a white binder out of a drawer, and slid it across the table to Aunt Alexis and me.

"You may want to alert the rest of your family and begin making final plans. Now, we may get lucky, we may not get that far down the road. We've pumped his stomach and this could turn around. But, you should be prepared for it not to. I'm very sorry."

I looked across the table at the doctor and I felt absolutely numb. All of my tears had dried up and I felt like an empty corn husk. I heard myself ask him a question, but I never felt my lips move.

"What percentage of survival are you giving him right now?"

"Honestly, ma'am, I can't answer that. I've never seen anyone come back from something like this. But he's hanging in there so we'll just have to wait it out and see."

I'm not sure if I was in shock or just dazed, but I sat there, not saying a word. Aunt Alexis spoke up and thanked him for the information as he exited the room. I think we prayed together before we rejoined the rest of the family. Upon opening the door of the small meeting room where the doctor had just told us we might want to start making final plans for Jeff, I looked over the nurses' station and saw Jeff in an emergency bay. There were wires, tubes, beeping monitors, and IV bags everywhere, the nurses moving all around him. His eyes were closed, his lips parted by the tube going down his throat. His shirt had been ripped open. I turned my head and could see Emory bouncing on Aunt Erica's lap through a small window in the double doors. I looked back at Jeff. The tears spilled over like a pot just coming to a rolling boil.

Where was the chapter in that motherhood manual that detailed how to explain to your child that her father tried to kill himself because she ended their relationship? I needed a step-by-step manual and a survival guide because I couldn't guarantee that even *I* would make it through this one without help.

Aunt Alexis and I alerted the rest of the family and at about 1:30

a.m., we all headed home. There was nothing for us to do, and I had to get Emory to bed. Yes, that sweet girl who had just endured a day I prayed she'd never remember, was still awake, still happy, still giggling. I thanked God for sending me a child who somehow instinctively understood the weight of a moment, and just chilled. I also asked him to bless me with enough money to pay for her therapy to undo all of this when she was older. As we drove home I passed by the CVS on the corner, where I'd found Jeff. The irony was not lost on me that the same place I went when I was trying to save his life when we first started dating, is the same place I went to save his life when we finally stopped dating. I stared at it as we drove by—the red letters lit up. X marks the spot—except it didn't. The spot where Jeff had almost died just hours earlier wasn't marked at all. There was no evidence that death came to visit that CVS the night before.

I told myself I'd never shop at CVS again.

I haven't.

MOMS DON'T HAVE TIME FOR BREAKDOWNS

Between unemployment and food stamps, I was making it by the skin of my teeth. Jobless and without Jeff's small income, I didn't have room for extras, fanfare, or midday crying sessions. Once I ended things with Jeff I did what I do best, I hit the autopilot button. I put my head down and forged ahead. What choice did I have? Giving up wasn't an option. But, I couldn't help but be consumed with wondering how I got here. I did everything you're told to do so you don't end up sitting in the public assistance office waiting for someone to call your name. I went to college, graduated top of my class, got a job in my career field, and bought a house. Of course, I did get knocked up after two months of dating someone. I skipped that rule, and now here I was, sitting in the food stamp office with other women who probably thought they did almost all the right things too.

"Nice purse. Are those your nails?"

The judgment from the public assistance office intake workers was subtle yet rich and dripping with "oh, how the mighty have fallen." But if this is what I had to endure until I got our lives back on track, so be it.

Approximately three weeks after Jeff's suicide attempt, I was still going strong. I hadn't cried again since that night, the lights were still on, and I had been on what seemed to be a very promising job interview with the Houston Food Bank. I was feeling good, and Emory was doing great with her in-home therapies. Three days a week we had visits from a physical therapist, a speech therapist, and an occupational therapist. She was fitted for ankle-foot orthotics and had received a donated "ladybug chair," which supported her back and allowed her to sit upright while she played and watched television. We were good, or so I thought.

We sat at the table for dinner, as we did every night, and I was helicoptering Emory's ravioli into her wide-open mouth, also, as I always did. Around bite number six, Emory pushed the helicopter hand away and turned her face. I tried again, and again the same response. I did the thing most parents do—switched to a choo-choo train because obviously if air transportation wasn't working to get her to eat, land transportation would surely do the trick. I was wrong. That train flew off the tracks faster than Patti LaBelle's shoes at a Verzuz show. Emory was not having it. That's when I felt it. My heart began to race, and I couldn't catch my breath. I pleaded with Emory to eat the ravioli, and she just kept pushing it away. My pleading escalated to tears and pleadings in between giant gulps of air I was struggling to take in, but my girl wasn't budging. I erupted. I slammed my hand down on the table and yelled at my child.

"Just eat the goddamn ravioli!"

She jumped in her high chair and burst into tears. I knew I'd scared her half to death. Truthfully, I'd scared myself too, but it was too late. I was scream-crying and couldn't stop. I needed help and I needed it fast because I knew this feeling. It was the exact same feeling I'd felt before—that creeping up my spine, wrapping itself around my throat anxiety that showed up when I was trapped in the throes of postpartum depression. I refused to go back there so this time, I called for help. With trembling fingers and eyes I could barely see through, I called the only person I could think of—Lizzie, my first husband's cousin. I got to keep her in the divorce, and we were as close as sisters. Five minutes later, Lizzie was at my kitchen table chugga-chugging ravioli into Emory's mouth while I cried like a baby on the couch no more than ten feet away. She cleaned Emory up after dinner, changed her into her pajamas, gave her a bottle, and put her to bed. Then she just sat with me. With nothing but the sound of my sniffles filling the silence we sat on the couch for hours. Lizzie, cuddling my legs that were curled into the fetal position, finally broke the silence.

"Wanna talk about it?"

"I don't know."

"Well, what happened? I mean, how does one go from ravioli to losing their shit in less than ten minutes?"

I had to break my solemn disposition to laugh. That was Lizzie—blunt, honest, and funny as fuck.

"Shut up. Don't make me laugh. I'm sad!"

"Well, duh. I can see that. But why are you sad? What happened? Is it Jeff?"

And I just started sobbing all over again.

"Lizzie, what have I done? What have I done? He tried to kill himself, Lizzie! And I found him—half dead! Me! I found him!"

I realized that this was it. The chicken that was Jeff's attempted suicide and my decision to become a single mother had finally come home to roost and, in its roosting, it decided to shut my shit all the way down. It rendered me incapable of speaking or thinking clearly—and even parenting. It plucked me of every piece of armor I had and left me raw and exposed to every hurt I'd been pushing down over the last three weeks. There was no room for embarrassment, humility, or walking away from this. The hurt and anger demanded I acknowledge its existence, and didn't care if it had to turn my daughter's dinner time routine into a scene out of *Raising Arizona*. Lizzie, bless her heart, acknowledged the shit show she had willingly walked into but was not about to let me wallow in it.

"Yes, you did. You found him. But if you hadn't found him, he'd be dead, so you actually saved his life. You did what you felt you had to do and he did what he felt he needed to do to . . . whatever the fuck that was. Who knows why guys do what the fuck they do? Why did Will dump me? I dunno! I'm *foine*! Look, men are idiots and we are not responsible for their bullshit. Ain't nobody got time for that!"

I sat up looking at Lizzie like she had two heads. With a balled-up Kleenex held up to my nose and puffy eyes, I uttered, "Lizzie . . . did you really just go from Jeff's suicide attempt to talking about how fine you are?"

"I sure did. Why you actin' brand new? You act like you don't know who I am!"

I rolled my red, puffy eyes and laughed.

"I fucking love you, Lizzie. Thank you, girl. I don't think I would have made it through this night without you."

"Sure you would have! Actually, I take that back. You absolutely would not have made it through without me."

"Bitch, get out my house," I cackled.

"Bitch, you know you love me."

She was right. We exchanged good nights, and I closed the door behind her. I surveyed the scene before me. A mere two hours beforehand I'd been losing my shit over some ravioli and scaring the love of Jesus out of my child. Now, my house was quiet, my kitchen was clean, and I could breathe. I thanked God for Lizzie as I made my way down the hall to check on Emory. Her bedroom door creaked open, and the glow from her butterfly night-light lit the room in a dim haze. I stood over this sweet, loving little girl, asleep in her crib. She was about to be thirteen months old, and she was barely thirteen pounds. Apparently it was not uncommon for children with athetoid cerebral palsy and bilateral schizencephaly to be smaller than typical. Her body was in constant motion, trying to regulate itself, monitor itself, control itself, motivate itself—she burned through calories like they were Scooby Snacks. I looked at this teeny tiny human that came from *my* body—mine—and all I could see was her perfection. She was perfect in every way possible, designed exactly as she was supposed to be, and for some reason, I had been entrusted to care for this little person. And I think after much convincing, she actually chose me to be her mama. At least that's how I believe it, and how I've always imagined it. In my head, she and God were hanging out in heaven, or wherever God hangs out, flipping through the big book of souls trying to figure out who she should go to. They came to my page and she flat out said "pass." God paused and said, "Actually . . . this might be the one."

"Nope. Can't be. She doesn't even know that dude, God."

"True, she doesn't. But she'll come to know herself, and that's what's important."

"By way of me? Nah. I'm good. Pass. Hard pass."

"No, no . . . it'll be good. I promise. She's loads of fun and her future—I mean—just *look* at these pages! Look at what you'll be getting!"

And, while letting out a deep sigh, she would reply, "Alright, then . . . put me in, Coach. I'm ready."

And this is how this teeny tiny human came to be mine. Now it was up to me to make sure I kept her safe, happy, and healthy, and apparently keep *myself* open to learning a thing or two. I just had to figure out how to get us through this situation we were in, but I could start working on that in the morning. It had been a long day and an even longer three weeks. I was finally released from that anger, that hurt, and could breathe a little bit. I quietly lowered the frame on Emory's crib and nuzzled my nose into her hair. She smelled of Pink lotion and Baby Magic; tears filled my eyes again. Jeff had insisted we use Baby Magic lotion on her because he loved the smell. I let my nose rest there a moment. I could inhale her all day.

"Good night, munchkin," I whispered into her hair. "Mommy loves you so much. I don't know exactly how we're going to get through this, but I promise you we will. I will do whatever I have to do to make sure we're okay—you're okay. I promise."

I wiped my tears before they dripped onto her scalp, running the risk of startling her awake, kissed her head, and tiptoed out of her room, leaving her gently snoring in the glow of her night-light. As I drifted off to sleep I held this thought close: *Tomorrow is a new day, and I can always start again.*

I can always start again.

*

Jeff was released from the hospital a few weeks later. Upon being discharged from the hospital, Jeff did not have stable housing—no place he could say was home. For a short period of time he slept in a vehicle, and at one point he stayed with relatives, but all of these were short-lived until Bunny finally decided to take him in. We may not get along (trust and believe, she has every reason not to be a fan) but I'll tell you, she has a bigger heart than I'll ever have. Or, maybe she just *actually* loved him, and couldn't bear to see her children's father homeless while in dire health. And trust, he was absolutely in dire health. That suicide attempt wreaked havoc on Jeff's body and he could not regulate his sugar or blood pressure no matter how hard he tried. The peritoneal dialysis now caused him excruciating pain, and because of this, his moods were even less stable. Understandable, yes, but I couldn't have that in my home, around my child. I couldn't. No matter how cruel and unkind it sounds, like I left my daughter's father out there twisting in the wind while my daughter and I lived in a four-bedroom home, I was trying to move forward. For me, that would have been ten steps back.

Now, for what it's worth, Jeff did try to help as best he could. He couldn't offer financial assistance because he was no longer able to work, but he also didn't want us to be homeless. The thought of his daughter being homeless brought him to tears whenever we discussed it, and he was terrified that I would move back to Arizona with her. He called me one day and told me he had a friend that was willing to take Emory and I in until we found an affordable place to live. I declined. I didn't know this friend and there was no way I was going to move my disabled daughter and I into a stranger's house, in a part of town I was unfamiliar with, and with zero support. It was not feasible and would not solve our problem of stability and security. Every phone call ended with him asking me if I was going to move back to Arizona with our daughter, and every time I assured him that was not my plan. And it wasn't. I truly had no intention of moving back to the land of whiteness. As a Black woman raising a Black child, it was incredibly important that I raise my child somewhere she could see people that looked like her every day. It was important to me that she have the experience of growing up with her Black siblings, Black cousins, and Black aunts and uncles—which was something I didn't have.

I grew up mostly with the Puerto Rican side of my family, which, don't get me wrong, was bomb dot com. I take great pride in my Puerto Rican heritage and culture and had the *most* fun learning how to salsa dance with my Titi Mercedes in my Nana's living room, or eating Nana's *pasteles* every Christmas and trying to sneak cups of coquito with my cousins. To this day, if I'm flipping channels and hear Don Francisco's voice bellowing out, "*Sábado Gigaaaanteeeeeee,*" I'm stopping and watching. My childhood was steeped in Puerto Rican culture and tradition. But as I grew older I often felt it difficult to fit in with other Black kids. I didn't know all the latest rappers or double dutch moves—hell, I could barely double dutch! I didn't like greens, or catfish, or okra, and didn't know a thing about frying chicken. There was a lot about the Black experience I felt I missed out on just because I never felt like I could find my footing in a group that I so clearly belonged to—I didn't want the same for Emory. I wanted her to know her Blackness and experience the beauty of her Blackness full out, surrounded by her numerous gorgeous and talented family members in Houston.

I didn't have a Black community, or even a Black friend group that I belonged to in Tucson, so the thought of raising my child there— well, it had always been a hard NO for me, from the minute our plane touched down in 1988. So no, I truly had zero intention of moving back to Arizona. Aside from the lack of diversity, I didn't have the money to afford an apartment upon moving back, so that would mean I'd have to move in with my mom until I could get on my feet. Tell me—what thirty-three-year-old adult with a child *wants* to move in with their parent, as they try to raise their own child? The mental backflips I was doing trying to figure out how I would navigate the line between being the parent while simultaneously being the child was enough to send me into a mild panic. Nah. I was good. I'd figure it out.

And I worked hard at trying to figure it out, sending out resumes daily, gluing myself to job search sites while my daughter glued herself to *The Chica Show* on Sprout. However, the bank decided I wasn't figuring it out fast enough and decided to figure it out for me. In late July I received the official word: my house was going into preforeclosure. Unless I could come up with the balance owed from months of making partial payments, or sell it quickly and satisfy the loan, they would take it back and Emory and I would in fact, be homeless.

What the ever-loving fuck? How? How was this my life? How did this keep happening? *Why* did this keep happening? Didn't God see how damn hard I was working to get us back on track? Didn't he see that I had a disabled child? What the hell, God? What are you doing? I didn't sign up for this! I didn't sign up for any of this! What the actual fuck? I sat at my kitchen table and just stared at the letter from the bank for a good, long while. I didn't have anyone I could borrow the money from, and I certainly didn't have a 401k I could borrow from. I felt stuck in my situation. I called my mom and cried into the phone. If there was anyone on this planet who knew how to pivot and make something from nothing, it was my mom. She had had to pivot and make hard lefts more than a few times in her life, and somehow she always landed on her feet. She would know what I should do.

"Come home."

"No."

"Hear me out. Look . . . you're about to lose your home—"

"I'm not gonna lose my home."

"Just listen. You're about to lose your home, you don't have a job, and you don't really have a solid support system out there. Come back to Tucson, you and Emory can live with me until you can get on your feet and get a place for yourselves."

"I'm not moving back, Mom."

"Why?"

"Because I don't want to. I have a house here. I'll find a job and I'll make it work but there is no way I'm raising my child in Tucson."

"But what are you gonna do if you *don't* find a job? Then what? Are gonna move into a shelter with Emory?"

"You did."

"Ay, Adiba! Really? Yeah . . . okay . . . I did. But I didn't have a choice. I had to get away from your father and Nana wouldn't let me come home. I *had* to go to a shelter! But you don't have to—I'm offering you my home. You *have* a place you can go to that is safe—here."

I sighed. I really did not want to move back to Tucson and I certainly wasn't ready to give up on trying to make Houston work for us. I dug my heels in like the Scorpio I am.

"No, Mom. Moving back is not an option. Besides, her father is here and if it's possible, I'd like her to know him and have a relationship with him."

Mom sighed even deeper than I had a moment ago. It was that deep sigh that only moms sigh when they've about had it with your ass.

"Fine. But the offer stands. If you change your mind let me know."

"I will. But I don't plan on changing my mind. Sorry."

Famous last words.

*

Meeting with a realtor to sell the house you worked hard to get and even harder to win back in your divorce, only to lose it behind poor decisions and another man is . . . humiliating. At least it was for me. Telling her the story of how my home came to be, and now *not* be, forced me to take a long hard look at myself. As I heard myself telling her the story of my move to Texas up until the moment we were sitting at my kitchen table eating shrimp tacos and discussing the preforeclosure process, I found myself questioning the history and motivations behind every decision I'd made that led me to that point. Of course, I didn't question it too deeply because (a) shrimp tacos, and (b) who doesn't love a good old helping of self-denial. I could see a touch of where I'd made a left where

I should have turned right, but I wasn't yet in the place where I could say, "Yeah, girl—you were only concerned with your surface self and not dealing with your inner self and that's how you got here.

I still hadn't sought out a therapist. I wasn't trying to either. What I was trying to do was sell this house and get a job so I could move on from the nightmare I'd been living.

The realtor and I had a fine conversation. She handed me a Kleenex when I began to tear up in telling her about my situation, patiently answered all my questions about the bank, the market, and my credit, and then asked me some questions. Questions like if I had a place to move to if the house sold quickly . . . did I have a plan or path to move forward . . . and did Jeff know I was planning on selling the house. My answer to all of these was "no," and she just sat quietly and looked down at her hands. I told her that my mom had asked me to move home and take refuge in her house in Arizona until I could get back on my feet, but that I wasn't interested; that wasn't a path I wanted to walk down. I explained to her that the idea of simultaneously being the parent *and* the child was not something that seemed the slightest bit like a good idea—especially since my mom and I are both strong-willed, highly opinionated women. It just seemed like a recipe for disaster. Also, who in their right mind actually *wants* to move in with their parents when they're a full-on grown-ass adult? Moving home is not like winning the showcase on *The Price Is Right*. It's the consolation prize you get when you didn't look at everything in the showcase before bidding.

"Well, I wouldn't say it's quite that bad. I mean, you'll get more than a new toaster." She chuckled.

There was a beat of silence as we sat at my kitchen table. I traced the outline of the pleather insert on the tabletop with my fingertip.

"But you know, it might not be that bad. And, I can't guarantee that your house will sell before the preforeclosure period expires. If it doesn't, you'll be forced to move anyway . . . and if you don't have a place to go to . . ." Her voice trailed off. I listened to what she was saying, imagining every scenario possible. She wasn't wrong. There really was no guarantee that my house would sell quickly—the market was saturated with big, gorgeous new builds at roughly the same price my home was valued at. Who was going to buy a previously lived-in home when they could get sparkly and new for the same, if not lower, price? And the job offers were not coming in. I let out a heavy sigh and stared at the last bite of shrimp taco on my plate. I was full, but I was becoming emotional. I shoved that last bite in my mouth and between chews pushed out a muffled, "I'll think about it."

"That's all I'm saying. Just think about it. I'll call you later this week to see if you're ready to move forward in the process with me as your realtor, and if so, I'll bring the documents by for you to sign and we'll get right to work."

She stood and walked to the door, with me following a few steps behind. As she reached for the doorknob she paused and turned to me.

"Hang in there, honey. In the end, everything is going to be okay. You'll know what to do. And you know what, if it's not okay then it's not the end. Keep putting one foot in front of the other and see where the road takes you. Have a good night and squeeze that gorgeous girl of yours for me."

I thanked her for her time and her gracious words of wisdom and closed the door behind her. I had so much to think about and all of it felt like a twenty-ton anvil resting on my head. I had zero energy to further entertain the conversation I'd just had and decided to do the most mindless task I could think of: check the mail.

You know how they say "man plans, God laughs"? Well "they" are not wrong. Apparently, God was hell-bent on making me further entertain the conversation because in the mail, nestled in between the furniture advert from The Dump (Jeff's prior place of employment) and yet *another* letter from the bank, was a letter from the Texas Workforce Commission—the agency that handled my unemployment. Because life is fair and God has a sense of humor, the TWC was informing me that my unemployment was going to be running out in the next ninety days, and I wouldn't be eligible to reapply for more funds. Well, shit. And because God *really* fancies himself a comedian, I came back into my house only to find I'd missed call from . . . yep . . . you guessed it—my mom. Seriously God? Seriously? Ever hear of something called subtlety? It was so painfully obvious that God . . . the universe . . . something was telling me that I needed to move back home. I need to suck it up, put on my big girl panties, hold my head high, and just go home. Take shelter and refuge in the home of my mother, and maybe even rest a bit before picking up the torch again. I had been traveling a long, hard road for a mighty long time—rest might be good for my heart . . . my soul. Maybe this was what I needed to heal from . . . well . . . everything. But how would I do it? Yes, the logistics of moving back home seemed very simple on the surface—pack my house, rent a truck, drive home. But nothing is ever that simple—at least not for me.

Some months earlier, before the shit hit the proverbial fan, Bunny (Jeff's wife, in case you forgot) had been out of work for quite some time and was struggling pretty intensely. The kids would call us on the days they were scheduled to be with her and tell us there was no food in the house, or that there was only ramen, or mac and cheese, and they were hungry. Sometimes the electricity would be on the verge of being cut off. Regardless of what I felt for Bunny, I felt for her situation. I remembered not only seeing my mom struggle to make ends meet as a kid, but I also remembered being that kid, wondering what dinner might look like. Would it be rice again or would we have lucked into some sides. It was tough, and I knew what her family was going through—intimately. But one thing I can say about Bunny is that she was relentless. She had gone back to school and gotten her degree in the nursing field. She was determined to give her children a better life and a fresh start. She had applied for and accepted a position for a job in Dallas. It was an excellent opportunity for her to get back on her feet and give the kids a more stable home environment. I didn't like her, but I was happy for her, happy for her children. Jeff, on the other hand, not so much. He exploded in rage when he found out that she had accepted the job without consulting him, and vowed to make sure it didn't happen.

"Make sure *what* doesn't happen, Jeff?"

"Dallas! Dallas is not happening. She must be out of her mind to think she can just up and move my kids to Dallas! Fuck her—those are MY kids!"

Feeling sympathy for Bunny and their children, I tried to reason with him.

"Actually, Jeff, they're both of your children, and she's doing what she has to do to make sure they're taken care of. It's not like she's getting child support from you. She has to do this to keep a roof over their heads."

"Whose side are you on?!"

"I'm on your kids' side. This could be a great start for them, and they could really use some stability right about now. It hasn't been easy on them, being shuttled back and forth between our house and their mom's house. We don't get along—they deserve a break to just be kids."

But Jeff wasn't trying to hear me.

"If they need a break they can come here. She can go but fuck her if she thinks she's taking my kids to Dallas. I'll put a stop to that real quick!"

"How, Jeff? How are you gonna put a stop to it, Jeff? She already accepted the job and has started packing. She's told the kids and they're excited! You can't undo this—it's done!"

"Watch me!"

"Watch you *what*? What are you talking about?"

I had no idea how Jeff thought he could possibly stop Bunny from moving to Dallas with the children, nor any idea why he would want to. Didn't he understand it would be better for his children? Didn't that matter? Short answer: No.

"I'm talking about the courts. She wants to play dirty? Cool. I'll petition the court to stop her move, making it illegal for her to move my children out of Harris County!"

"What? Jeff! That's insane! Why would you do that? Those kids are suffering! Bunny is struggling! Why would you stop her from giving them a better life? Why?"

"'Cuz those are MY kids, Adiba. And she's not taking them anywhere!"

And with that, he did exactly what he said he was going to do. Nothing I did or said could convince him that he was in the wrong. He petitioned the court and got the move halted. Bunny lost the job opportunity she had, and the children continued to be hungry when they were at Bunny's house. Her situation didn't last long though. Like I said—she's relentless. She eventually found another job, in Houston, and slowly began to get back on her feet. But the damage had been done and the message had been sent loud and clear: Anyone who tried to take Jeff's kids away to give them a better life would be stopped dead in their tracks—stability be damned. And so there it was—there was no way I was going to be able to move home if Jeff knew about it. If Jeff had even the slightest idea that I was going to move out of state with Emory, he'd find a way to get a court to stop it, and we'd be just like Bunny—stuck. I couldn't take that risk, but I also knew exactly what it meant. My heart dropped to my stomach and I began to sob. I had to embody the best and the worst of both my parents. Like my father had done thirty-two years prior, I had to kidnap my own child. But like my mother, I had to do it for our survival.

Goddamn these generational curses.

Goddamn them.

*

It's a lot of work moving an entire four-bedroom house, a car, and a baby two and a half states away, in secret. Well, it takes a lot of planning, a lot of lying, a good amount of red wine, a very gracious godmother who loves you immensely, and three very hot firefighters who just happen to work with your daughter's equally hot firefighter godfather.

I set my move date as Labor Day, coincidentally, and my godmother arrived a few days before to pack up my house. For the month leading up to the move, I refused to let Jeff in my house, and I justified it by telling him that it was my house, and I didn't feel safe with him inside it. He saw the "For Sale" sign posted in my front yard and asked me, very pointedly, if I was selling the house and moving back to Arizona.

I lied and told him no—that I had to sell the house to avoid an official foreclosure. I mean, it wasn't a *whole* lie—just partly. When he asked me where I was going to live, I shrugged and told him I was looking for places in Cypress because it was imperative to Emory's future education that we stay in the school district. He gave me a long, hard stare but didn't push the issue. I don't know if he had a sneaking suspicion that I was up to something but didn't think I would actually do it or not, but the look on his face was enough for me to play it safe, keep my mouth shut, and move forward with my plans.

It had been decided with my mother that I was going to fly Emory out to Arizona with nothing more than a car seat, stroller, canister of formula, two bottles, and three changes of clothes, the night before I was set to pull out of Cypress, Texas, for good. I was absolutely terrified boarding the plane with Emory, my purse, and her diaper bag. Jeff had been calling all morning and not sure I'd be able to hold it together if I answered, I simply ignored his calls. I never answered and he never left a message but up until that plane was in the air, I was convinced he'd show up at the airport with the police and have me arrested for kidnapping. Luckily, this did not happen and though it was easily the hardest (and quickest) trip I'd ever taken, I was grateful to be able to have Emory safe in Arizona with my mom. Knowing that regardless of what would happen to me if Jeff found out before I loaded up the truck and headed out the next morning, Emory was out of harm's way, gave my anxious spirit a momentary sense of peace.

Morning came fast and by 8:00 a.m. the phone was ringing off the hook. By 9:30 a.m. I had four missed calls from Jeff and by 11:30 a.m. I was pulling out of my driveway—truck loaded, car hitched, godmother behind the wheel, and my heart in my throat. As we pulled away and headed toward the back of the subdivision to get onto the main road (fearing that if Jeff came in the front way, we'd pass him) I kept my eyes on the passenger side mirror. As we drove down Fry Road and headed toward the freeway, I stayed semislumped in my seat to avoid possibly being seen by him (should he be on the road), or by anyone who knew us. It wasn't until we passed San Antonio that I was finally able to let my shoulders fall a little bit, let my breathing recover from the semishallow pace I'd been keeping all morning, and sit up fully in my seat. I couldn't believe I'd done it—I'd really done it. I'd kidnapped my child and fled the state, only telling five people, none of whom were related to or were friends with Jeff. Wow. As a child I'd imagined a lot of things for my future. Dancing on Broadway, being a backup dancer for Janet Jackson, playing the violin in a Madonna video ("Papa Don't Preach" made me believe I could do it), even being a child psychologist (so basic in comparison, I know), but never once did I imagine I'd be "on the run" with my kid. I could be wrong but I don't know . . . I just don't think that's something people put on their vision boards.

But alas, there I was at 7:00 p.m. the next day pulling into Tucson— the place I vowed to never return to. Oddly though, as irritated as I was to be back, I was also so happy, so relieved, so grateful to have a place to return to. A place that was safe, a place I could move about freely with my child, a place that felt familiar even if I didn't want it to. Pulling into the parking lot of my mother's apartment complex, I noticed the sunset. If there's one thing I had to say I love about Tucson, it's the sunsets. They look like God melted an entire box of Crayola crayons and poured it out into the sky. Rich and brightly colored horizons that you swear don't naturally occur, except there they are—purple, fire orange, magenta. I looked at the great expanse of sky and all I could muster was a quiet "thank you" as I stared out the window. My thank you was directed at my godmother, who drove the entire distance from Houston, Texas, to Tucson, Arizona, but it was also directed at God. Yeah, that same God I'd railed against months earlier for essentially forcing me to move back home, I was now thanking him for delivering me home safely. Funny how that works sometimes—the things we eschew turn out to be the very things we need the most.

As I approached the courtyard of my mother's apartment I could hear Emory and her giggling inside. I was exhausted to the core—even my soul was exhausted, but that little girl's infectious laugh gave me life and it was all I could do to not take off in a full sprint to the front door.

I teared up when I hugged my mother and sobbed like . . . well . . . Emory, as soon as I got her in my arms. We had done it. We'd taken the first, very calculated steps in starting over, and though I had absolutely no idea what this new future held for us, I was certain it would be better than any fate that awaited us in Texas. It had to be. Well, it would be . . . after I told Jeff we were gone. One of the first things my mother asked me while I sat on her couch with Emory tucked into my arm like a football (I refused to put her down) was if I'd spoken with Jeff yet.

"No, Ma, not yet."

"So he still doesn't know you're gone?"

"Nope."

"And he doesn't know Emory is here?"

"Nope."

She and my godmother exchanged glances, neither of them saying anything to each other.

"When do you plan on telling him?"

"I don't know, Mom . . . never?"

"Adiba."

"Well, shit, Mom—I literally *just* left the man! Can I breathe and enjoy my peace for just a minute?"

It was as obvious as the nose on my face that I wasn't the least bit interested in having "the talk" with Jeff. I already knew how it would go—he'd ask me if I'd moved back home with Emory, I'd tell him yes, and then he'd proceed to call me every name under the sun, threaten to have me arrested, and hang up on me. It was textbook rage for Jeff— and I mean, rightfully so. Let somebody leave the state with my child and I find out *after* the fact? Oh, I'm snatching wigs faster than you can say the words "lace-front." Everybody's getting a beat down—your momma, your auntie, your little niece . . . everybody's catching these hands. So, I got it. Jeff had every reason to be furious with me, and though part of me hoped he would find a way to understand why I had to do it—you know, in the larger context of things, I was smart enough not to hold out hope. When dinner rolled around Tuesday night and

I still hadn't called him but I'd "missed" somewhere between ten and fifteen phone calls, my mother insisted, in the way only a mother can, that I call him and let him know I'd left.

"*Toma*," she said as she held my phone out to me.

I sat in her courtyard smoking a cigarette and just stared at her, not moving.

"*TOMA!*" she said again, this time with that serious Puerto Rican tone that basically said, "Take this or else that's your ass."

"I don't want it," I replied, still smoking my cigarette.

"Adiba, you have to talk to him. It's been three days now. He deserves to know where his—"

"He doesn't deserve to know shit! But you know what I deserve? I deserve to have as much peace as I need. *That's* what I deserve!"

And then she mom-handled me. It's this special talent that only moms have (and I swear Latin moms have it down to a science) in which they are able to convince you to do the one thing you have absolutely zero interest in doing, by laying the thickest, richest, most gut-wrenching guilt trip on you, and it usually has something to do with *your* childhood and *their* anguish. My mom pulled out the big guns and murdered me with guilt.

"You know, Adiba, when your father took you away from me for that month, and I had no idea where you were, it nearly killed me. All I could do was pray you were safe and alive. It was the worst pain I'd ever experienced. Remember how hard you cried last Saturday when you had to say goodbye to Emory even though you knew where she was going to be and with whom? Imagine doing that every day for *a month*. I know you're angry and scared but you have to ca—"

"*¡Ay, Dios mío! Ok! ¡Ya! ¡Ya! I'll call him! ¡Me caso en ná! ¡Coño!*"

"Watch your mouth. And . . . here . . . thank you."

As she walked inside the house I braced myself for the onslaught. I told myself that whatever he said didn't matter—they were just words, and I'd made the right decision. Sure as shit, the conversation went exactly as I'd predicted. He informed me of the different kinds of bitch that I was: dirty bitch, fucking bitch, lying bitch, and of course the more mundane and basic one: you bitch. He was furious, he was crying, and y'all, I'm not going to even try to convince you that I wasn't crying too. I was a sobbing, smoking mess. I understood why he was so upset, and even though I knew the response I was going to get from him before I even dialed his number, it still hurt immensely to hear it. It also broke my heart to have to tell his family and kids at the same time. Believe it or not, I never took them into account in making my decision to leave. I knew I couldn't tell them because the risk was too great, but I never thought about how they would react. Their anger was righteous and valid, and I deserved their fury, but I also desperately needed them to understand *why* I'd done it. I knew Jeff would never understand—he was too close to the situation. But I just knew that as mothers, his aunts would get it—they would be angry, but they would understand and be able to calm him down because we belonged to the sorority of mothers. I was one of them. But no, not at that moment. At that moment I was a traitor, an outsider, a villain, and there was no amount of *I'm sorry*'s or *let me explain*'s that was going to bring them to my side. They kinda-sorta, in a teeny tiny way understood, but the anger was too rich, the hurt too deep. His children were even worse, sobbing into the phone as they asked me how I could do that to them—how could I take their sister away from them without even letting them say goodbye. There was no love lost between Jeff's children and I, but they absolutely adored their little sister, and I had taken her away. I'd broken their hearts and probably ruined the relationship I had with Aunt Alexis and Aunt Erica—all unintentional consequences of trying to make a way out of no way.

When Jeff finally hung up on me, I felt like a shell of a human. I'd chain-smoked my way through the phone call of all phone calls, cried so much my eyes looked like chocolate marshmallows, and developed quite the gnarly headache. I shuffled myself to bed and vowed that tomorrow would be better, even if all it meant was I went the whole day without being called a bitch. A win is a win and I could use any, and all of the wins I could get.

*

Si quieres a ver la ultima chingona, mira a mi madre. (If you want to see the ultimate badass, look at my mom). My mom, bless her heart, took time off of work to stay with Emory so I could visit childcare centers, go on job interviews, and get Emory's early intervention programs set up. I give her a lot of flak for always trying to be in the know and asking questions that I deem "none of her business," but honestly, if it weren't for my mother, I wouldn't be the mother I am. With her assistance, in just under four weeks I found full-time work as a social worker with a behavioral health agency, childcare for Emory, and had an assessment set up for Emory with the Department of Developmental Disabilities. As I said, when shit hits the fan, I put my head down and go on autopilot. And when I say I go on autopilot I mean *everything* goes on autopilot—even my love life. Yep, you better believe I did what I always do and started dating an old flame shortly after moving back home.

Jack and I had dated my freshman year in high school, after meeting through mutual friends. He was white, a junior, and a football star, and I was Afro-Latin, a freshman, and a cheerleader. He was my first real boyfriend, and the first boy I ever went on a date with. When we were kids he was easy to talk to, kind, and funny—and twenty-some-odd years later, he was still the same easy guy to talk to. We would stay on the phone for hours after I'd put Emory to sleep. I'd sit on a chair outside my kitchen window and we'd marvel at the fact that we were both sitting under the same big sky, staring at the same bright moon, both counting shooting stars as we recounted the last two decades of our personal history. It didn't matter that I was getting eaten alive by mosquitoes. It didn't matter that he had school in the morning. All that mattered was that for the first time, in an inexplicably long time, there was a slight air of lightness in my life, and things felt . . . less hard.

When my phone rang and I saw Jack's name pop up on the screen, the breath in my lungs didn't feel so hot, so thick, and so heavy. I knew I was falling for him. I'd been tricked into loving someone who wasn't even available for me to love. Or, if I keep it all the way real, I found myself in a relationship I had no business being in because I didn't trust my gut. As a consequence of that decision, I starved myself damn near to death craving emotional intimacy. Then here comes Jack, who didn't judge me, was honest with me from our very first conversation about his less than stellar past that included extensive drug use and prison time, and openly shared stories about his concerns raising his half-Black daughter as a single parent. I don't think Jeff had ever been honest with me about anything ever. Finally something felt easy.

I was single, he was single, and I clearly hadn't learned my lesson when it came to jumping from one relationship to the next without so much as two full period cycles between them. But in my defense, this relationship had a whole *three* period cycles between the start of it and the end of Jeff. Granted, for two of those cycles I was still in Texas but still—three! It was a goddamn record!

By April of the following year, I was moving into a place of my own, Jeff was still cursing me out (but doing so from Texas, and no longer threatening to have the courts make me bring her back), and Emory, at twenty-two months, was saying her first word—Elmo. No, it wasn't mom, but given the events of the previous seven months, I was just glad it wasn't "dirty bitch." In May I wrote my first children's book, *Meet ClaraBelle Blue*, for my daughter because representation and diversity were sorely lacking on bookshelves, and I was contemplating actually publishing it for public consumption. Things felt good—*Life* felt good, and it was about damn time. I was still dating the same guy and the sex was pretty good, so I guess you could say I was feeling myself. But then, because God is who God is, he decided once again, to show me just how funny he is. In June 2011, almost a year to the day when I lost my job in Texas, I lost my job in Tucson.

I was working as a behavioral health specialist for children that had special mental, emotional, and behavioral health care needs, but I was *also* missing work to care for my own child who had special physical and neurological healthcare needs. The day I lost my job was an odd one, for sure. I had been running late since I'd opened my eyes that morning, and in rushing out the door did not realize I didn't have my work planner with me. If you know anything at all about social work, you know that your work planner is basically the bible. You write your notes in it, schedule all of your home visits, court appearances, and child-family team meetings in it, and basically guard it with your life. I woke up and immediately remembered that I had a scheduled meeting with my supervisor and *her* supervisor at the end of my day, and I knew it wasn't going to be a good one. I had already been called into my boss's office once to discuss my attendance and the whole time all I could think was, *um, didn't you just miss almost a week of work because your fucking dog had a seizure?* I guessed that this conversation was to discuss my attendance, again, and the fact that I wasn't meeting my monthly "points requirement," meaning I wasn't billing enough services per child on my caseload, and I was correct. However, to make matters worse, I was late to the meeting because I had to run to Jack's house to pick up my work planner, where I had left it the night before, I called to let them know I was going to be late, and why, and that was the match that sent the whole thing up in smoke. I lost my job almost as soon as I sat down, and to add insult to injury, the company denied me unemployment. That, my friends, is a special kind of cruelty.

But that cruelty changed my life.

I moved in with Jack because once again I lost my home, but I also began actively pursuing a way to bring *Meet ClaraBelle Blue* to the world, at my cousin's urging. I'd written a book for Emory, and he convinced me that other children like Emory needed to see themselves represented in the books they read. I, in turn, convinced myself that I was worth far more than any employer thought they wanted to pay me—and that my daughter's life and well-being trumped all of that. I went full speed ahead, working with an art student, and conceptualizing what the book could look like, but I still needed to make money. I took a micro-time job[37] with a local homebuilder—a woman—the only woman in the field, and it turned out that she had much the same beginning in motherhood that I did. She was a single mom with two

---

37. I worked six hours a week. MICRO. TIME.

children, living in a two-bedroom trailer when she began offering roof coatings to her neighbors. She kept going, expanding her knowledge base, and eventually became the only female contractor in Tucson—and a millionaire. If she could do it, I knew I could do it. Granted, our circumstances and the optics of them were different—she, an attractive white woman, inherently had a touch easier time "getting in the room," but we were both women, both single moms, both from very humble beginnings. And both hell-bent on making the best life possible for our children. Terry, if you're reading this, thank you for being what I needed to see when I needed to see it.

By 2012, after a year and a half of dating, Jack and I broke up. Turns out that just because you're a fat guy, it doesn't mean that you're necessarily attracted to a fat girl, even if said fat girl is the same weight she was when she initially began dating said fat guy. Actually, up until a more slender girl entered the picture, said fat guy always told this fat girl how pretty and sexy he thought she was. This whole event left me devastated, and I did something that I never thought I'd ever do and have vowed to never do again. He tried to break up with me because he was no longer attracted to me, and I begged him to stay with me, using the line loved and used by moms of preteens everywhere: "Beauty is only skin deep. It's the heart that matters." I even signed us up for couples therapy so that *we* could work through *his* fatphobia. Not my internalized fatphobia, only his. Who does that? Who begs someone to accept them as they are and then begs them not to leave? A person like me does that. A person whose self-esteem is so heartbreakingly low and wants to be "chosen" so badly they believe no one will ever love them so they hold on to whatever it is they currently have, even if it is dangerously toxic and demoralizing for them. Definitely not one of my finer moments in life, but looking back I can see how that experience helped to build and shape the relationship I have with my body today. Am I thankful for it? Hell no. I'm just barely to a place where I can tell this story without cursing his name, but I can see why it had to play out the way it did.

In the end, ironically, I ended up breaking up with Jack. Not due to weight and size issues, but due to his increasing irritability and bad temper, and my own shortness with his daughter. She was the sweetest child, but she also had undiagnosed ADHD/ADD, and at the time I didn't have the bandwidth to learn about it nor the know-how to help her through it. Jack and I eventually just became two unhealthy sides of the same toxic coin.

Jack let me keep the apartment out of the goodness of his heart. He knew it would be easier for him to find an apartment that met his and his daughter's needs than it would be for me. I was able to afford the apartment using the disability payments Emory received from Jeff, and her own disability checks, but after paying the rent, there was only about sixty dollars left every month. The pay I received from the construction company came to $264/month, and that combined amount was supposed to cover the water bill, gas bill, electricity, and transportation. Thank God I no longer had a car payment[38], but I couldn't pay for much else. I began not sleeping due to the stress of the ever-persistent question: How do I make ends meet? The ends weren't even *close* to touching. They were about as far apart from each other as Kim K. is from her natural skin color (yeah, I said it). I called my best friend, Faith, one day in tears. I didn't have money to get diapers for Emory, I was on my last one, and I didn't know what to do. I'd just made a payment on my electricity and gas bills, but couldn't pay the water bill, and I had just under a quarter tank of gas in my car and Emory had numerous doctor's appointments across town the next day. If it wasn't for food stamps (yes, again), we wouldn't have been eating either. I felt like I was failing at all things motherhood. Faith reassured me that I was a great mother—I was making sure we had a roof over our heads, that Emory was getting the best medical care in town, and she was loved. She told me those were the makings of a great mother— the rest was logistics. I took slight solace in her words and felt a huge relief when she told me she was sending me a check for twenty-five

---

38. Thank you, Uncle Sam, for those tax returns, and my godmother for that loan!

dollars every month so I could get the BIG box of diapers. Up to that point I'd been getting the small packs because it was all I could afford if I wanted to put gas in my car to get Emory to and from child-care and her doctor appointments. That little bit—that twenty-five dollars—made a difference, albeit a temporary one, in feeling like I could provide for my child.

You know, it's late at night when the fear, anguish, and feelings of failure seep in. It's when I'm lying in bed doing mental math, trying to figure out what bill I can skip this month so that I have a little bit extra for necessities like soap, shampoo, toilet paper, and toothpaste. One night the anguish overtook me, and I found myself on the floor, crying my eyes out and whisper screaming at God—asking him what he wanted from me. What lesson was he trying to teach me by break-ing me at every turn? Why would he give me a child that needed so much from me, and then not give me a way to provide? I was so angry at God, myself, and the situation that I did something that I never thought I would do, and to this day am still in shock that I did it in the first place.

In my senior year of college, I did an internship at a children's shelter called Casa de Los Niños. They took all babies and children, regardless of ability, and housed them until they were either reunited with their birth families or placed in a foster home. I still knew the director of social work there and the on-site social worker. It was a secure location with loving employees. I knew if I took Emory there, she would be safe, she would be cared for, she'd have enough food to eat and diapers to wear, and maybe, just maybe she'd be adopted out to a wonderful family who could afford to care for her. She was two, and cute as a button—she'd be snatched up by a good family pretty quickly. As I sat on my floor, eyes blurry and overflowing with tears, I picked up my phone and dialed the number to the shelter. Emory deserved better than what I was giving her. She deserved the very best that life had to offer her—I was failing her, and I knew it. This seemed like the most loving thing I could possibly do for her, you know? Give her a chance at a better life because it wasn't happening with me. For some reason, God just stopped listening to me, or so it seemed. I stared at the number on my phone screen, my thumb hovering just above the "dial" button, and wept until I couldn't see the screen anymore. Then I put the phone down. I couldn't do it. I knew she deserved better, but I couldn't knowingly give my baby away. I couldn't.

And that's when God proved he had been listening to me and seeing me all along.

At that very moment, a song I hadn't heard in ages, and never really paid much attention to, began playing in my head. Now, I don't know if you're familiar with the gospel singing sensation, Mary Mary, but they had a song called "Can't Give Up Now," and the chorus of that song blared in my head like someone was holding speakers right in front of my face.

I just can't give up now
I've come too far from where
I started from
Nobody told me
The road would be easy
And I don't believe He's brought me this far
To leave me

The only thing I can attribute that song popping into my head at that precise time is God. You don't have to believe like I do, or even believe in a higher power, but you can't tell *me* that God didn't see me that night, on that floor, about to give his gift away. I took it as a very clear sign that he was reminding me that he was there, had always been there, and that he absolutely did not bring me that far (even if it didn't seem too far removed from my situation in Texas), just to leave me.[39]

39. Side note: While editing this book I heard Oprah say this in one of her Super Soul Sunday podcasts. When she was on a plane that ran the risk of crashing over the Pacific Ocean and Lady O was internally *freaking out,* she said Steadman took her hand and told her she'd be fine—that God didn't bring her all this way just to leave her. This was just further confirmation to me that God has his hand all up and through my life. I, too, have a deep fear of flying over the ocean . . . me and Lady O. Look at

And in that moment, I chose to believe the lyrics. I chose to believe that I wasn't going through this alone and trust the idea that it was all for a bigger picture, a larger purpose. I just had to keep trusting and putting one foot in front of the other. I crawled back into bed, shoulders still heaving from trying to catch my breath between sobs, but assured that somehow, we were going to be okay.

It seemed as if that's all God was waiting for. I know—it probably sounds crazy. But I grew up in the church, and while my relationship with the church is fraught, at best, my relationship with God has *mostly* been solid. I may not have always understood the motivations behind certain situations, but I've always known if I just hung in there, it would all make sense in the end. This situation proved to be no different. The next day I received a call from a local agency I had called for utility help, and they informed me that they would be able to pay my gas bill. Another agency called to let me know that a local church was going to cover my electricity bill. A week later I interviewed for a job with more pay, more hours, and closer to my daughter's doctor appointments. On my way home from the interview for that job, I put in an application for an adorable casita that was not only walking distance from the job but also had all utilities included. Bonus: the rent was the exact amount I was receiving from Emory's and Jeff's disability payments, which meant that my paychecks could go toward things like gas in my car, household necessities, diapers—maybe even a Christmas tree *and* presents, instead of having them donated like we'd had to do the year prior. I got the job *and* the apartment within a week of each other, and my landlord agreed to let me out of my lease, without penalty.

Listen, when Black folks say things like "look at God," "won't He do it," and "God is good all the time, and all the time God is good," *this* is what we mean. You can try until you're blue in the face, but you will never convince me that God was not all up and through that

---

us. No . . .look at me, trying to be friends with Oprah. I hope she's reading this. We should be friends, Oprah. Hit ya girl up!

tribulation, just waiting for me to realize that he'd never left me to begin with.

Oh, and that little children's book I wrote—with the help of two ridiculously talented Latinx art students, I self-published that bad boy[40] and was able to have it printed with a loan from my illustrator's dad and my tax return. Since my book launch in 2013, I have independently sold over six thousand copies of *Meet ClaraBelle Blue*, made a career out of speaking around the country about the importance of diversity, accessibility, and inclusion in the classroom, on the bookshelves, on television, and in life, *and* started my company, RocketChair Productions to expand my work and mission into children's television and film.

Look. At. God.

---

40. Yes, *Meet ClaraBelle Blue* was rejected by quite a few publishing companies, and is still being rejected today. But that's okay, it obviously didn't stop me, and it's obviously a fan favorite, so the joke's on them.

CAUTION: HAZARDOUS MATERIALS PRESENT

"Will she ever be normal?"

"So, what's wrong with her?"

"Oh, bless her poor heart!"

"It's so good of you, mom, to take her outside . . . you know . . . out in public." (Said as he was literally petting the top of my child's head.)

"Can I lay hands on her and pray for her healing?"

"Is she sick?"

"Will she ever be . . . okay?"

"She's such a beautiful girl, despite being handicapped."

"She goes to school? Wow! Good for you, mom!"

"What is her life expectancy? My friend's brother had CP and he died when he was very young."

And the list goes on and on of the most fucked up, insensitive, and egregious things I've heard from complete strangers, mostly (99.99 percent) white, concerning my child. And before you throw this book across the room and accuse me of being mean, or "playing the race card," and not giving people a fair shake, or decide to rattle off an email to me telling me that they're probably just curious and not trying to be mean, please don't. We are almost a quarter-century into the 2000s, and in the throes of the biggest fight for civil rights our generation has ever seen. You can't open a newspaper or turn on the television without hearing or reading the words "Black Lives Matter Movement." If for only that reason, folks should have enough sense to think about how the words they're about to say to a Black woman and her Black child might land. Not to mention that my child is disabled. But her disability is not deafness; she can hear these things. And people assuming she cannot because she is disabled, or assuming she can't understand what they're saying because of her disability is honestly the most ableist thing I've ever experienced. I'm not saying don't say anything at all—we're friendly and my daughter loves meeting new people. But maybe say it in your head first. If you wouldn't mind someone saying it to or about *your* kid, then, by all means, approach! However, past experience tells me this doesn't happen. And you know, I didn't want to go there but I can't talk about this thing that makes my eye twitch without addressing the historical context of all of this. Historically, as in during the slave trade, Black people (men, women, and children alike) were treated as chattel. Completely stripped of our dignity and rights, we were physically inspected—hands in our hair, hands roaming all over our skin, teeth bared and fingers in our mouths to check for gum and tooth health. Our genitals fondled; breasts lifted. We were spoken *about* but never spoken *to*, so it is not such a far reach to understand why (a) we don't EVER want you touching our hair; and (b) I would take such umbrage with someone talking *about* my child, as if she isn't a whole-ass human being sitting right next to me.

Secondly, when I hear phrases like I heard from the older gentleman who thought he was well within his right for praising the fact I took her "out in public," I am instantly reminded of the not so distant past when people with disabilities were taken from their parents and sent to live in homes, and often abused. In 1907 the Immigration Act was passed which forbade families from entering the United States if they had a family member with a disability, for fear that the US would become a "country of defectives."[41] Then there were the "Ugly Laws," adopted by some cities in the United States, which basically stated that if you or any person in your family was "diseased, maimed, mutilated or disfigured in any way," you were not to be seen in public. It was considered illegal. Chicago was the last city to remove this law from their books—in 1974. Y'all, I was born in 1977. We are not that far removed from this history. And this older gentleman was old enough to remember when Hitler went on his eugenics tirade in his efforts to create the perfect master race and murdered not just Jews, but gays, lesbians, disabled folks, the mentally ill, and allies and caregivers. So, for him to dare put his hands on my child *while* making this statement—well #sorrynotsorry, I saw red. I told him it was quite asinine to think I would not take my child out in public, and before I could continue, Emory came through with a quick slap to his hand with her one good arm. Y'all, when I tell you it took everything in me not to crack up laughing in this man's face . . . but he had it coming. He yanked his hand back so fast and just stared at her in shock. When he looked at me all I could say was, "She hates when people touch her head. Do it and draw back a nub." He harrumphed and shuffled away. I gave Em a high five and we carried on about our business, me enjoying my coconut milk chai tea latte, and she, her birthday cake pop. Between you and I, I secretly wished she'd punched him right in the balls. It was a straight shot, and it would have shut him right up.

Sadly, the worst thing someone has ever said to me about Emory didn't come from a stranger on the street. It came from the director of her childcare center—yes, the person charged with her early childhood education. When we moved back to Tucson, I had a very difficult time finding a quality early childhood education center for Emory. Places either weren't accessible, didn't have enough staff to properly ensure she'd get the assistance she needed, or staff wasn't trained to

    41. "A Brief Timeline of the History of Disabilities: The Shameful Treatment of People with Disabilities"; https://sailhelps.org/a-brief-timeline-of-the-history-of-disabilities-the-shameful-treatment-of-people-with-disabilities/

work with children with disabilities. I finally found one and though I wasn't incredibly impressed by the aesthetics of the place, they said they followed a Reggio Emilia[42] learning philosophy, and this was important to me. Plus, I had to start work and this was my only option—it would have to do.

She was one and a half when I enrolled her and they advised they didn't have room in the one-year-old room for her just yet, so they'd have to put her in the infant room until a space opened up. Again, I didn't have other options, so I agreed to this arrangement with the caveat being that as soon as a one-year-old kid graduated to the two-year-old room, she would move up. Things were going along fine until a few months in I began to question when a space would be opening up. I was told they had space but they didn't know if they had the staff that could work with her *and* the other kids at the same time. Because I had previously worked for a childcare resource and referral agency, I knew what the state mandated for ratios, and advised that per state regulations, they did. They agreed to work out a schedule that would allow Em and one of the teachers from the infant room to go into the one-year-old room after nap time, and spend the last few hours of the day with her age-appropriate peers. This wasn't ideal, but I felt it was better than nothing. Emory had just gotten her new stander and was beginning to learn a bit about independent play and supportive play. I was excited for her to be in the big-girl room, as we called it, learning from and playing with her peers. However, my mom (who would often pick Emory up from childcare for me due to my long hours) began to tell me that more often than not, when she would go to pick Emory up, she would find her in the infant room, and when she would question as to whether or not she had spent any time in the one-year-old room, there was often an excuse of "ran out of time," "not enough staff," or "she was too tired today."

42.   Child-centered, interest-based approach to learning that takes culture into account when teaching

One day I got home earlier than usual, and my mom was just returning with Emory. She informed me that yet again, Emory had spent the day in the infant room. Now to give you some perspective here, Emory started at this particular childcare center in October 2010, when she was eighteen months old. It was now May 2011— Emory was now two years old, and still could not even get time with kids *literally* half her age. I was livid. I had just put my purse down but I picked it right back up, kissed Emory on the forehead, instructed my mom to give her ravioli for dinner, and drove myself right across the street to the childcare center. They only knew me as Emory's mom, but they were about to meet Adiba: the mom with zero fucks left to give.

When I walked in, it was close to closing time. I asked to speak to the director and was informed she was on a call. I told them I'd wait—it was important. I could see her through the window behind the receptionist, and she could see me. We made eye contact and as soon as she saw the look on my face I read her lips: "Hey, I gotta go. I think I have an angry parent waiting for me." All I could think was, *Oh, honey, you have no idea what angry is but you gon' learn today.* She came out, greeted me, and led me back to her office.

"Ohmigosh, we just love little Emory so much! She is just the sweetest, cutest little thing!"

"Yes, I love my child too. I'm quite fond of her actually," I said, taking the seat across the desk from her.

"Well, the feeling is mutual! How can I help you today?"

"Well, my mom just informed me that once again, Emory did not go into the one-year-old room today. Can you tell me why?"

"Oh . . . so yes . . . I've been meaning to call you about that." She fidgeted with a pen on her desk.

"Oh, have you?"

"Yes. So, we actually *can't* accommodate Emory in the one-year-old room."

I shifted in my seat, crossing my legs.

"And why is that?"

"Well, she's not walking yet, and our policy is that to be in the one-year-old room, children must be walking independently."

I paused a moment before responding. Did she just say what I think she said?

"Huh. Children must be *walking independently* in order to be in the one-year-old room?"

"Yes."

"And that's your policy."

"Yes, ma'am."

"Hmmmm . . . Okay. And can you help me understand what walking independently has to do with learning ABCs, one-two-threes, colors, shapes, animal sounds, and how to share your toys? Last I checked one was not a requirement for the other."

Now *she* shifted back into her seat and looked down at her desk. She was so uncomfortable, and I did not care. I was glad she was uncomfortable. She was crazy if she thought I was just going to sit back and let her deny my child an education.

"Well, technically you're right. One does not negate the other, but it is our center policy that the children must be walking. It's a state mandate and since we are licensed by the state, our corporate policy has to follow state rules. If we don't, we could be fined. Also, Emory's stander. It's just not safe."

"Not safe? Not safe for whom?"

"Well, the other children. It's pretty cumbersome, and you know, these kiddos are so little and just got steady on their feet. One of them could easily trip over one of the wheels, fall, and get really injured. It's a safety hazard."

This woman had absolutely no idea what fresh hell she had just opened up for her center with that statement. A safety hazard? A FUCK-ING SAFETY HAZARD? In my head, I punched this woman right smack in the middle of her face and told her that now *I* was the motherfuck-ing safety hazard. However, I have couth and a clean record, so I opted to use my words instead.

"Children trip on *air*," I said flatly while maintaining eye contact. She laughed nervously.

"And I'm sorry but did you just refer to my child as a '*safety hazard*'?"

"No! I would never refer to Emory as a safety hazard—just her stander."

There was that nervous laughter again. I drummed my nails on the arm of my chair and stared at her. My blood was boiling with rage. This woman really thought she could not only deny my child access to a fair educational experience but also low-key *insult* my child to my face? I wanted to snatch her bald and maybe let her face get really cozy with my fist, but I had to keep it cool. I don't look good in orange so there was no way I could go to jail.

"You mean the stander that is an extension of my child? That stander?"

"Yes . . . No. Just the stander—*not* Emory."

"Uh-huh. Okay. And you say it's a state mandate that children in the one-year-old room must be walking?"

"Yes, ma'am."

Pause.

Do you remember a few chapters up I mentioned how my best friend says there's a certain look I give when shit's about to go down? The raised eyebrow? Well, let's just say it was all the way up as I listened to this woman stick to her story. Continue.

"And you also say that if the state mandate is not adhered to, you could be fined? Am I understanding you correctly?"

"Yes, Ms. Nelson. I'm sorry. I wish there was more I could do."

"Yes, well, me too. I'll be searching for new childcare for Emory when I get home. She'll be here, with her stander, until I find one."

"I'm sorry. I know you're upset. I wish there was more I could do!"

"Oh, you've done plenty. Trust . . . PLENTY. I'll see you tomorrow."

I didn't even bother to say goodbye. I let myself out of her office and immediately got on the phone. She had messed with the wrong kid.

*

If you want to get eaten alive, mess with a bear cub. That mama bear will come out of nowhere and wreck your entire life. They will make you regret ever owning a teddy bear or even eating Teddy Grahams. I'm that kind of mama bear. Mess with my child and you'll regret it—as I think most of us mamas are. Except for some reason, this center director didn't get the memo and kept poking and poking and poking. And this mama bear was hungry.

The next morning I got on the phone with the executive director of the agency I had previously worked for. Susan, a fellow New Yorker, was not one to fuck with. She rarely looked at you when you walked into her office because she was either eyeball deep in policy around early childhood education, or rattling off an email to the state about the insulting lack of funding offered to low-income families unable to afford quality early childhood education. She told you what the deal was and didn't give a rat's ass if your feelings got hurt. Susan also knew people—powerful people in high-up, decision-making positions in the state's childcare center licensing department. If anyone could help right this situation, it was Susan. And she did not fail to deliver. A week later the center received an "impromptu visit" from the state licensing office and numerous sanctions and fines were levied against them. And wouldn't you know it, all of the sudden Emory started spending much more time in the one-year-old room, and not a single milk-drunk toddler fell and busted their face open because of her stander. They may have tripped over an ant, but Emory didn't have a damn thing to do with that.

Susan also gave me a referral to a much better childcare agency, one that was fully inclusive and also employed a Reggio Emilia/Maria Montessori approach to learning. I'll never forget my first phone call with Lela, the director of the Children's Achievement Center. She listened as I explained what had happened with Emory at the other center, and how upset it made me. I told her what I wanted for my child, what my hopes were, and what I was looking for in a childcare center, and I'll never forget her words to me.

"Well, first of all let me just say this—your child is not a safety hazard. That's a load of bull. She and all of her equipment will be welcome here. What she doesn't have or cannot get we can refer you to a local organization that can make it for her, and it can be here with her. If any of her home-based therapists would like to come and work with her here, they are welcome. It would be really great if that happened, actually, that way our teachers can also learn how best to work with her, and the other children can see it. It creates a real community in the classroom."

I was silent. I couldn't believe what I was hearing. A childcare center that valued my child, and saw her as a child, capable of learning and encouraged her learning. They didn't see her as something to be placed in a corner and out of the way so other kids stayed safe, like a piece of furniture with sharp corners. Finally, I spoke—but not without the biggest lump in my throat.

"I'm sorry, did you just say that my child isn't a safety hazard?"

"Yes, I did."

"And she could bring her equipment with her, and actually use it in the classroom?

"Absolutely. We want her to use it in the classroom."

"Would she be in a class with her age-appropriate peers, or would she have to start in the infant room?"

"Oh, God no! She's two years old, so she'd be in one of our one-to-two-year-old rooms. We have two infant rooms, four one-to-two-year-old rooms, and two three-to-five-year-old rooms."

And then I was just crying. I was in shock—it was such a stark difference from where Emory was at the moment. They valued my daughter and hadn't even met her yet. I immediately put her on the waiting list and told myself we could hold on for the six months we'd have to wait before a spot opened up. But like I said earlier, the universe is holding my girl so close. About three weeks later I got a call from Lela—a spot had just opened up. It was mine if I still wanted it. The tears flowed hard and fast. My baby, my sweet, sweet girl, with whom I'd had the rockiest start but would now move entire tractor-trailers for if the situation demanded, was finally going to get what she rightfully deserved. Emory started at the Children's Achievement Center without incident, and I began to see this little girl blossom. She went from this shy, quiet girl who didn't really know how to interact with other children her age, to engaging in story time, and trying to copy the hand motions to "The Wheels on the Bus." Her silly, sweet personality began to shine, and pretty soon, everyone in that center, parents included, was as in love with her as I was. Emory stayed there until it was time for her to start kindergarten, and when she left, she was assessed as being above grade level in intelligence, and I have absolutely no doubt that a big part of that was due to the fact the Children's Achievement Center saw her as a whole human being. They believed in her right to dignity, and autonomy, and basic humanity. I shed a few tears during her "graduation ceremony" as I watched her and all of her classmates do a performance to the *Frozen* theme song, "Let It Go." Yes, it was time to let my baby go—go into the big kid school—and shine like the bright star that she was (and still is).

A few years later I received a collection notice from the "safety hazard preschool" for $478—my balance owed for disenrolling Emory midmonth, four years prior. I contemplated returning the bill to them with a note attached that said, "This notice is a safety hazard to my mental and emotional well-being. Cease and desist, please," but in the end I decided it wasn't worth my energy. I tossed it in the trash and went back to helping Emory with her homework—working on the small tray that was attached to her stander.

A JEW & AN AFRO-LATINA MEET IN A BAR

When I was twenty, and long before Jeff and Emory were even blips on my radar, my girlfriend Serena and I went to a bar that had a palm reader in the back. Me, having grown up very religious but against a backdrop of mysticism and metaphysics, was familiar with how it worked, but was admittedly, a little bit freaked out by it. Serena, on the other hand, was all for it and all but jumped in this woman's lap and facepalmed her in excitement. The woman read Serena's palm and then turned to me.

"Would you like a reading tonight, young lady?"

Me? The daughter of a bible-thumping, pray without ceasing, cast all your cares upon the Lord ordained minister? Get my palms read and my tarot cards pulled? Shiiiiiiiiiit, I might as well have just pulled up a seat next to Judas and told Jesus "Yo, I'm next homey." Tarot and reading of palms were things of the occult as far as my mom was concerned, and I was *never* to dabble in that. I don't think it helped that my dad dabbled in the metaphysical world. Her daughter following in the footsteps of her abuser? Yeah, she was not down for that AT. ALL. If she knew I was even contemplating it I'd probably have gotten a lecture about how Satan will use anybody and anything to lure us away from God, and a whole list of scriptures to read.

"Ummmm, I dunno . . . " I mumbled to her, peering at her through squinty eyes. I wasn't sure this white woman was the real deal. Here was my experience with palm and tarot readers: Hector, the very gay, very Puerto Rican neighbor who would periodically come to my Titi Ana's house when I was a kid, Walter Mercado (*Bendición, Walter. ¡Con mucho, mucho amor!*), Miss Cleo, Oda Mae Brown, and Dionne Warwick's Psychic Friends Network. Notice anything about these folks? I'll help you—they ain't white. My point of reference for those with "the sight" were people of color, not a white lady in a bar wearing a turban. But, after much cajoling by Serena, I agreed to let her do it. I placed my hand in hers and struggled not to pull my hand away as she traced the lines with her fingernails.

"Interesting . . . " she began.

"You're going to have two children from a relationship, but the relationship is not going to work out. Later in life you're going to meet a very nice man—a nerdy man—like, 'pocket protector, computer geek' nerdy man, but you're going to fall in love with him because of how nice he is, and how well he treats your children."

"Huh. What color is he?"

That was my test. At the time I was mostly dating white guys and so if she said he was Black, I'd know she was a fake.

"Ummmm . . . I see a Black man . . . and I see the letter J . . . I keep seeing a J . . ."

I smirked at Serena and turned back to the fortune-teller.

"Ah, nope. I pretty much date white guys soooooo . . . "

"I can only tell you what I see."

"Okay, cool, no harm no foul. Here's your five dollars. I'll *see* myself out," and with that, I placed my money on the table and left the bar, Serena chiding me about being rude. I didn't put much stock in Serena's scolding me, and even though I didn't believe anything that lady had just said to me, I found that I thought about her words for most of the night. A nerdy guy, computer geek, I had two kids from a previous relationship, the letter J.

Huh.

That was 1997.

Fast forward sixteen years: I was a single mom to *one* child[43], fresh out of a shit show of a relationship with a bona fide sociopath, heartbroken, and in my bathroom crying and praying for God to either send me someone kind or leave me the fuck alone because this shit wasn't funny anymore. Enter eHarmony. Apparently in one of my more relationship ragey moments of the past, I had registered on the site and promptly forgotten about it. Now, you may be wondering why I had even signed up on an online dating site in the first place. Well, first of all, I'm an Afro-Latin woman living in Tucson, Arizona. If you live in Tucson, I really don't need to say much more—you already know what that statement means. But for those of you who *don't* live here, let me give you a glimpse into what dating is like here.

You're out at the bar with your friends, you see a hot guy across the bar and after much eye-fucking, you call him over. Y'all get into a conversation and find out you have numerous friends in common because *Tucson*. You talk some more and discover that you went to the same high school, a few years apart. Oh wow! Small world! No—small Tucson. Two shots later you find out that three weeks prior, you slept with his cousin and his mom is the gynecologist who treated your yeast infection last year. THAT is dating in Tucson. Also, Tucson is only 4 percent Black and I can go an entire week and never see another person that looks like me. So, if I had any chance of finding a brotha in these streets, online dating was my last and only hope. That being said, I wasn't actively running these online streets, so I was pretty shocked when a pictureless message landed in my inbox from eHarmony. I honestly can't even tell you what it said, but I can tell you what it *didn't* say. It didn't say, "Damn, baby, you so fine," "What's a beautiful girl like

---

43. Ho-ly shit. I just realized . . . I was pregnant with twins . . . by Jeff . . . A BLACK MAN . . . this white lady may have known her shit after all. Sorry for my rudeness white palm reader in Tucson in 1997.

you doing looking for love online," or "Hey, Miss Lady"—all things I'd been approached with on other dating sites in the past, so he already had my attention. I couldn't see his photo because I refused to pay to date (dumb—I know), but at that moment, his words on my screen were sufficient. *And*, it just so happened that it was a free communication weekend, so I was able to respond. But I didn't. At least not right away. I needed to check out his profile first. He was divorced—I'd have to check court records because I was not going down *that* road again. His name was Scott. He owned his own business. He liked to ski and play racquetball and described himself as humble and open-minded. *Okaaaaaay*, I thought to myself, *I can do this!*[44]

We corresponded over the weekend, and because I am a creature of habit, I did what I had done in every prior relationship: I failed to set boundaries, launched into a series of marathon emails, and asked to continue the conversation outside of the eHarmony site. Should I have done this? Of course not! I was fresh out of a pseudorelationship that left me questioning my intelligence, my worth, my beauty—hell, my whole-ass self! But as I said, I needed kindness, and this man *didn't* call me "baby," talked to me like I had a shred of intelligence, and seemed genuinely harmless. *SO* harmless I agreed to a lunch date after four days of emailing back and forth.

WHO WAS I?

I was a woman who just wanted someone to make me feel like I was worthy. Just be nice to me, pay me some attention and I would love you forever. Also, in hindsight, I can plainly say that I had a desperate need to be chosen and to be seen as beautiful. I spent my childhood wanting to be chosen by my father, who chose drugs instead. Well, that's only half true. In a way, he sort of chose me, but in the way a parent who simultaneously chooses drugs does.

My father, Emory Oxford Nelson, a.k.a Brian, adored me. I have

---

44. Folks, never think you can do this after merely reading a dating profile. Trust me on this one. Also, maybe don't respond to a message from someone on a dating website while you're still reeling from your previous relationship. Again, trust me on this one.

been told by friends of his, and family members that I was the world to him. The sun, moon, and stars—I hung them all, in his eyes. He wanted to name me Queen, because that's what I was to him, a regal queen in infant form. However, this same man, who was completely and utterly enamored with his own daughter, was also addicted to cocaine, liked to smoke pot, and played around with the hot drug of the day: acid. Because of this, choosing me in all the wrong ways looked like kidnapping me at one year of age, attempting to kidnap me again at two years of age, and threatening to kill me with a screwdriver, also at two years of age. I think Rick James said it best—"Cocaine is a hell of a drug." So is acid. So is PCP. When my father *stopped* choosing me, that looked like no visits at Grandma Ann's house where Mom allowed supervised visits, no phone calls, no letters or birthday cards. No dad to take me to a father-daughter dance or tell me how amazing I was when some boy at school made me cry. It was like I didn't exist.

In junior high I wanted to be chosen by the boys I went to school with, but instead they chose to tell me I was ugly, that my skin was too dark, my hair was nappy, that they could fit entire rolls of quarters between my front teeth. I'd spent my entire life wanting to be chosen, and this was no different. Toward the end of my previous relationship, I had learned that my "boyfriend" had chosen me, and about four other women. If we had agreed to an open relationship, I would have had no problem with this, but we did not. We were exclusive, or so I thought. So, yes, I felt like I needed to be chosen to be special, so that I might reclaim *some* semblance of self-worth; I jumped at any glimmer of light indicating that that could be a possibility.

Y'all, this is absolutely NO WAY to go into a relationship—not with your partner, your friends, your vibrator—nothing and nobody should get any less than the whole you that you've put countless hours of work into. It's not fair to them, to you, or anything that might come about as a result of said relationship. But this is what many of us do—we relationship hop in an effort to feel better. One day, during a session with my therapist, we decided to take a trip down memory lane and count the number of relationships I'd had, and how much time had passed between the end of one and the start of the next. Folks, what I'm about to tell you is sad, sad, sad, but in tallying it all up, we realized that since I'd turned sixteen I'd had a total of ten relationships, with no more than thirty days between the ending of one and the starting of the next. *Thirty days!* Basically, I'd stay single long enough to confirm I hadn't gotten knocked up by the last guy, and then jump right back out there to test my luck again. How sad is that? But I digress. Back to faceless dating.

A few days before our lunch date I asked him to send me a photo since I didn't have access to his pictures on eHarmony. He did and my honest to God first thought was, *Well, he looks like a serial killer.* It was a photo of him, sweaty, on a Ferris wheel at the county fair. Wisps of his hair were matted to his forehead, his head was tilted back, and his eyes were half-closed. I told myself to stop being so judgmental, and that it was just lunch. And that's exactly what it was—just lunch. But even at just lunch, it was clear (and painfully obvious to the older white lady who continued to stare at us as we ate) that we were different in every possible way. Case in point: because Scott is who he is—steady, neutral, low vibe—he showed up dressed in head-to-toe beige. Beige checkered shirt, beige dockers, a beige Boy Scout–style belt, beige socks, and beige walking sneakers. Because I am who *I* am, I showed up in a black-and-white ruffle-neck dress, red patent leather pumps, red patent leather skinny belt at the waist, and a super cute vintage black-and-red handbag. Absolutely nothing about me was beige. Not even my bra and panties. However, the conversation was easy, and it flowed as we blabbed our way through enchiladas and burritos, him making corny jokes, me laughing like a schoolgirl (because honestly, I love corny jokes). I realized as our *just lunch* was coming to a close that it was the first time in a long time that I had really laughed, and I didn't want to stop laughing. I didn't want to stop feeling good. I didn't want to stop being the center of someone's attention. I needed that at that moment, so I asked him if he would like to walk the mall with me.

Y'all . . . I was not wearing mall-walking shoes and my feet were screamin'! But I wasn't about to hobble away from the best feeling I'd had in, well, thirty days. So, we meandered through the mall, my toes cursing the day I was born with every step, and continued our dance of corny joke/giggle, corny joke/giggle. Everything was going along nicely, and I was feeling good, but I wasn't sure there was any real spark—until he was walking me to my car. Searching for words to say because insecure me was uncomfortable with silence on a first date, I decided to ask him about his eating habits. Specifically, if he liked junk food. Awkward, yes, but it turned out that he did like junk food and that his favorite kind was . . . wait for it . . . CHOCOLATE. Honestly, the big deal isn't the fact that he said chocolate, but rather how he said chocolate. This man, who up to this point had shown zero evidence of having any swag, looked dead into the face of the chocolate-brown woman standing in front of him, smiled, and said chocolate like it was the most decadent thing on earth. Like I was the most decadent thing on earth. I caught my breath and began to choke on the air in my lungs.

"Um, did you just say chocolate?"

"I did."

Goddamn! This man refused to break eye contact. I don't know what he was *trying* to do, but whatever he was doing was working. My heartbeat quickened a little bit and I swear my vulva had a pulse. I gathered just enough wits to hit him with some sass.

"Oop! Okay! I see you, sir! You ain't slick!"

Captain Beige! This was not a corny joke; he was actively trying to let me know he was down with my brown. And that, my friends, was all it took to convince me that I should see that man again. Now in hindsight, I should not have been okay with this white man likening me to food. The historical context of likening Black people to anything other than a human being is ridiculous, not to mention the use of Black bodies as slave labor to create some of the worlds' most favorite and decadent chocolate goodies is becoming more and more known in the mainstream. But pay attention to where my headspace was. He could have likened me to a damn coke bottle, and I would have been okay with it. I needed niceness and kindness and to feel desirable, and he was giving it to me in droves. So much so that my low self-esteem convinced me that he was the one after only our second date.

The date was to be at a local creperie in the middle of monsoon season, in downtown Tucson. I dropped my daughter off at my girl Jen's house and proceeded to gush about just how excited I was for date number two. However, just as I was about to walk out the door, Jen's husband called and advised that he might need her to come pick him up from the airport because his outbound flight might get canceled. I panicked at the thought of having to call Scott and cancel our date, and so Jen suggested I just tell him I would be late until she knew more. When I called to let him know, he was remarkably chill about the whole thing and responded with an easy "No problem, just keep me posted." I ended up calling him three more times, having to adjust my ETA, and each time his voice stayed just as calm as could be, and he'd say, "No problem. I'll see you when you get here." I. Was. Floored. Who was this man? How was he staying so chill? My nerves and attitude were not set up that way. I was of the mindset that if you can't handle your shit and be on time, on the *second date*, then there wasn't going to be a second date. Was that the ideal way to be? No. But I grew up in the era of *Waiting to Exhale* and Angela Basset burning cars and shit. I had zero time for a man's bullshit (although clearly that was a lie since I'd dated a sociopath for damn near a year, and had put up with plenty of bullshit from other men over the years). By the time I finally got to the creperie, almost ninety minutes had passed, but there he was, sitting cool as a cucumber, wearing a Hawaiian shirt a la *Magnum PI*, black jorts, and sneakers. Again, I thought, *Adiba, don't be so judgmental. He's nice.* And so we sat, and we chatted, and while we waited for our food, we played UNO, and in playing UNO, I decided he was "the one." Yep. You read that right. A child's card game was the litmus test I placed on my heart and decided he was the man I was going to marry.[45] How does one know, over a game of Uno, you ask? Well, it went something like this:

"Draw two."

---

45. Are you keeping track here? A little bit of flirting got me to date number two, and a child's card game got me to believing he was "the one." I won't even be mad if you judge me right now. Shit, *I'M* judging me.

Scott quietly drew two cards from the stack.

Me, in a giddy, sing-songy voice: "Reverse back to me . . ."

I gingerly placed down a Wild Draw Four.

"Yellow!"

Scott, inhaling sharply, begins to pick card after card from the deck until he finally lays down a solitary yellow five.

Me, throwing down my card with all the boss bitch attitude I can muster, "Draw two aaaand UNOOOO, BITCH!"

Okay, so what you *must* know about me is that I am KING shit-talker when it comes to UNO. I will talk shit to you, your mama, your kids— hell, I'll talk shit to Jesus if he wants to throw down some janky-ass cards. Nobody's off-limits when I'm playing UNO! I have taken all the cards out of my own child's hand because I didn't like what she was putting down, looked her dead in her eye, and proclaimed, "Girl, I will end you—put down another Wild Draw Four card . . . g'head. I dare you." So this man who I was on my second date with was not getting a pass. NOPE. Well, let me just tell you—he had my number because right as I picked up my glass of water and eyed him over the rim, this dude put down a Draw Two, and followed it up with a Wild Draw Four, picked a color I did not have in my hand, looked at me and said, "Oh, I got your UNO."

I did not stop drinking my water.

This man, whom I'd once mused looked like a serial killer, who had the fashion sense of a mole rat and the heart of a saint, had not only just checked the boss bitch right out of me but also beat me at my own game, in the kindest, most understated way possible. And that was it. That's all it took. Right then and there, in a creperie on Fourth Avenue in downtown Tucson, on a hot, sticky, muggy monsoon day in August, I decided he was my man.

Do I recommend this? HELL NO! In what world do we decide our fate by playing Chutes n' Ladders or Candyland? I mean, can you imagine? You spin a four and find yourself facing down a "chute," and your date looks at you and says, "Nah baby—spin again," and at that very moment you say, "Yep! Dassit! He's the one! This man told me to "spin again' so I didn't have to go down the chute. *Obviously* it's a sign he's the one for me." How ridiculous does that sound? So ridiculous that it couldn't possibly be true? Well, get ready to judge my ass because honey, it's true. This is *exactly* what I did. Because I was giddy with excitement, I called my best friend *as* I drove to Jen's house, to proudly proclaim that I had just had crepes with the man I was going to marry. I am a thousand percent sure that I must have sounded like a maniac. Why she didn't reach through the phone and smack the crap out of me, I'll never know.

Actually, not true.

I know exactly why. Because she knew it would have done no good. My friends know that once I get an idea in my head about a possible love interest you might as well buy stock in Kleenex because I won't let it go until I break my own heart, or they break it for me. Am I a glutton for punishment? Yes. Yes, I am. Well, I used to be, but we'll get to that later.

So yes, I staked my claim on this man whom I'd only eaten a burrito with, looked at some cats at the mall pet shop with, had some crepes with, and played a child's card game with. But on the real, Scott was, and is, one of the gentlest souls I've ever met. He would never hurt a fly (seriously—I used to have to yell like my face was on fire just to get him to kill the desert critters that would find their way into our home. *Kill it! Kill it! KIIIIIIIILL IIIIIIIIIIIIT!!*), and always acted with what he believed was good intention. And it was for all of these reasons, and also how he loved my child, that I did actually fall in love and marry him two years later in what I can only describe as my dream wedding. It truly was perfect—Emory walked down the aisle using her gait trainer, my lipstick lasted the entire night, and I only mildly embarrassed myself during our toast (damn champagne, beer, cocktail spree I went on two minutes prior to our toast). I remember, at some point in the night thinking back to that palm reader from my early twenties. She'd called it. Here he was, my pocket protector–wearing computer nerd, who loved my kid from my previous relationship—and the two J's she saw—his sons—Joshua and Jeremy. It was a dream day, and there isn't a single thing I would change about it. However, getting to that day wasn't quite what I would describe as perfect. There were many, *many* clashes between him and I, *and* his sons and I once we all lived under the same roof. I had never lived with three men, much less three white men, and they had never lived with a Black woman, much less a Black woman with a disabled child. We each had vastly different lived experiences, and you can rest assured that every damn difference was on full display those first few months.

Our first night of living together I had the misfortune of walking down the hallway only to come eyeball to penis with his eighteen-year-old son as he exited the bathroom naked. I couldn't unsee that. His boys, ages thirteen and eighteen, were not used to picking up after themselves and they would leave their plates on the table after eating dinner. I would tell them they needed to put their plates in the sink, and I'd get attitude because (a) I was expecting them to do something no one else expected of them; (b) I wasn't their parent; and (c) I *told* them to put their plates in the sink, as opposed to asking them to do it. Now, could I have *asked* them to pick up after themselves? Sure, of course I could have. But it was completely lost on me that they'd never had to do this, and so my instruction registered as a command as opposed to how I meant it, which was purely instruction because "why should I even *have* to tell you—you're not small children." And therein lay the distinction. I was raised by a single, Puerto Rican mom who raised me to be independent because she had no choice. Not knowing if you're going to live to see tomorrow changes how you parent, so I was raised to know how to take care of myself at a very young age. That meant I knew how to clean, do my own laundry, cook certain meals, and pick up after myself as early as six years old. We did not have a cleaning lady, my mother did not have a 401K. We were not about that life. And while Scott, himself, did not grow up with a cleaning lady, he *did* grow up in a two-parent household. The house he came home from the hospital to is the same house he left for college from. His parents were both educators with a pension. Subsequently, his children had much of the same upbringing, with the added bonus of a cleaning lady, so in hindsight, I can completely understand how to them, the idea of this woman who definitely was not their mother, asking them to do damn near anything was seen as an egregious violation of their civil liberties. However, at the moment I thought they were entitled brats, and because I hadn't started down the lovely road of therapy where I learned I didn't have to say *all* the things that popped into my head AS they popped into my head, I made it known just how entitled I thought they were. And because of that I can tell you with absolute certainty that starting a sentence with "slave days are over," when talking to white men and boys is never going to get you the response you're looking for.

There were also a fair number of arguments between Scott and I around me having passionate responses to some of the more racist-leaning or misogynistic things his sons would say. Again, I'm not one to keep my mouth shut (about anything), and if I heard some ridiculous white male privilege bullshit coming out of their mouths, or just bullshit in general, I would call them on it. If there was talk about people wanting a handout instead of "pulling themselves up by their bootstraps," I reminded them about the racist ideologies our country is founded upon, and how the chips are unevenly stacked so pulling oneself by the bootstraps is never really a thing you can do if you never got the boot or the strap to begin with. When one would rant about how a woman's place is in the home taking care of the children, I would chime in with, "A woman's place is wherever she damn well wants to be." I didn't think twice about it because the way I saw it, I was preparing them for the world they were going to go out into someday; a world where you can't just say whatever you want without consequences.

Let me make something very clear.

I was wrong for doing that. Dead wrong. These boys were children—teenagers, but boys, so essentially children. And not even *my* children. They hadn't experienced life's hardships, nor had they had any real-life experiences that could shape their views on the world around them. Also, these children were white males. They actually, very literally *could* say whatever they wanted and pay zero consequences. The odds were always going to be in their favor, and instead of using the instances as teachable moments and inquiring as to why they felt the way they felt, or why they felt so comfortable making such cavalier and offensive statements, I jumped down their throats, thus confirming the trope that the media has made so popular of not only "the angry Black woman," but also "the evil stepmother." While I had (and still have) every reason to be angry, I am not proud of how I responded to Scott's sons at times.

Do you think I stopped there though? Nope. It never failed that after storming out of whichever room the offense had taken place in, I'd slam the door behind me and launch into a full-on argument with Scott about how he'd raised entitled, racist, sexist children, and how appalled I was that rather than checking them on their behavior, he was checking *me* for what he called "overreacting." In his defense, he was not wrong—I should have been "responding." Instead, I reacted — in front of his children. But let me tell you, friends—if you want to see a woman's head spin 180 degrees on her neck, tell her she's overreacting, mid-argument. I wanted to snap him in two like a goddamn Slim Jim. I *wasn't* overreacting when I was speaking (yelling?) to him—I was simply reacting to the litany of offenses that were being espoused in my presence, and none of these men/boys were used to being checked on the things they said, much less checked by a Black woman. However, again, I was dealing with his children. Did I (and do I still) have the right to be angry? Absolutely—about what they'd said and how they'd said it. And about the fact that it seemed like I was getting zero support. But I was the adult, and furthermore, I was the adult who had no relation to his children aside from the fact that I was dating their dad.

These kinds of arguments with his children went on for the length of our three-year marriage, and for three years I continued to react instead of respond. Now mind you, some of the reactions were warranted, like when, while driving home from school, his youngest made a "joke" about getting Black people to show up someplace by having fried chicken and watermelon available, and I kicked him out of my car. Or when he refused to respect the privacy of my bedroom, so

I took his bedroom door off the hinges. I stand by every time I kicked him out of my car for being disrespectful, but I don't stand by how I consistently and unapologetically reacted by yelling, slamming doors, and even once getting in the face of a child who (a) was clearly trying to get a rise out of me by calling me a cunt, (b) was probably struggling with the fact that his dad had moved on from his mom, and (c) was a child. I am not proud of some of the ways I handled certain situations, and in my defense, I had no idea how to be a stepparent to young, white boys. However, what I should have never done was try to parent them as if they were my own. These children had grown up in a world where they had little to no expectations of behavior, and in a society that was tailor-made for them, specifically. Yet here I was trying to "prepare them for the world" with hard lessons and even harder truths as if they were young Black boys. They were not, and this was a losing game. I just didn't know it yet.

*

Right around our second year of marriage I noticed a shift. A year prior I had asked Scott if he would be okay with me quitting my two part-time jobs, and give me five years to focus on building my writing career. He agreed to it, and a year and a half later my writing career was beginning to take off. I was getting pieces in the *Huffington Post*, was a staff writer for *Ravishly* magazine and our local weekly paper, and I had a style column in *3story Magazine*. I was beginning to become more well known in Tucson and had even added some spots on our local NPR affiliate—including a commercial for PBS Arizona. I was feeling fantastic about the way things were finally on the upswing and decided to put it out into the universe, and the land of Facebook, that I wanted to do a TED Talk before I turned forty. At that moment I was thirty-nine. No sooner than five minutes after I announced my desires to Facebook, I was being introduced via Messenger to the woman who ran TEDxTucson. Six months later I was on stage living out the very thing I'd manifested. That is also the very first time I felt the twinge of a shift in our marriage. As soon as I finished my talk and exited stage right, I was overcome with emotion and couldn't stop crying. Deep heavy sobs that sunk me all the way to the floor in the backstage restroom. I felt as though the universe had given me a second gift of purpose. I understood in that very moment how else I could reach people and I felt the power of the moment. It was unlike anything I'd ever felt, and exhilarating feels like much too small a word for it. However, when the show was over and I emerged from backstage to share with him what I'd experienced he seemed less than enthused. Instead of "I'm so proud of you," or "Wow, babe—you did so great! That's really incredible!" I got a lackluster "That's great," and a strong "can we go now" vibe. And just like that, the joy, the thrill, the over the moon natural high of the moment was gone. I could tell that he was annoyed that people wanted to talk to me, and I wanted to talk to them. When I shared with him that I'd met the wife of one of the speakers, and she was so moved by my talk that she wanted to buy copies of my children's book for all the teachers in her school, I got, "That's cool." I tried with everything I had in me to stay in the moment, maintain my high, but I felt the pull of his energy, and I went down with it. I had no way of knowing it at the moment, but it was truly the beginning of the end.

My TEDx Talk led to me partnering up with Stephen, a business genius and investor who saw a huge future, almost as big as a future I saw, for *Meet ClaraBelle Blue*. However, before we could do any work, I told Stephen I'd need to discuss this new venture with my husband. It was going to be a major undertaking, and I couldn't move forward on it without discussing with him what it would mean for our family. I discussed it with Scott, being very open and forthright about what this might look like—lots of long nights, less time with him and the family, less energy for sex—but that it wouldn't be forever. When we met, he owned his own business, so he knew what kind of dedication this would require. I told him that I needed to know that he was okay with it and that he fully understood what we were walking into—what *I* was walking into. He gave me his blessing and with that, Stephen and I began having phone calls and video meetings and shooting emails back and forth daily. I was building a website and learning about business philosophy, all while continuing to write for various outlets. My days bled into my nights and admittedly, as predicted, I was spending less time with Scott. I would tell him I'd be done working by ten o'clock, and ten would roll into midnight, and midnight would roll into one fifteen in the morning, and I'd crawl into bed as quietly as I could so as not to wake him, only to hear a voice in the darkness say, "You don't have to be quiet, I'm awake." I would apologize for working later than planned and be met with silence. It was awkward and uncomfortable, but I didn't know what else to do. I was finally going to be able to really get my dreams for my children's book off the ground, and I had someone who actually had the connections and money to help me make it happen. I could not half-ass this, and even if I could, I wouldn't because that's just not who I am. So, my days consisted of me waking up at 4:00 a.m. to get some work and emails done before Emory woke up, then from 6:00 a.m. to 8:30 a.m. I was in mom mode: making breakfast, getting her dressed, packing lunches, packing backpacks, and getting both her and Scott's youngest son to school. Then home and working from 8:30 a.m. to 2:45 p.m. when I had to leave to pick kids up from school, and back in mom/wife mode from 3:45 to 6:00 p.m., when Emory would go to sleep. And from about 6:30 p.m. to oftentimes midnight, I would head into my she-shed and continue working.

Now, if you're looking at that timeline and saying to yourself, "Wait a minute. This chick didn't once mention spending time with her husband," you're absolutely right. I didn't mention it. I didn't mention it because it didn't happen. I dove headfirst into building my business because *that's how you build a business.* You hustle your ass off, and you make sacrifices and in the end, you hope and pray it was all worth it. At least that's how I did it. And yeah, I guess you could say I sacrificed my marriage for my business, and on its face, that statement would not be wrong. But I would ask you to look at it from the perspective of a woman who was finally getting the opportunity to make her dreams come true—why would she not put everything she had into making it happen, and why would her husband, her helpmate, the one who's supposed to be her ride-or-die, have a problem with it when she did? Those first couple of months were not easy, but I kept telling myself that in the end, it would have all been worth it.

Little did I know that a short time later the universe was going to make me prove just how worth it this opportunity really was.

Two months after starting the business with Stephen, the entire bottom fell out. The morning we were to meet at our respective banks to set up the business account and get the LLC on file with the bank, Stephen had a massive stroke (from which he has never fully recovered) that landed him in the intensive care unit. I no longer had an investor. If I no longer had an investor, I no longer had a business. If I no longer had a business . . . The word devastated is an understatement of epic proportions. Fear and sadness rolled through my body like a tsunami, enveloping me before I could even plan my escape route. I'll never know Scott's real feelings about this sudden turn of events, but I remember him being (rightfully) concerned about Stephen and saying something like "these things happen . . . very rarely do businesses get off the ground . . . any number of things can keep them from growing." Scott, for all of the wonderful things he was (and still is), was not an optimist. I remember thinking at that moment that he had lied on his eHarmony profile. I told my best friend I felt like I had been duped. He wasn't an optimist; he was a dream crusher. But he isn't. He's just a realist. He doesn't dream like I dream, and that's okay, but at that moment I needed him to be a dream resuscitator. I needed him to hold my dream that was gasping for air, in the palm of his hands, and massage it back to life—or at least help me figure out how to do so. We both realize, now, that this may have been the beginning of his depression as far as our marriage was concerned. Even if he had wanted to be more supportive, his depression was coloring his view of everything. The fact that I was no longer able to give him the attention I had been able to give him the previous four years (and to be honest, wasn't willing to give him because dammit, what about MY dreams) translated to me rejecting him and not making him a priority. To an extent he was not wrong. I *wasn't* making him a priority, and I took no issue with

telling him as much. We had many arguments that ended with me telling him that he was not always going to be number one on my list of
priorities; that sometimes Emory would be number one, sometimes
my work was going to be number one, and still other times my health
was going to be number one, and he was going to have to be okay with
that. I yelled at him to stop treating me like I was his ex-wife (being
snippy, dismissive, avoidant, argumentative), and he told me I wasn't
listening to him. His ex-wife was also a writer, but unlike me, did not
build a career out of it, and for this he was resentful. I was a writer, and
I was building a career out of it, and for this he was also resentful. We
argued about the importance of my work and what I thought success
would and could look like, and he refused to acknowledge that not all
success is measured monetarily. I became incredibly emotional, telling
him that he didn't value my work or see the importance of what I was
trying to do, and he told me I used my tears as weapons. We were dying
a slow death, and even though he provided a life for us that enabled me
to embark on my career with minimal distractions (we had a cleaning
lady and a housekeeper), my career actually became a major distraction
in our marriage. It became the avenue for his depression to bubble to
the top, as if it had been fermenting for months, until it was poised and
ready to rot us from the inside out.

Then it did.

For my fortieth birthday we planned a trip to Mexico City. We had
been in therapy together for the past three months, and while it didn't
necessarily feel like we were making progress, it did feel like a trip to a
completely different country would be a nice reprieve and let some of
the air out of our consistently contentious interactions. Mark my words:
when your therapist tells you in your first session that while you are
very linear in your communication style, your partner is rather circu-
lar, and that's a big part of the reason you can't understand each other,
no amount of distance between you and your therapists' suede couch is
going to magically fix your issues. We started arguing the week before
we left for the trip and didn't stop until . . . well . . . we just didn't stop.
Everything from bad Google directions to buying handmade jewelry

from a child street vendor was up for eye rolls and hollers. The straw that broke the camel's back (on this particular trip) was when Scott continuously yelled at me in the middle of the DMZ plaza, and while I counted backward from ten, and took deep breaths (to keep from clawing his face off), he interrupted me to yell-ask me if I was done yet.

Y'all. When I tell you it was eighty-five degrees outside and I immediately went ice cold . . . in that one instant, I saw his whole life flash before my eyes. Why *my* eyes, you ask? Because in my mind I was about to stomp his ass out. You know how in the movies some egregious thing will happen to a woman, and while she is pleasantly smiling at the offending party, she's smiling at the camera, showing all her teeth, and quietly murdering him in her mind while sipping a glass of red wine? Well in that very moment, I was that lady and I was poised to end him right then and there. However, I don't look good in prison couture and my idea of a good time is *not* ending up in a Mexican prison while on vacation. So I did the next best thing—I walked away—sparing both our lives. The funny thing, he was so busy yelling at me he didn't realize I had walked away until I was halfway down the street. And when he caught up to me, I got yelled at for walking away from him. We didn't speak for the rest of that afternoon, and that night I lay awake in our tiny hotel room, listening to the bass-thumping house music pouring out into the streets from the nightclub across the way. I wanted desperately to be anywhere but there, in Mexico City, with him.

He didn't return to therapy with me after that trip, and though I wish I could say that we somehow managed to work through our issues, that just isn't the case. Things got worse and worse. The speaking dwindled down to "Good morning" and "What time will you be home" and "How was your day." The hugs became shoulders that brushed each other in passing. The sex became "that thing we used to do." We were foreign entities to each other, but even through all of that, I loved him. I continued going to therapy, but not to learn how to heal myself, but to learn what things I could do to try and make our marriage more sustainable, us more amenable to each other. How could I word things better, how could I motivate myself to want to hug him since his love language was physical touch and mine was acts of service and words of affirmation—none of which we were giving to each other. How could I make myself smaller so he might feel bigger in my life? I was trying desperately to heal and fix something that was (at the time) broken beyond repair, and I realize now that I wasn't trying to heal it because I loved him, though that's what I told myself. At the root of it all, I was trying to heal it because (a) I was scared of what it would mean if I *didn't* heal it; and (b) I was too scared to begin healing myself. I'm going to say this, and I hope this helps someone: DO NOT STAY SEATED AT A TABLE WHERE YOU ARE NOT BEING FED. It doesn't matter how beautiful the house is, how fine the china is, how crystal blue the pool out back is. If that table is set, and you are seated, and your plate remains empty, regardless of how long you are sitting there, get up, leave, and make a table for yourself. Don't go looking for *another* table to be served at—make your own. Fix your own plate, nourish your own soul. So often we know exactly what it is we need to feel fulfilled and like a whole human being, but we settle for the bare minimum because a little bit of something is better than nothing, right? Wrong. The bare minimum is just that—THE BARE MINIMUM— just enough to get by. And what I came to realize during this time in my marriage is that I am on this earth to do more than just "get by," and so I need all the fuel the universe wants to offer me so that I can be every bit as EXTRA as I know I am. And trust and believe—I *am* extra— today. I am extra kind to myself, extra loving to myself, extra forgiving with myself; and because of this, I am able to be extra everything with everybody else. But it had to start with me. I had to decide to settle for not just more but extra. By May of 2019 I think we both knew the end was close. During an argument I told him that the way he had been approaching our marriage the last few years was akin to someone who had been wearing the wrong prescription glasses for years. Even though he gave his eyes a break for a few years when it was time to get a new prescription (remarry), he just put the same glasses back on, and lo and behold, he still couldn't see clearly. He had a new wife but he was still behaving in the same ways that led to the downfall of his first marriage because he couldn't see me. He continued to regard me through old, smudged, dirty glasses, and wondered why nothing looked different, and why he kept bumping into things and breaking them. "Well," I told him, "you keep treating your new wife like she's your old wife. You became so accustomed to those old wife glasses that when things got rough, rather than attempt to correct your vision (therapy), you just kept those same old glasses on, and expected everything to be fine. Well, sir, everything is not fine, and everything has not been fine for quite some time." At that moment, I knew in my heart that I was done. By July of 2019, Scott and I decided it was time to let the marriage go.

*

It is never easy to walk away from forever. There were so many fears and so many questions on my end. Where would Emory and I live? How would I support us since he was the major (major!) breadwinner? How would we tell Emory that her mom, and the only man she'd known as "dad" were no longer going to be living together, she wasn't going to see him every day, we were no longer going to be husband and wife. That was probably the hardest part of it all—the feeling that I was doing it again—taking my daughter away from her father, making the decision, yet again, to be a single parent. I didn't want that for my daughter, but I had to weigh what was more important for her to see. Was it more important for her to see a woman who looked like her know and claim her worth, step out on faith and say, "I deserve to be loved and seen and appreciated," and commit to her own healing journey, all while build-ing a career she believed in? Or was it more important that she grew up seeing her mom and dad under the same roof every day, even if they barely spoke to each other? I had to decide which was going to serve her more as she grew into a young, Black, disabled woman. My friends had to remind me constantly that I was not going to fall, that I had a whole community of support that would not let me, and that I was stronger than I was giving myself credit for. They had to remind me of the career I had already begun to build for myself, and the career that was forming on the horizon. They had to remind me of the parable of the quarters. The parable of the quarters is this: you can only have so many in your hand at one time; the value and quantity of these quarters will not change. But if you're willing to let go of the quarters, your hand is now free to hold hundred-dollar bills. Not only can you hold more hundred-dollar bills than you can quarters, but those hundreds are worth exponentially more than the small number of quarters you can hold. You simply have to be willing to let go and trust that the universe will give you more. I remembered all of these things and found a beautiful apartment for us to live in. Scott and I came to an amicable agreement for alimony—one that ensured our daughter's way of life would not change. And on the day I was moving out of our home, I received an email from my agent that would change the rest of my and Emory's lives—for the better. I let go of the quarters and my first hundred-dollar bill found its way right to my palm. At that moment I knew beyond a shadow of a doubt that I'd be okay—we'd be okay. I had jumped and prayed for wings on the way down . . . and this was the beginning of me taking flight. Even though I had checked out of my marriage (emotionally) six months prior, my heart still had some major healing to do. I had some major habits to break and some major habits to learn, like how to respond and not react, how to acknowledge fear and fiction, but stick to the facts, how to trust my gut, and listen deeply to my intuition. How to be present (I am a consummate daydreamer and future caster). How to name the things I am feeling, as I am feeling them, and how to identify where the feelings are stemming from (which is almost *always* deep-seated emotional trauma). How to detach from that trauma and not carry it with me in my knapsack of life. How to honor the little me that never felt strong or beautiful or safe or worthy, and let her know that she is all of those things today, right now, and forever. And if I ever wanted to love again, I mean really deeply, in the truest sense of the word, love again, it was crucial that I learn to love myself—every part of myself—even my shadow self. And let me tell you, my shadow self is one petty-ass bitch. I'm a Scorpio through and through so my shadow self can be vicious.

But I had to learn to look at her for who she is—a lot of times she is my protector. My own, fiercely loyal ride or die. She wants to save me from all the things I am fairly sure are out to get me. However, she is also the Queen of the Spiral. When something goes the least bit awry, I can count on her to be right there in my ear telling me all the things I did wrong to mess things up. She will concoct whole ass stories that have absolutely nothing to do with the actual truth, and before I know it I'll find myself in tears, over a story my shadow-self concocted. But again, I have to love her. I have to love her enough to tell her, "Honey, that's not true. Fact over fiction—what are the facts?"

It took a lot of therapy, and a lot of journaling to even get me to the point where I could even *say* the word "love" again. I'll never forget the time I was cleaning my house listening to music and the India Arie song "Ready for Love" came on. I immediately skipped the song and said out loud to absolutely no one: "Oh, hell no, I'm not!" It was such a reflexive response I had no choice but to laugh at myself, but that's when I realized that I was finally getting to a place where I was truly *knowing* myself. I began meditating, and I made a list of affirmations that I said out loud, every morning, while I drank my tea.

I am beautiful, inside and out.

I am strong—across the board.

I am all the beautiful parts of my father.

I am worthy of love.

I am respectable.

I am loveable.

I am desirable.

I am not in financial need or struggle.

I am a great friend.

I am a highly sought-after speaker.

I am a great mom who gives more than the bare minimum to my daughter.

I am an exceptional partner.

I boldly ask for the things I want, and assuredly decline the things I don't.

I am enough for me and everyone else.

I am walking in my purpose daily.

I am highly intuitive and trust my gut.

I am not dispensable.

I am love.

I also began to write messages to myself on my bathroom mirror. Things like:

"You are not dispensable. If it leaves your life, it simply was not meant for you."

"Healing is a continuum. You will not come undone."

"The only thing you can control is yourself. That's it."

"Follow the leader. SPOILER ALERT: The leader is NOT YOU. Trust the process."

"Walls are a trauma response. You are no longer being traumatized, and vulnerability can actually lead you to safety."

"It is not your job to fix people."

Doing these affirmations and seeing these messages every day, several times a day, played a huge role in my growth and healing. It also played a major role in helping me get comfortable with the idea of loving someone again. I was nowhere near ready to do it any time soon, but I was getting clearer and clearer about what kind of love I would accept in my life—what kind of love I was going to call in. On November 11, 2019, I wrote this in my journal:

Love—I call to myself a deep, honest, fulfilling, respectful love. One that demands no less than my whole self, and one that refuses to show up as less than what my soul and heart need but is authentic in its showing up. I call to myself a love/lover that values emotional intimacy and emotional vulnerability in themselves and in me. I call a love/lover that values my independence as much as their own but knows my heart is a safe space for them. I call to myself a confident lover, who is as gentle as he is adventurous, someone who relishes learning my body and allows me to relish his. I call to my heart a lover who understands what it means to

be, and wants to be, my partner. I call to myself a healing love; a
love that is home. I welcome all of this into my life.

I welcomed all of this into my life, but more than anything I welcomed genuine male friendship. I needed to learn how to just be friends with men, and I needed to go much longer than thirty days before entering into my next relationship. I was determined to break that cycle my therapist and I had identified that one fateful day in her office. I had to be more than just the thirty-day rebound queen. I was moving along in my life, healing and loving myself exquisitely (and exclusively), when three months later, after a three-hour conversation with this fine brotha who had left his bowl at my dinner party a few nights earlier, said a few simple words to me as he walked me to my car.

"For real though . . . can we be friends?"

Because I am painfully awkward and don't know how to be anything other than a smart ass, I quipped back. "Well, I'm kind of on hashtag team no new friends right now, but you did say you can make a mean steak and a girl gotta eat, so yeah . . . we can be friends."

He smiled and walked back to his car. As I settled myself into my big old mama van, I whispered to the universe, "What just happened?" I swear I heard her whisper back, "You're welcome."

FAMILY KEEPSAKES

Excerpt from "Mother to Son"
by Langston Hughes

> *Don't you set down on the steps*
> *'Cause you finds it's kinder hard.*
> *Don't you fall now—*
> *For I'se still goin', honey,*
> *I'se still climbin',*
> *And life for me ain't been no crystal stair.*

My mother had "Mother to Son" on our refrigerator all throughout my junior high and high school years. She even had me memorize it when I was twelve and auditioned for the part of Raylene in August Wilson's *Fences*. I never quite understood what Langston Hughes was trying to say. Who has crystal stairs? One good slip and fall and you would literally die either from shards of crystal slicing you to pieces or head trauma on the way down. I didn't get it then. But now, it's crystal clear (pun intended).

This was my mother's way of encouraging me to never stop dreaming, never stop striving and wanting for more, even when she couldn't provide more. It was *our* life, *our* story, staring me in the face every day. I couldn't so much as grab a glass of Kool-Aid without reading it. Now, I realize that much like it was my mother's story as I was growing up, it has also been mine as I've embarked on my own journey through motherhood. Motherhood hasn't been a crystal stair by any stretch of the imagination. There have been more splinters and tacks than I can count on both of my hands, but to be honest, many of those splinters and tacks have greatly influenced how I move through the world—some for the better, some not so much. In some ways, much like if you leave a splinter in your skin for too long and your body absorbs it and creates scar tissue around it, I've done the same thing.

My therapist, Katie, likens my life traumas to splinters and thorns that I've held on to for far too long. So long, I've built a hedge of protection around myself, making certain areas of my heart and life seemingly impenetrable. She's not wrong. I have definitely built a nice, cozy little fortress for myself. And I had been quite comfortable with it until Katie felt the need to inform me (as she always does) that due to my wall of protection, I had been living and acting in a way that signified I was still in survival mode, and I didn't have to be. I no longer had to exist, create, or even love, from a place of scarcity, of lack, want, and desire. She also decided it would be in my best interest to inform me that because I was living my life that way, I was robbing Emory of the opportunity to experience the whole, beautiful, healing Adiba, and I was robbing myself of experiencing that woman too.

Damn, Katie. Way to fuck a mom up.

But that's why I love her. Like me, she pulls no punches, but unlike me, she doesn't roll her eyes, suck her teeth, and curse in Spanish when she does it. She was right. By building up scar tissue on top of scar tissue, I have been teaching Emory that we don't deal with our hurts, we just push through them. Which on some levels is good because she needs to know that we can do hard things. But what she really needs to help her develop and nurture her own wholeness is to see me pull out those splinters, let down the fortress, be vulnerable. The women in my family do not do this—still. We are a frighteningly strong brood of women, locking away our hurts and pains and secrets and curses—from the world, from each other, from ourselves. Our bodies and hearts, so filled with splinters and fragments of our lives that we try to piece them together as a form of survival. And we have passed these curses masquerading as "strength" down, through our actions, our thought processes, our DNA, from generation to generation, cycle after cycle. We go into the fortress and then teach our children how to navigate it instead of finding the light and guiding them to it. The fortress keeps me locked in, and that is not what I want for her. We are not doing that anymore. I am not doing that anymore. The curses stop here. She's already lost her father, who died at the age of thirty-eight just like he predicted. These generational curses didn't start with me and Jeff, but this is where they end. The fragmented life stops here.

Instead of trauma, fear of abandonment, and a fear-based mentality, I will leave only the finest keepsakes for my daughter to pass down. I leave with her permission to be unapologetically *herself.* When I started burlesque, Emory was my motivation. How could I teach her to love the body that God gave her until I, a fat Black woman with kinky hair and a gap in her front teeth, embraced my own? I pass down to Emory liberation and self-belief. The kind that finds you standing on stage dressed as a naughty housewife, grinding and shaking while burning a hypothetical cheating man's clothes, *and* the kind of liberation and self-belief that pushes you to write, publish, and promote a children's book that publishing companies continue to reject, because fuck them[46]. The locking of ourselves in the fortress stops here with me, with Emory, with us.

---

46. That probably just cost me any future children's book deals for *Meet ClaraBelle Blue.* *shrug*

In so many ways she is already locked in—locked into a society that is not set up to meet her needs, locked into a health care system that determines when and if she can have new rehabilitative equipment or even just basic daily living needs for hygiene. From age nine to eleven, even her voice was locked inside of her because the state of Arizona denied her a communication device for almost two years. If I want Emory to view herself as a whole human being, and if I want others to regard her as such (and not a disabled person they can speak about, around, or worse, not speak to at all), I have to model what that looks like. And believe me—there are days that it would be so much easier to just parade around town as a shell of a woman. As an Afro-Latin woman raising an Afro-Latin girl-child who is *also* disabled, life can be absolutely draining in these days and times. I have to worry about teachers not taking the time to learn her communication skills and deeming her a "problem kid with behaviors," because it is a known and proven fact that Black and Brown children with disabilities often have higher suspension and expulsion rates than their white counterparts.[47] I worry about when she gets older and some love interest (or person in general) decides they can take advantage of her sexually because she's not as strong as they are, or cannot communicate that she is not giving consent. And then there is law enforcement and the ever-growing issue of domestic terrorists who would love nothing more than to wipe the country clean of people like my daughter.

I shield her from as much of it as I can. I act as her fortress as I build my own light-filled fortress (even though Katie is constantly

---

47. "Nationwide, the proportion of African American students who experienced ten days or fewer in-school suspensions/expulsions is twice as large as that of their white peers, and three times as much as that of their Hispanic peers. In eight states, over 60 percent of students with disabilities disciplined in the 2016–17 school year were black. In states such as Mississippi and Louisiana, African American students make up approximately 40 percent to 50 percent of the total served in special education, but over 70 percent of students subjected to disciplinary removals totaling more than ten days are African American."—*Special Ed Discipline Disparities: The Numbers Reveal The Need For Positive Practices*, www.nsba.org/ASBJ/2019/August/Special-Education-Disparities

reminding me of why I shouldn't), because ain't that a mother? We protect our babies from the ugliness of the world, while we simultaneously gird them up to deal with the ugliness of the world. So no, motherhood hasn't always been a crystal stair, but hey, we're still here . . . we're still climbin'. And you know, I've been blessed to have many people climb alongside me, push from behind me, and extend a hand to pull me up to the next stair when I wasn't sure that I would, or even could make it. There have been fine-ass brothas who asked if we could be friends, and then showed me that loving and being loved, *really* loved, isn't scary when you learn to love yourself first. I have a therapist who leaves the most mind-blowing breadcrumbs for me to find on my journey back to me so that I can walk alongside my daughter as she begins her own journey to herself, a mother who stopped at nothing to make sure I became the woman writing this book today, and friends—oh the friends, the mentors, the people who simply "put me in the room" or floated my name in a room full of decision-makers. My community who allows me to be whole, allows me to fuck up, and looks out for Emory as if she was born to the whole of Tucson. All of these people, and this community, have walked these stairs with me and my daughter, and I am grateful beyond words.

Do I know what the future has in store for us? Was Michael Jackson's nose real?

Y'all, I have no idea what the future holds for me and Emory. When she was ten, she was diagnosed with an acute seizure disorder, and though her neurologist and I have managed to keep it in check with medication, because nature is going to nature, even with meds, she still has an increase in seizure activity in the week leading up to and during her menstrual cycle. I've sat through two major surgeries with this child and nothing terrifies me or breaks my heart as much as holding her hand through a seizure does. And every time she has one, my eyes dart from her eyes to her lips and back again—are her eyes rolling back in her head, are her lips turning blue, is she foaming at the mouth, all while trying to time the seizure. And recently, they've been getting longer, and more intense, and my heart hurts more and more for her because dammit—doesn't she have enough to deal with? But I hold her hand through every single one, and I tell her it's okay, and mommy's here, and just breathe—because yes, she stops breathing when she's seizing. And when it passes, she pulls me in for the tightest headlock hug as if to say, "Thank you for getting me through that." So yes, this too, is a step on our staircase. But it's not the only step, no. We're just barely getting started on this climb. We're only twelve steps in!

So what's going to carry us up the rest of these stairs besides therapists, mothers, and friends who refuse to let us be anything other than our whole, human selves? Beyoncé dance parties in the kitchen and Drake dance parties in the car. *Oprah's Super Soul Sundays* for me, and *Down to Earth* with Zac Efron for Emory. Masturbation for me and if she's smart, masturbation for Emory (quit freaking out, Mom, everybody does it, it's healthy, and it's a great sleep aid/stress reliever/time passer). And wine. Copious amounts of wine—for me, not my kid. Because like Langston's mama, life for me ain't been no crystal stair, and honestly, I don't expect it to ever be. I'm sure there will be thorns and splinters I'll encounter as I continue to rise— as Emory continues to rise. Remember—God thinks he's funny AF. But it's cool. I've got the tools (thank you, therapy), the knowledge (thank you, Mama), the hustle (thank you, life), the love for self (thank you, me), and the love of others (thank you, friends, family, and community) that will get me through this beautiful comedy of errors. We'll take the thorns and splinters—one seizure, one headlock hug, one stair at a time.

ACKNOWLEDGMENTS

A good friend will bail you out of jail. A best friend will bring a shovel and a flashlight. Saying I've needed bailing out over the course of my life would be an understatement of epic proportions. This book would not have been possible without my squad. To each and every one of you, thank you.

First and foremost, I absolutely MUST give thanks to God, Jah, Jehovah Jireh, Allah, The Universe, The Great I Am, My Number One Homey, My Ace. You're a regular-ass comedian, but can't nobody tell me that you're not real. You have had me from day one—zygote stage. You refuse to let me fail no matter how damn hard I try. The love and gratitude run so deep, so I'll just leave it with "good lookin' out, homey."

Mom. Ma. Mama. Never Mommy, Madre, or Mami. Mother when I'm thoroughly annoyed. But above all of that, you are my Day One—literally and figuratively. You are the walking embodiment of a "ride or die" when it comes to me. You have *literally* almost died numerous times while being my mother, both at the hands of my father and your own health. Each time you stared death in the face, you asked God to just let you live to get me to adulthood. Well, here we are, forty-some-odd years later, I'm a whole-ass adult, and you're still kicking. Our relationship to each other was forged in the fire and in the fight for survival. You saved my life, and you left an abuser—and you did it because you love me. I do not regret the missed tickles and cuddles, because those are not the only things that mean "love." I watch you give Em all the unbridled love and affection you couldn't give me as a child because we were living in survival mode, and I know that's your way of showing me love too. Also, Mom, look at what you did! I know you tend to feel bad about the conditions we sometimes lived in when I was growing up, but Ma . . . *Ma* . . . look!! Look! At! What! You! Did! I wouldn't and couldn't be the mother, friend, and woman that I am were it not for you. I mean, I might be biased but I'd say you did aight!

To Mammy—I don't even know what to say because everything I said to Mom, I can say to you. There simply are no words to describe the love I have for you. You filled a hole in my six-year-old heart. A hole I didn't even know I had. And you continue to fill it. Thank you for being everything I've needed when I've needed it.

Back in junior high, it was me and Faith—all day every day. Walking from my house to her house singing En Vogue's "Hold On" at the top of our lungs like *we were* En Vogue. Thank you to my #BFSLD-ITWW Faith, the only white girl I know who knows every Mariah Carey song, worships at the altar of Mary J. Blige, and will proudly list Guy's "Let's Chill" as the only slow jam that matters. Thank you for your pranks that kept me laughing (and crying that one time) over these thirty-some-odd years, and for making sure I never take myself too seriously. You're still the first person I tell all my firsts to, my calm in every storm and neither friend nor sister can ever begin to fully capture what you are to me.

Tess, thank you for being Emory's "Faith." One day, I'll catch you sneaking Em out of the house. I'll ground you both because I can do that, and then I'll thank God for giving me a "bonus daughter," and my daughter a friend—no . . . a sister like you.

I hated you because my college boyfriend thought you were hot. Yet somehow, Morgenstarr, decades later I cannot imagine my life without you in it. We are two awkward Black girls peas in a pod. We've always joked that you're the conspiracy theory, love-is-dead cynic and I'm the free love, there's got to be a better way, look at the hummingbird in the tree moon child. Maybe we're both somehow right. I will never understand how one of the highest-ranking women in the United States Air Force, a mom to my two gorgeous nieces, and an aspiring philanthropist, somehow always finds time for me and my shenanigans. And yet here you are. How lucky am I?

Everyone has that one friend who just is. There's no need for an explanation of how you met because you've known each other over lifetimes, and it shows. To my tour guide, thank you for the lifetimes passed and the lifetimes to come. So much healing has also taken place since you became a part of my life, and a lot of that healing helped me write this book. Thank you hardly fits.

And last but certainly not least, to my relentless agent, Jess, who had dreams for me that I didn't even think to dream and has forged new paths in my life that were never on my radar. You've gone from agent to friend, Jess, and I love you dearly. You've changed my life. My editor, Kelly, who cosigned every unapologetic move in this book, and then doubled down with "folks can Google what they don't know." Thank you so much for embracing me, and this book, and seeing it through to the end with me. I knew I hand-picked you for a reason. Jill Scott, without you there may not be a baby to have made me a mother, which means there may not be this book, so I must give you your propers. I stand firm though—back child support, fa real.

If I have forgotten to thank you here, charge it to my head and not my heart. I mean this, I thank each of you for seeing me and loving me—flaws and all.